BEHIND THE VEIL IN PERSIA AND TURKISH ARABIA

LECTOR HOUSE PUBLIC DOMAIN WORKS

BEHIND THE VEIL IN PERSIA AND TURKISH ARABIA

M. E. HUME-GRIFFITH,
A. HUME-GRIFFITH

ISBN: 978-93-90314-19-5

Published: 1909

LECTOR HOUSE LLP
E-MAIL: lectorpublishing@gmail.com

THE AUTHOR AND HER HUSBAND IN BAKHTIAN COSTUME

Dr. Hume-Griffith's dress is that of a chief, and is of blue cloth lined with red flannel: and the lady's is of richly-brocaded velvet, and her head-coverings are of very pretty muslin, embroidered with silk.

BEHIND THE VEIL IN PERSIA AND TURKISH ARABIA

AN ACCOUNT OF AN ENGLISHWOMAN'S EIGHT YEARS' RESIDENCE AMONGST THE WOMEN OF THE EAST

BY

M. E. HUME-GRIFFITH

WITH NARRATIVES OF EXPERIENCES IN BOTH COUNTRIES
BY
A. HUME-GRIFFITH, M.D., D.P.H.

WITH 37 ILLUSTRATIONS AND A MAP

1909

I DEDICATE

THIS BOOK

TO
MY HUSBAND

**IN LOVING REMEMBRANCE OF
EIGHT HAPPY YEARS
1900–1908**

PREFACE

I have endeavoured in this book to give some account of that inner life of the East of which a traveller, however keen-sighted and intelligent, seldom gains more than a passing glimpse. In a residence of eight years in Persia and Turkish Arabia I have become intimate with a large circle of friends whose life is passed behind the veil, and as the wife of a medical missionary I have had unusual opportunities of winning their confidence and becoming acquainted with their thoughts. Of direct missionary effort I have said very little, but I hope that the picture I have given may arouse interest in lives spent amongst surroundings so different from our own.

It is impossible for any one, however unversed in politics, who has lived so long in Mesopotamia, not to be deeply interested in the future of the country. While all Europe has been filled with astonishment at the bloodless revolution in Turkey, we who have become familiar with its inner life are touched with a feeling of admiration and something akin to awe. Whatever misgivings there may be as to the permanence of this reformation we hope and trust that it will endure.

Of one imminent change the effect is likely to be far-reaching. The new government has secured the services of Sir William Wilcox as their adviser in great irrigation schemes. Irrigation in Mesopotamia will change the whole face of the country; vast stretches of desert will be transformed into a garden, ruined villages will be restored, a new kingdom may be born, and Babylon possibly rebuilt. Mosul, practically on the site of ancient Nineveh, will become easy of access from Europe by means of the Baghdad railway and the restored navigation of the Tigris. Its waste places may be filled with corn, and the city be crowned once more with some of its ancient glory.

I should like to take this opportunity of thanking all those who have kindly allowed me to use their photographs, amongst them the Rev. C. H. Stileman, Dr. Saati of Mosul, and the Publishing Department of the Church Missionary Society.

I am indebted to Professor Brown's valuable book entitled "A Year amongst the Persians" for information on the Babi religion, and to Sir A. H. Layard's classical work on the excavations of Nineveh, which I have frequently had occasion to consult.

M. E. H.-G.

CONTENTS

PART I

CHAPTER I

EARLY IMPRESSIONS

CHAPTER II

KERMAN

CHAPTER III

PERSIAN INDUSTRIES

CHAPTER IV

THE CLIMATE OF PERSIA

CHAPTER V

HOLIDAYS IN PERSIA

CHAPTER VI

SOCIAL LIFE IN PERSIA

CHAPTER VII

THE WOMEN OF PERSIA

CHAPTER VIII

MORE ABOUT PERSIAN WOMEN

CHAPTER IX

SOME POINTS IN THE MOSLEM FAITH

CHAPTER X

OTHER RELIGIOUS SECTS

CHAPTER XI

DESERT DELIGHTS

CHAPTER XII

PERSIAN MEDICAL MISSIONS

CHAPTER XIII

PIONEER MEDICAL MISSION WORK IN KERMAN

CHAPTER XIV

MEDICAL MISSION WORK IN YEZD

PART II

CHAPTER I

THE CITY OF NINEVEH

CHAPTER II

THE PEOPLE OF MOSUL

CHAPTER IX

MANNERS AND SUPERSTITIONS IN MOSUL

CHAPTER X

THE YEZIDEES

CHAPTER XI

TRAVELLING IN THE DESERT

CHAPTER XII

THE PLEASURES OF DESERT TRAVELLING

CHAPTER XIII

PIONEER MEDICAL MISSION WORK IN MOSUL (NINEVEH)

LIST OF ILLUSTRATIONS

BEHIND THE VEIL IN PERSIA
AND TURKISH ARABIA

PART I

"So, after the sore torments of the route,
Toothache and headache, and the ache of mind,
And huddled sleep and smarting wakefulness,
And night and day, and hunger sick at food,
And twenty-fold relays, and packages
To be unlocked, and passports to be found,
And heavy well-kept landscape—we are glad
Because we entered (Persia) in the Sun."

D. G. ROSSETTI.

CHAPTER I

EARLY IMPRESSIONS

*Start for Persia — Arrival at Isphahan — Departure for Kerman — The Land of
the Lion and the Sun — A rainy day and its effects — Eclipse — Locusts —
Sand-storms — Land of cats — Modes of conveyance — Inhabitants.*

> "'Tis the sight of a lifetime to behold
> The great shorn sun as you see it now
> Across eight miles of undulant gold
> That widens landward, weltered and rolled
> With patches of shadow and crimson stains."
>
> LOWELL.

> "Shadow maker, shadow slayer, arrowing light from clime to clime."
>
> LORD TENNYSON.

Our life in Persia extended over a period of three years, dating from the spring of 1900 to that of 1903.

It was with great joy I heard the news, early in February of 1900, that my husband had been appointed by the Church Missionary Society to open medical work in Kerman, and that we were to start almost at once. Within a month we were married, had bought our outfit, bid sorrowful farewells to our relations and friends, and started for the romantic land of Persia. From London to Isphahan took us just nine weeks, as we were delayed by illness for some weeks both in Russia and in the Persian Desert. However, on 9th May we entered the beautiful city of Isphahan, to find a warm welcome awaiting us from friends there. This place will always have a very warm corner in my heart, for it was there we made our first home. The doctor in charge of the work at Julfa (the Christian quarter of Isphahan) having left on furlough, my husband was asked to remain there till his return, which he accordingly did. It was not till the following spring that we left for Kerman. Thus our first impressions of this land of light and darkness were gathered from Isphahan and its neighbourhood. There is no after time so full of interest to those who live abroad as the first year spent in a new life and country, gleaning fresh ideas, seeing new sights, gaining experiences often dearly bought, but which must be purchased ere the newcomer can settle down to life in the East with any comfort or peace of mind.

The native servants love to obtain posts with fresh comers, knowing that for the first few months, at any rate, they will have an exceedingly good time, being able to make a huge *medâqal* (profit) from the unsuspecting Feringhi. I sigh to think of the many ways in which we were cheated those first few months of our life in Persia, but no one breathed a word to us, realising that our eyes would be opened only too soon, and that experience was the most effectual teacher. It is a strange fact that all housekeepers new to the land think their servants are perfect till they find out, perhaps when too late, their foolish delusion.

From the very first my heart went out in affection to the dear Moslem women, and now, after eight years spent amongst them, I can truly say that my love has deepened, and my sympathies become enlarged, for these charming but, alas, too often unhappy followers of Mohammed.

Our knowledge of Persia extends especially to three cities, in each of which we spent a year. Isphahan, as we have seen, was our first home, then came a year at Kerman, a distance of some 500 miles separating the two cities. Finally we spent a very happy year at Yezd, that City of Sand, situated midway between Isphahan and Kerman. Of each of these cities we shall hear more in other chapters.

Persia has well been called the Land of the Lion and the Sun. Certainly the latter name is well deserved, for the sun is almost always shining, and without the brilliant sunshine we should hardly recognise it as the land of Persia.

The symbol of the Lion and the Sun originated in the days when the Zoro-astrians were the inhabitants of the land. The Sun, being the emblem of the Fire Worshippers, was taken as their national badge. The Lion was added later because Ali, the grandson of Mohammed, was called "The Lion of God." The woman's face in the Sun was inserted some years later by one of the Persian kings as a tribute to his favourite wife.

The sunshine of Persia forms one of its greatest attractions. Even in winter the dull, cloudy days are few and far between. When by chance a rainy day does come, the people are so surprised and taken aback that they seem paralysed for the time being, and are unable to go about their usual business.

The remembrance of our first experience of a rainy day still lingers in my memory. We had awakened one morning much later than usual to find the sky clouded over and the rain coming down in torrents. I was surprised to find that we had not been called as usual, but imagined the servants had forgotten to do so. Upon entering the dining-room, what was my surprise to find no preparations for a meal. Calling the servant, I asked him why breakfast was not ready. At this he seemed quite hurt, as he answered, "But, Khanum (lady), it is raining!" This fact was to his mind quite sufficient reason for everything. As long as the rain lasted the servants could be prevailed upon to do nothing except crouch over the fire and shiver! The moment the rain ceased and the sun once more shone out they resumed their normal state.

This constant sunshine is a great boon to the beggars and poor, helping to make life endurable for them; they need very little clothing, as a rule, to enable them to keep warm. So long as they can lie and bask in the sunshine, picking up bread enough to sustain life, they trouble very little about working or earning money.

There is only one place where there is very little sunshine, and that is in the hearts and lives of the people. Especially, perhaps, is this true in the case of the women of the land, as we shall see presently.

A Persian gentleman once visited England, and on his return to his native country was questioned by his friends as to which was the better land to live in. His reply was to the effect that in England the houses were grander, the scenery more beautiful, but that there was no sunshine! This lack, to his mind, far outweighed all the other advantages which might belong to England, and his friends decided that, after all, Persia was the better country to live in.

When there happens to be a cloudy day or night in summer, the result is anything but cooling, for the air becomes terribly oppressive, it is almost impossible to breathe, and during the night it is quite useless to think of or hope for sleep till the clouds have rolled away.

The natives are very much alarmed when an eclipse of the sun takes place, as they are afraid they are going to lose their benefactor. Once, while we were in Yezd, the sun was eclipsed. Suddenly hundreds of guns and cannons were fired off from all parts of the town. We ran out to see what had happened, and were met by our frightened servants carrying their guns, who told us that an enormous fish was trying to swallow the sun, and that they hoped, by making a terrific noise, to frighten it away! Great was their joy and relief when the shadow began to pass from the sun.

Sand-storms are terrible trials in Persia. Quite suddenly, without any warning, the light disappears, clouds upon clouds of dust come rushing in. Before you have time to shut all the doors and windows, everything in the house is covered with a fine white dust. Sand-storms are disagreeable and trying to the patience when they find you in the house, but when you are caught in a heavy sand-storm out in the desert, it is often a source of great danger. If riding, the only possible thing to do is to dismount, cover your head and face as well as possible, turn your back to the storm, and hope for the best.

At other times the light is obliterated in the daytime by a swarm of locusts passing overhead. Till I saw this myself I could hardly believe it was possible for these little insects to obscure the light of the sun as they did. One day in Kerman we were just ready to set off for a ride, when suddenly the light vanished, and I thought a fearful thunderstorm was about to burst upon us. On looking up we saw what appeared to be a huge black cloud hovering overhead: presently this descended and resolved itself into myriads of flying insects. As some fell to the earth we found them to be locusts from two to three inches long. The natives were dreadfully alarmed lest they should settle on their fields, as it was springtime, and the ground was already green with promise of harvest. Had the locusts settled, it would have meant ruin and starvation to many. Fortunately, they passed over that time.

We have seen that Persia is a land of sunshine, we must not forget that it is also a land of cats.

I was amused the other day to see how differently two people can see the same thing. In the course of a conversation with a friend who was for some years in Persia, I asked him if he did not admire the Persian cats very much. "Never saw one," was his answer, and he maintained that the whole time he was in Persia he never saw a long-haired cat. My experience was quite the reverse, for I hardly remember ever seeing an ordinary short-haired one during the three years we were in Persia. We had some beautiful white ones, but they were very delicate, and generally came to an untimely end. We tried to take one to Kerman, but it met with a sad death when only half way there.

Cats are exported on quite a large scale to India and other places. They are taken to the coast by horse-dealers, who tether them in much the same way as they do their horses.

One of the late Shahs is said to have been very devoted to cats, and always took one with him when he travelled, a special baggage animal being reserved for the cage of this favourite pet.

There are many ways of journeying in Persia, and the would-be traveller can take his choice according to his own ideas of comfort and convenience. To my mind the most pleasant way of all is to have your own horses for riding, and thus be able to set your own pace and not have to be bound down to the slow, wearying, never-changing rate of the caravan.

For those who do not care for, or are not strong enough for riding, there are many conveyances. Here, again, the traveller has quite a large choice of good things. First of all there is the "kajâvah." This consists of two cage-like boxes, suspended one on each side of the animal: the interior of these boxes sometimes boasts of a little low seat, but as a rule is innocent of any such luxury. Two people of about the same weight must sit on each side, or the result is disastrous. I remember once being with a large caravan. In one of these kajâvahs was travelling a Government official and his wife. He was very tiny, she was quite the reverse, the result being that the little man was generally up in the air while the opposite side of the kajâvah was weighed down nearly to the ground. They tried all manner of experiments in their endeavour to strike the balance, gathering stones and depositing them in the lighter side, tying bags of fuel, &c., to the outside of the kajâvah, but all of no avail. At last, in disgust and anger, the woman jumped out without giving her husband any warning: the result to onlookers was ludicrous! The wife refused all that day again to enter the kajâvah, preferring to walk, till one of the muleteers offered her a seat on the top of one of the baggage mules. The little man was soon balanced with stones picked up by the wayside, and travelled for the rest of that day in peace and comfort. At the end of the stage, however, his wife would not speak to him or cook his dinner for him! and the man (who was quite the reverse of an ordinary Moslem man) came to one of my husband's assistants, begging him to act as mediator. In this case the man and woman seem to have exchanged places as regards character, the wife being decidedly the master, and he, poor man, looked as if he hardly dared call his soul his own. Even amongst Moslems there doubtless are some strong-minded women.

I have travelled many miles in one of these kajâvahs, finding them very comfortable and restful, after riding for hours. My husband had a pair specially made for me, with seats inside, and nicely cushioned: these always went with us on our journeys in Persia, so that, when I tired of riding, I could rest awhile. While I was not using them our servants had to take my place, a favour they did not always appreciate. When travelling by night, I have slept for hours at a stretch in one of these kajâvahs, the steady measured walk of the mule favouring slumber. Sometimes, however, the monotony is broken by the mule suddenly dropping on to its front knees, and you find yourself deposited on the ground, shot out like an arrow from its bow.

If this form of conveyance does not appeal to the traveller then there is the "takhtiravan." This is a most luxurious mode of conveyance, and is, as a rule, only used by invalids or high-class Moslem ladies. It consists of a box, with doors and windows, measuring about six or seven feet by four in length and five in height. The top is covered with heavy felt or some material which will keep out the sun or the rain, according to which season of the year you are travelling in. Inside is placed a mattress with plenty of cushions: the whole is built on shafts which are slung between two mules, one in front and one behind. The motion is rather like that of a rolling ship, and, unless the occupant is a good sailor, the experience is not always a pleasant one. I once travelled for a week in one of these conveyances, and on arriving at our destination found my back was a mass of bruises. The takhtiravan is very good for night travelling, as you can lie flat down and sleep, provided the animals keep in step and the road is good. On an uneven road the sensation is not too comfortable.

We once had a never-to-be-forgotten week of torture in a springless wagon; it really was too terrible. Oh, the jolting, the jarring, and the bone shaking! Each day the misery increased, till every bone in our bodies was bruised and aching, and every nerve racked to its utmost. I should not recommend this mode of conveyance to any one contemplating a journey in Persia. When we first went to the Land of the Lion and the Sun, carriages were very scarce and very expensive south of Teheran. Now they are becoming much more generally used, at any rate as far as Isphahan. When we left Kerman in 1902 we drove to Yezd in a carriage kindly lent to us by one of the Kerman native gentlemen. Albeit the wheels came off occasionally and various other accidents took place, still it was a very luxurious way of travelling, comparatively speaking. Then, when we finally left Persia in 1903, we drove from Isphahan to Teheran in a private carriage belonging to a friend who lent it to us for the journey; so that I fully expect by now that travelling by carriage has become quite the ordinary mode of journeying in Persia.

PERSIAN CONVEYANCES

The takhtiravan is a slow but comfortable conveyance for travelling in. It is a species of sedan-chair, slung on two long poles; to these shafts mules are harnessed, one in front and the other behind. The Kajâvahs are a much less luxurious mode of travelling. They consist of two cage-like boxes slung one on each side of the mule. If the animal is sure-footed and the balance of the boxes maintained, the sensation of riding in them is not unpleasant.

The last part of that drive into Teheran has left a vivid remembrance on my mind. It was a Saturday, and we were very desirous of reaching Teheran that night, otherwise it meant spending Sunday at a village near the city, as we did not like travelling on that day. So we determined to push on at all costs. To add to our difficulties it began to pour with rain soon after starting in the morning, and continued a steady drench the whole day. Long before we reached the end of our stage we were both wet through to the skin. Sunset found us still some twenty miles out of Teheran, and, the horses beginning to show signs of fatigue, we perforce had to rest them for a while. When we were within five miles or so of the city, we found the road all flooded, and it was difficult to know where the road ended and the ditch began which ran parallel to the road on both sides. It was by then pitch dark, so there was nothing to be done but let the horses take their own way, hoping their instincts would lead them and us safely. All went well till we were within sight of the lights of Teheran, when suddenly smash went the carriage, and down fell the horses into a deep ditch. One poor horse (our own, which we were taking to Teheran to sell) never moved, and we thought he was dead. I jumped down from the dogcart and landed in the ditch nearly up to my waist in water! The lamps had gone out, and we were in total darkness. We called and called for help but no one came, so my husband and I walked on a little to see if we could find any one to help, leaving the horses and carriage in charge of the driver, who was half beside himself with fear.

A HALT FOR LUNCH

The midday break in the day's march is always welcome and refreshing, especially when it is possible to rest in the luxury of shade.

Presently we came across a little wayside coffee-house, and found some men who were willing to go and help extricate the poor horses from their dangerous position, while we walked on to the gate of the city and waited in the porter's lodge. After about an hour the carriage came along, the horses looking none the worse for their escapade. Our kind friends of the American Mission were waiting up, and had prepared hot baths and hot drinks for us, knowing that if we did arrive that night at all we should be in a terrible plight. Thanks to their kindness and thoughtfulness, we suffered no harm from our damp and adventurous drive.

The inhabitants of Persia are: Moslems, the Persians of to-day; Zoroastrians (Parsees), the Persians of yesterday; Armenians, and Jews. Of the two former I will not speak now, as we shall make their acquaintance a little later. A few words will suffice for Armenians and Jews. The former were brought from Julfa in Armenia many years ago by some former Shah on account of their industry and workmanship. He gave them a suburb of Isphahan to live in, and very soon a large Armenian settlement sprang up. Julfa of Persia is about three miles from Isphahan.

Here all the Armenians live, and until quite lately the Europeans also, as it was not considered safe for them to reside in Isphahan. However, of late years this is all changed, most of the Europeans now having houses in Isphahan.

The Armenians are very clever workmen in all crafts and trades. Also to their shame be it said that they are the wine and spirit makers for the Isphahanis. A true Moslem is not allowed to make or drink wine. Thanks to the Armenians, however, the temptation is ever at hand ready for him, with plenty of opportunities afforded him of indulging in secret.

The Armenians make very good assistants for hospital work, some of them turning out quite good doctors. One young fellow was with my husband for two years. After we left he went to India, where he took a medical course, and is now a fully qualified doctor practising in India. They have plenty of "push" in them, and once they make up their minds to get on, no obstacle is too great for them to overcome.

The Jews of Persia are a miserably poor, degraded class of people. Their lot is a very hard one; despised and oppressed by the Moslems, hated and cursed by all, their life is not enviable. They are to be found everywhere, in Isphahan, Yezd, Kerman, and many other cities. My heart often ached for these poor, wretched people as they flocked to the dispensaries. Fortunately for them, there is a Mission amongst the Jews in Persia which helps in no small way to brighten the lives of the poor, downtrodden people.

We have taken a fleeting glance at the Land of the Lion and the Sun; we must now try and become more intimately acquainted with some of its towns and their inhabitants.

CHAPTER II

KERMAN

Short history of Kerman — Its overthrow — City of beggars — Story of the fort — The jackal's "tale of woe."

"A little red worm — the gard'ner's special dread."

V. FANE.

The first view we had of Kerman was a very picturesque one. We had been travelling for about twenty days, and on Easter Eve reached a lovely garden some four or five hours' ride from Kerman, and here we decided to stay for Easter Day. Early on Monday morning we started for the last stage of our journey. Just as the sun was rising we came to the top of a hill, and there away in the distance lay the city of Kerman, the city towards which our hopes and thoughts had been tending for so long, as it was the goal to which we had been pressing for the past twelve months, and which we fondly hoped was to have been our home for many years; but God ordered otherwise.

Kerman is a very interesting old city, having passed through many vicissitudes and seen many changes during its varied and chequered history. It is also a very pretty place, especially as seen from a short distance, surrounded on three sides by the eternal mountains, with their ever-changing shades and shadows, and forming a magnificent background to the city nestling at their feet. On the fourth side the desert stretches away to Yezd and Isphahan.

Kerman is said to have derived its name from a Persian word Kerm, meaning a worm, and the legend connected with it is as follows. The princess who founded the city was one day walking with her followers over the site of the future town, and plucked an apple from a tree: upon eating it she found to her disgust and annoyance a worm at its core. As she threw it away in anger, she declared that the new city should be called Kerm-an, a worm. Kerman is certainly a very ancient city: the inhabitants claim that it was a large town in the time of Solomon. Whether this is so I do not know. The first time it is mentioned in history is by Herodotus. Alexander is said to have marched his army through Kerman on his way to India, and Cyrus passed that way on his return from India. Perhaps few places have suffered more at the hands of invaders than Kerman. It has been sacked at least six times, and in 1794 the city was almost entirely destroyed by Agha Mohammed Khan. The city was bravely defended by the prince-governor, who was one of the last of the Zend dynasty; he sustained a long and severe siege, till two-thirds of his troops had perished from starvation, and then the city was betrayed treacherously into the hands of the enemy and its brave defenders obliged to flee, only to meet with a cruel death some two years later from the hands of the same oppressor. This incarnation of cruelty, Agha Mohammed Khan, gave the city over to the will of his soldiers, who resembled their leader in cruelty and barbarity. There was no compassion in his heart, and he would listen to none of the entreaties of the unfortunate inhabitants for mercy, nor would he withdraw his troops from the city till he had received a gift of twenty thousand pairs of human eyes. When these were brought to him, he insisted on counting them over himself to see if the number was correct, and is reported to have said to the trembling man who carried the baskets piled high with these awful trophies: "It is a good thing the number is correct; if it had not been, *your* eyes would have gone to make up the exact number." The city never recovered from this terrible blow, and to-day Kerman is a byword among Persians for its poverty and extraordinary number of beggars. If you were to ride through the bazaars you would be struck by the tremendous number of beggars, all holding out their hands, beseeching you for the love of God to give them a copper.

There is a quaint saying among the beggars which one hears very often; it is as follows:—

"Khuda guft, 'Beddeh,'
Shaitan guft, 'Neddeh'"

(God says, "Give"; Satan says, "Don't give").

Just outside Kerman are the remains of two old fortresses, the larger of which is called the *Galah i Doukhta*, or the Fort of the Maiden, doubtless on account of the story connected with it.

These fortresses were built on small hills, and so alike are they in formation and colour to the soil that it is difficult to see where the castle begins and the hill ends. Between these two old fortresses lie the ruins of ancient Kerman. This city was the last to fall under the Moslem sway in its invasion of Persia, and the legend connected with it is interesting.

The city was surrounded on all hands by the Moslem invaders, and it seemed as if the enemy would be obliged to retreat, as its defenders had withdrawn themselves into the castles or fortresses already mentioned. These had been well provisioned for a long siege in case of need, and also were connected with the outer world by means of underground passages, known only to those in the castles. All, perhaps, might have gone well but for the fact that there lived in the fortress a beautiful woman—alas! as treacherous as beautiful. She was the idolised daughter of the king of the castle; nothing was too good for this loved and spoilt beauty. Her father showered gifts upon her—gold, jewellery, silks, all were hers; and it is said that just before the siege began her father had planned and designed a beautiful garden for her, such as never had been seen before.

Being so loved and such a favourite of all, she was allowed to roam at will within the castle walls, and often beguiled the time by watching the besiegers who lay far below in the plain. One day her attention was attracted by a handsome Arab general, who always seemed to be foremost in all that was going on, leading his men into the most dangerous and exposed parts. Where the arrows fell fastest and most often, there this Arab prince was sure to be seen, always brave and courageous. His bravery, added to his good looks, so appealed to this spoilt and petted woman that she immediately fell in love with him. Day by day this love increased, till her whole soul was afire with all the abandon of an Eastern love, and she felt that nothing could or should keep her from her hero. "Love" soon found means of communicating with the object of its affection, for love is stronger than barred or barricaded fortresses. By some means, known only to herself and one other, she gave this Arab to understand that if only he would promise to marry her, she would deliver the castle into his hands.

The Eastern as well as the Western agree that "All is fair in love and war," so this general of the East consented to this plan, and agreed to accept victory at the hands of treachery.

Accordingly, all was arranged satisfactorily to both parties, and one dark, moonless night the deed was done. The lady of the castle, the idolised and beloved of all, became the betrayer of her people. After all had retired to rest that night, and the sentinels were lost in the dense darkness, she stealthily crept out of the castle, safely passed the sleeping men supposed to be on guard, and opened the secret gate to her lover and his soldiers—the enemies of her father and her country. A terrible massacre ensued, in which the father was slain, fortunately dying without the knowledge of his daughter's base action. The prince-general had given strict orders to his men that on no account was the girl to be touched during the attack on the castle, but that she was to be conducted to a place of safety till all was over. At last, in the early hours of the morning, the general had time to think of his ward.

Tired out with his work of bloodshed and slaughter, but rejoicing in his unexpected victory, he sent for the girl to find out the reason of her willingness to thus betray her own people and land into the hands of the enemy. When brought into his presence he was amazed at the beauty and loveliness of the girl before him, and his heart went out in great love and admiration towards her. She, still thinking only of her own wicked infatuation, was congratulating herself that *now* her heart's desire was to be granted her, and she would soon become the wife of the man so long idealised and idolised. But alas! for her fair hopes.

The general, notwithstanding her beauty, desired to find out what her motive was for doing as she had done, and so he plied her with questions. "Was she very unhappy?" "Was her father very cruel to her?" or "Had she done this to avenge herself for some wrong?" To all these she replied in the negative. "Then, in the name of wonder, *what* was your reason for sacrificing father, home, country and all?" cried the general. "For love of you," answered the now frightened girl, and she then told him how kind her father had been to her, how he had done all in his power to make her happy, and how nothing was ever denied her that he could possibly procure, but assured him that all this was as nothing to her compared to the great love which she felt towards him, her lover, and ended by beseeching him, now that she had sacrificed all for him, not to cast her away.

At this the general was so disgusted and enraged with her, that he determined that she must die, and cast about in his mind for some means of death worthy of her selfishness and wickedness, "for," said he, "you are not a woman, you are a fiend, and therefore must die."

He therefore ordered his men to bind her with cords, face downwards, on to the back of a wild horse, and to turn horse and its rider into the desert. This order was carried out amidst heartrending cries and entreaties for mercy from the girl, but to all the general paid no heed, declaring that she was only suffering a just death for the abominable behaviour to her own people. The soldiers followed the horse for some distance into the desert to prevent its returning, and thus perished the beautiful traitress of Kerman.

I may say here that this form of death is not unknown even now in Persia, and I heard a story of a man who treated his wife in much the same way, only the idea was perhaps a little more diabolical. He was angry with her for some reason, and desired to rid himself of her, so he caught a cow, and kept it shut up without water for some days. Then he bound his wife under the body of the animal and sent it off. Of course the cow made for the nearest stream, and we can imagine better than describe the fate of the poor woman.

The Kerman of to-day is a large walled-in city of about forty thousand souls. This wall is pierced by some dozen gates, some of which are in good repair, but others are fast falling into ruin. In fact, most of the buildings in Kerman, as well as other parts of Persia, are "kharab shodeh"—that is, either in ruins, or fast falling into that state. The "kharab" buildings outside the town are the abode of jackals, hyænas, owls, and other creatures of the desert.

The story of how the jackals came to be inhabiters of the desert is told by the Kermanis with great gusto, and they quite sympathise with them in their banishment from the civilisation of town life. When in Kerman our house was outside the city, so we had the full benefit of the cries and wailings of these jackals, and at first it used to make me feel quite creepy, but after a time we became more accustomed to the weird music of the night, and missed the evening concerts when absent from Kerman. Sometimes the jackals would come right up into our garden, at other times their howling would come from the desert, like the far-away cry of a soul in torment, or the wailing of the banshee; but all night and every night the wailing, wailing went on, always crying for what they had not and never could have—never satisfied, and always letting people know the fact!

The story of the dispute between the jackals and the dogs of Kerman was told me soon after our arrival there. It is said that, in olden days, the jackals were the domesticated pets of the inhabitants of the town, and lived quite happily and contentedly in their respective homes, always enjoying security and peace within the closed gates, while the dogs had to be content to be dwellers of the desert and ruins, outside the walls of the city. One day the dogs awoke to the fact that the jackals had much the better time of it, and they did not see why this unequal state of things should remain. They were tired of being always outsiders, always short of food, and exposed to all the chances of wind and weather—so they resolved to make a great effort to obtain a position *inside* the gates, where there was plenty of everything. Being Socialists, they believed in the maxim of "share and share alike," so they called a committee to consider by what means they could oust the jackals from their comfortable quarters and install themselves in their places. After due thought and much discussion, they determined to send some leading representatives to the city to interview the jackals. This they accordingly did, telling them that many of the dogs had been ill, and the doctor had ordered change of air for three days. Would not the noble jackals allow their humble neighbours the dogs to exchange places with them just for three days, in order that the invalids might have a chance of recovering their strength and health. At the same time they enlarged upon the beauties of the desert air, which they said would be so good for those who had been cooped up in the stifling city for so long. The jackals, after long and careful consideration, agreed to this proposition, arranging to leave their comfortable homes for three days only, at the expiration of which time all were to return to their original places.

The next night the change was accomplished, and in the morning the people were all surprised to see dogs where the night before there had been jackals. However, they did not object very much. At the end of the three nights, the jackals came to the gates of the city and demanded admission, longing to return to their own haunts and homes, having found three days in the desert quite enough, there being no comparison between the comforts of the town and the dreariness and cold of the outside life. The dogs appreciated the change so much that they answered, "No, thank you, we prefer to stay where we are, and do not wish ever to return to the desert." So the poor jackals saw that they had been fooled, and went away sad and sorrowful, and every night since then have come howling for admission to the gates, and on the dogs answering "No," they go away wailing. And that is the reason why every night we can hear the howling and wailing of these disappointed creatures. And they will probably go on howling and wailing till the end of time, for the dogs are never likely to wish to return to the desert life.

Such is the legend of the jackals and the dogs of Kerman.

CHAPTER III

PERSIAN INDUSTRIES

Carpet-making — How to tell a good carpet — How to make a carpet — The cry of the children — Shawl manufactures — Calico-printing — Brass-work — Agricultural industries — Water disputes — Kanâts — Poppy crops — Wheat and corn — Tobacco-growing.

Saying in Persia — "One plum gets colour by looking at another."

"Do ye hear the children weeping, O my brothers,
Ere the sorrow comes with years;
They are leaning their young heads against their mothers,
And that cannot stop their tears;
... the child's sob in the silence curses deeper
Than the strong man in his wrath."

E. B. Browning.

The subject of the industries of Persia is such an extensive one that I cannot even attempt to discuss it here at any great length. I only wish to describe a few of the manufactures and industries which came under our notice while in Persia.

By far the most interesting of them all, to my mind, are the carpet manufactories to be found in many parts. Very few Europeans live for any length of time in Persia or other carpet-manufacturing countries without being affected by the carpet craze. They may try to fight against it, but they are almost sure to succumb, sooner or later!

When choosing a carpet the first thing to do is to make sure that the colours are fast. This is done by moistening a handkerchief or small piece of white cloth and rubbing the carpet. If the slightest tinge of colour comes off, the carpet is not a good one. So much depends upon the nature and durability of dyes used. In olden days, the only dyes used were indigo, madder, and vine leaves. From these three ingredients they were able to mix and make most delicate and artistic shades, all of which were "fast" colours. Now, however, the aniline dyes are so commonly used that it is difficult to find a carpet in which all the colours are permanent. Europeans are often deceived when buying carpets, but natives seldom! When the latter invests in a carpet he expects it to last the whole of his lifetime, and not only of his life, but also of that of his children, grandchildren, and great-grandchildren, and perchance be more valuable at the end of that period than the day he purchased it. As a rule he realises his expectations. When a native buys a new carpet the first thing he does with it is to put it down in the bazaars for all the traffic to pass over it. The more muddy and filthy the shoes of the passers-by, the greater will be the beauty of the carpet afterwards, provided the colours are fast. This statement may perhaps refer more especially to Syria and Turkish Arabia, but I believe it is also true of Persia. I have, myself, often seen carpets laid down in this way in the bazaars of Damascus, Beyrout, Baghdad, and Mosul. I could never quite make up my mind to allow our carpets to be subjected to this treatment, though my husband always assured me it was the only way for the carpets to acquire that beautiful silky gloss, so dear to the heart of the carpet-lover. As a matter of fact that gloss is maintained by the native custom of leaving the shoes at the door. The constant walking upon the carpet with bare or stockinged feet tends to bring about this desirable finish: whilst, on the other hand, our barbarous custom of wearing dirty shoes in a room is not so good for the carpet, nor are tables and chairs great carpet-improvers. Before the time of exporting carpets from Persia in any great number only good carpets were made, but now the demand is so great that to keep up the supply a good deal of shoddy work is manufactured and sent out of the country.

To be a good judge of a carpet you need to be quite an expert. Many things have to be taken into consideration. First the dyes, as we have already seen; then the number of stitches to the inch must be counted, and it is said that a good carpet contains about 10,000 stitches to the square foot, while some of the better ones have as many as 40,000. Another point to notice is to see whether both ends are the same width. This is done by doubling the carpet: if the ends do not coincide it is not a well-made carpet. Then, again, it should lie perfectly flat on the floor, otherwise it will crease in a very short time, and be worthless. My husband had a beautiful Kerman carpet given to him once: it was valued at £20, and, but for the fact that it does not lie flat on the floor, would be worth a good deal more. As it is, we have to keep it hanging on the wall, where it cannot get "rucked" or creased.

Prices vary, of course, according to the size and make of the carpets. Very fair ones, the size of an ordinary hearthrug, can be had from £2, 10s. to £8 or £10. Silk ones cost a great deal more, but are worth the money. A small silk rug can be bought for £50, but they can be obtained any price up to £500 or £1000. A mixture of wool and silk is now made to suit the European market, but is not so durable as the pure silk ones. It is generally acknowledged that the Kurdistan carpets are the best: they are the most expensive, being about £3 the square yard. The chief attraction of these lies in the fact that they are alike on both sides, and are very smooth and fine. Next to these come those made at Kerman, the design being quite different to those of Kurdistan. In the Kerman carpets it is not at all uncommon to find figures of men and animals, sometimes almost life size. Whilst in Kerman we visited one or two of the carpet manufactories, and were very much interested in watching the process.

All carpets are, of course, made without machinery of any kind. The warp is stretched on a loom, which is merely a frame. The woof consists of short threads woven and knotted by hand without the aid of a shuttle. When a row is finished it is pressed tightly to the rest of the web by means of a comb inserted into the warp. The "pile" is regulated by the amount clipped off. For a velvet pile the woof is clipped very close, till a perfectly smooth, even surface is obtained. The weaver does not see the pattern as he works, as he sits with the reverse side of the web towards him. The looms are generally kept in an underground vaulted room, often with water running through the centre. At each loom three or four workers sit, according to the size of the carpet. Sometimes the workers consist of one man and two children, and occasionally the owner uses boys and girls only for the weaving, one man acting as overseer to the children.

I sat on the high stool by the side of a tiny girl whose fingers were working away so fast I could hardly follow her movements. The overseer was walking up and down the room, calling out instructions to the workers. To me it sounded a horrible, incoherent jumble, but the children seemed to understand it perfectly. The overseer held in his hand a paper, from which he was apparently reading out instructions. Not having a very thorough knowledge of the Persian language, it was impossible to follow, but as far as I could make out it was something as follows: To No. 1. Three blue threads, one white, two green; No. 2. Four yellow, one white; and so on, each child repeating after the "master" the instructions given. As it was all said in a high-pitched monotone, the result was confusing and deafening, but there the little weavers sit, day in, day out, week after week, in this damp, gloomy cellar, kept hard at it by the unrelenting overseer.

The children are taken on as "weavers" when very young, some even starting when five or six years old. Their hours of work are from sunrise to sunset in the summer, and until two or three hours after sunset in the winter, and they are paid at the enormous rate of about 2d. a day, sometimes starting with even less, whilst learning the work.

The consequence of this abominable sweating system is that to-day there are hundreds of little children in Kerman, from eight to nine years of age, confirmed cripples from rheumatism and other diseases. From sitting so long in one position, while still of tender years, amid such damp surroundings, their little feet and hands become knotted and deformed. They can no longer earn their daily bread, so perforce must help to swell the great multitude of beggars who throng the streets and bazaars of Kerman.

I once saw a little girl about seven years old sitting by the roadside just outside our house. On asking her why she was sitting there all alone, her reply was, "Mother sent me to my work (carpet-weaving), but my feet hurt me so, I can't walk." She was waiting there whilst a companion in work and sorrow ran to try and find some one who would carry her friend to the workroom.

When we think of the sufferings of these hundreds of poor innocent children, do not our hearts ache with sadness for them? Surely the "Cry of the Children" of Kerman will go up to God, and He will have mercy.

In the meantime, because people want cheap Persian carpets, these little martyrs must be willing to sacrifice childhood's happy days, health, aye, and often life itself, on the altar of cheapness.

Major (now Colonel) Phillott, then acting British Consul in Kerman, was so horrified at what he saw of the state of these little sufferers, that he determined to start a loom of his own, employing men only to do the weaving. This he accordingly did, finding, of course, that the expense was enormous, as men's wages were so much higher than the children's, and also that they would not consent to such long hours. So long as children are to be had for a mere nominal wage, so long will the weavers use them, caring nothing for their sorrows, only bent on making money—the god of the Persian.

A NOVEL DRYING-GROUND

The dry bed of the river at Isphahan is used in summer-time as a drying-ground for curtains and printed cloths, which are manufactured in the city.

A soft kind of felt carpet is also made in Persia, specially in Isphahan and Yezd. These are called Namads. The materials used are wools of all kinds, chiefly camel's hair. The colour is a light ochre shade of brown, and there is generally a pattern woven in the centre of different colours, red predominating. Some of these Namads are an inch or more in thickness, and are delightfully soft for walking on. They make a splendid foundation in a room for laying carpets on. There is yet another kind of rug much used, called the Galeem. These are much cheaper than carpets, and are suitable for rough use, such as travelling. They wash well, but do not improve with use as carpets do, having no pile.

There are still shawl-manufactories to be seen in Kerman, though they are rapidly on the decrease. The best kind of shawl sells for fifty tumans (about £10) each, but there are others less expensive, which resemble the famous Cashmere shawls of India. These "shawls" are given as coats of honour by the governor or other high official, and are sought after and valued by all. They are woven in much the same manner as the carpets, and are made from the under hair of a special kind of white goat called "koork," which is only found in the neighbourhood of Kerman.

PERSIAN MODE OF IRRIGATION

The ox, who patiently walks up and down the inclined passage, draws up from the well a large skin of water, or sometimes an iron bucket, which empties itself into trenches prepared beforehand.

The silks of Persia are very pretty and durable. They are woven principally at Yezd, Kashan, and Resht. The latter place is noted, too, for its patchwork and embroidery. This work consists of tiny pieces of cloth pieced together into some floral or other design. I had two or three pieces of this work given me by a Persian gentleman of high rank. One is a study in red, and the other consists chiefly of black and green, enlivened here and there by bright patches of other colours.

Another rather interesting industry to be seen in Isphahan is the calico-printing; this is done by means of blocks, and, as a rule, one design covers the whole piece. These prints are used very much as curtains, table-cloths, &c., and have the advantage of being inexpensive. The natives often use them as shrouds for the dead, for which purpose special ones are manufactured, bearing suitable quotations from the Koran.

During the summer in Isphahan the bed of the river may be seen covered with these prints, laid out to dry in the sun after having gone through the process of dyeing and "blocking."

Space forbids my mentioning all the many other articles manufactured in Persia—the brass-work of Isphahan, copper-work of Kashan, silver of both Isphahan and Shiraz, mosaic also from Shiraz. But enough has been said to show that the Persians are a very clever and artistic race of people, and considering the primitiveness of their methods and implements, the results are astonishingly beautiful and charming. The agricultural industries of Persia, too, are considerable—the water supply necessary for these being a fruitful source of quarrelling and fighting, which sometimes leads even to murder. The labourers whose duty it is to look after the watering of the crops are armed with long spades, for the purpose of digging trenches and clearing a way for the water, &c. In a dispute these spades become very formidable weapons, and many a broken head have they caused.

Often when riding in the desert we have met a company of these men returning from their labours, each carrying his murderous-looking implement on his shoulder, and in the gloaming they resembled an army of soldiers marching. The water supply is very often conducted into a town or village from the mountains by means of kanâts, or long underground passages. Pits are dug at a distance of about 25 feet apart, each one being connected with the other by a subterranean passage, and so on till the place is reached where the water is needed. Sometimes these tunnels extend for many miles, and as the mouth of each pit is surrounded by mounds of earth thrown up, it gives the appearance of a succession of huge mole-hills running across the country. Great loss of life is associated with the sinking of these shafts from the constant falling in of the sides; on this account very high wages are given to compensate for probable loss of life.

One of the principal crops around Isphahan is that of the poppy. It is a beautiful sight to see field after field of these lovely white flowers, stretching away for miles, maybe. How sad to think that such beauty should lead to misery, wretchedness, and degradation! When the poppy is ripe, the "head" is scratched at sunset with a kind of comb in three places; from these gashes the opium oozes out. It is then collected in the morning before sunrise, dried, and rolled into cakes ready either for use in the country or for export. It is calculated that about 8000 cases of opium, each case containing some 200 cakes, are exported from Persia every year.

Although the growth of opium enriches those directly concerned, yet it tends to impoverish the country; for the ground which before was cultivated with wheat and corn is now required for the poppy, thus making grain much dearer.

There is also a large quantity of tobacco grown in Persia, which is used for the "kalian" (or water-pipe) and cigarette smoking. The best kind is grown in the neighbourhood of Shiraz.

Wheat and barley are largely grown, and are always reaped with the sickle. The land is very fertile, and with very little trouble a good crop is obtained, provided the water supply is good.

It has been said of Persia that "it is only necessary to tickle the land and it will laugh into blossom."

CHAPTER IV

THE CLIMATE OF PERSIA

*Resht, Teheran, Isphahan—Dryness of atmosphere—Cellars—Roof life—
Children attacked by jackals—Chequered history of work in Kerman.*

"The climate's delicate, the air most sweet."

Shakespeare.

When speaking of the climate of Persia, Cyrus is supposed to have said, "People perish with cold at one point, while they are suffocated with heat at another," and this may be applied equally well to the climate of Persia to-day, for every town has a different climate according to its height above sea-level. When we land on Persian soil from the Caspian we find ourselves some feet below sea-level, consequently the climate is very damp, and vegetation is profuse. The rainfall in Resht is so great that the wells are often overflowing, rain falling during quite two-thirds of the year. Always having thought of Persia as a very dry, parched land, our surprise was very great on reaching Resht, the port on the Caspian, to see such lovely forests of trees, and flowers in abundance, both wild and cultivated. Primroses, anemones, periwinkles, cyclamen, and many other kinds of flowers, all were in bloom as we drove through Resht on our way to Isphahan. The ferns, too, were splendid, maiden-hair and ox-tongue being especially beautiful. With all these homelike flowers and ferns around us, we could hardly realise that we were not driving through some dear Devonshire lane in Old England. But as we mounted, higher and ever higher over the Elburz Mountains, we soon lost this English type of scenery. The climate became dry and warm, till by the time we reached Teheran we were thankful indeed for the shelter of the comfortable quarters of our American friends, who extended to us the most hospitable kindness during our stay in that city. The climate of Teheran is very good; its winters are pleasantly cold, and the summer heat is not so overpoweringly great as in other places. Then, too, there are lovely summer gardens near at hand, whither the residents can retire during the warm months of the year. And for those who love the mountain heights there is the beautiful and picturesque Mount Demavend, rising some 19,400 feet above sea-level. This mountain adds greatly to the beauty of Teheran, both as regards its scenery and climate. It stands as a sentinel guarding the valley in which Teheran lies, and has an ever-changing beauty of its own, with its eternal snows catching and reflecting all the radiant hues of the rising and setting sun. It also forms a most valuable health resort and summer retreat for all the heat-wearied ones of the neighbourhood. This is the highest mountain in Persia, but there are many others from 10,000 to 13,000 feet high, so, if necessary, a cool climate is to be found at all times of the year. Once over the Elburz, the whole of Persia is a high plateau land, till we descend once more to the shores of the Persian Gulf.

Isphahan has a very pleasant climate; the winters are cold and bright, and it is possible to enjoy sitting out in the sunshine most of the winter months. The mornings and evenings are cold, but the days are delightful during the sunshine. The atmosphere here, as elsewhere in Persia, is very dry, and one's skin gets very cracked and "chapped," not from the cold, but from the dryness of the air. This is the cause, too, of much "nerve" trouble amongst the Europeans, especially, perhaps, with the ladies. In the winter the natives warm themselves and their rooms by means of a "korsi" (literally, a chair). This "korsi" is a contrivance for giving warmth at a minimum cost. A hole is dug in the floor of the room in which the whole family live. Into this hole is put a clay or iron firepan full of lighted charcoal: above this, the "korsi," a wooden frame varying in size according to the number of the family, is placed, and over all is spread a large "lahaf" or padded quilt. All round the "korsi" are placed soft mattresses and cushions, and here the family pass the time eating, sleeping, talking; the "korsi" acting as a dining-table and the "lahaf" as a covering by day and night. This arrangement is very unhealthy, but the natives love it, and the more friends and relations they can gather round the "korsi" the happier they are.

The summers at Isphahan are rather warm, but there are many places near by, which are cool, pleasant, and within easy distance for those whose business keeps them in the vicinity of the town during the hot season.

There is always plenty of ice to be had during the summer here—perhaps not always of the cleanest, but still good enough for the purpose of cooling fruits and drinks. The native method of making ice is rather clever. A "yakh khaneh" or ice-house is generally situated outside the town or near some running water: a trench is dug some two or three feet deep, and a wall from twenty to forty feet is built facing north and south, thus shielding the trench from all rays of the sun. As soon as frost sets in, an inch or two of water is let into the trench: this freezes during the night, and the next day more water is diverted into the hole, on top of the ice. This is repeated several days in succession, till about a foot or more of ice is formed. This is then broken up and stored in deep caverns or wells for use during the summer. The process is continued as long as the frost lasts, and thus there is generally enough to keep the town supplied with ice during the great heat. Well-to-do Persians have their own "yakh khanehs," and others use them for a means of livelihood. If the supply runs short before the hot season is over, frozen snow is brought from the mountains; but this is very expensive, as it has to be brought such a long distance.

Yezd has a much warmer "hot season" than Isphahan, and the heat is much more trying and of longer duration. The houses are essentially summer houses. The winters being shorter and much less severe, little attention is paid to the comforts necessary for cold weather, but everything is considered which will add to the coolness and airiness of the houses.

As a traveller approaches Yezd he cannot fail to be struck by the number of tall "chimneys" rising from the city, and he almost fancies he is approaching some large manufacturing town, and speculates perhaps as to the nature of the manufactures possible in such a sandy city of the desert. But as he draws nearer he sees there is no smoke rising from these "chimneys," and so concludes that, after all, they are not for manufacturing purposes. What, then, is the purpose of all those tall, square, chimney-like buildings, appearing from the roofs of nearly all the dwelling-places of Yezd? They are air shafts, built with the hope of bringing a little cool air into the houses during the hot season, when the atmosphere below is so stifling that it seems impossible to breathe. These structures are called "bâd geers," or "wind-catchers." There was a very large one connected with the house in which we lived in Yezd, and even on the hottest days, some air was always to be felt coming from the "bâd geer." It was so arranged in our house that after the air had been caught and brought down by means of the chimney, it passed over a "hoze" (tank of water), and in this way was cooled before circulating through the house. Another aid to bearing the heat in Yezd is the custom of spending the middle part of the day underground in cellars.

Some of these cellars are quite palatial, the walls and floors being made from the famous Yezd marble, which closely resembles alabaster. One such I remember very well: it was a room about 40 feet by 30 feet, very lofty, and lit from the top by windows on a level with the ground above. In the centre of this room was a "hoze" (water tank), of which the Persians are so fond, and rising from the water was a fountain capable of playing to the height of 30 feet; a large bowl turned upside down had been fixed on the ceiling to catch the spray and prevent it from becoming damp. Here the inmates of the house took their mid-day siesta, and very charmingly cool it was compared to the upstairs world. Some cellars are not at all healthy, and, if slept in during the day, the sleepers are very liable to contract malaria or some other fever. When dry and well ventilated no harm seems to come from this custom of retiring underground during the great heat of the day, and certainly a good cellar is a great boon to a European, and a great blessing when the thermometer registers 110 in the shade upstairs, while in the cellar it rarely goes above 86 or 90 degrees.

Scorpions, centipedes, tarantulas, and suchlike creatures have a good time in Yezd. The climate agrees with them, and they thrive and enjoy life to an alarming extent. One day my husband killed three scorpions within the hour, two of which were the poisonous black kind. Tarantulas abounded inside the house and out. They always seemed to make a point of running across my path during prayer times; to say the least it is very disconcerting to see one of these creatures glide softly past you with the evident intention of seeking shelter under your skirt! Our cat always used to make a dart directly he saw any of these tarantulas, just to draw our attention to them, but he would never kill one.

From life in the cellar we pass to life on the roof. This was often the most enjoyable part of the day. It is lovely, when the heat of the day is over, to lie and watch the stars, knowing that the same stars were watching over our loved ones in the Homeland.

A CHIMNEY OF YEZD

These tall chimney-like buildings are air-shafts, constructed with the hope of bringing any cool air which may be circulating above the houses into the rooms below. The above is a photo of the house in which we lived in Yezd.

Sleeping on the roof had its disadvantages as well as its attractions and advantages. One great disadvantage is the fact that the sun wakes you up so early; another, the talking and singing which goes on all round you from the adjoining roofs, often make it difficult to sleep. In addition there is this very serious drawback, that often the jackals visit the roofs of the houses at night, seeking for something wherewith to appease their hunger, and if they cannot find anything else to satisfy them will attack sleeping children. On several occasions poor little mites have been brought to the hospital terribly mutilated and torn by the jackals, some just slightly bitten on the face, others so mauled and eaten as to be quite unrecognisable. One especially sad case I remember; the poor mother was wild with grief, for her child, a baby of only a few weeks old, had been almost eaten up by these abominable creatures.

A KORSI OR HEATING CONTRIVANCE

In a hole made in the floor a pan of lighted charcoal is placed. This is covered by the Korsi, a wooden frame varying in size according to the family; and over this again is spread the lahaf or padded quilt. This arrangement serves as a table, and is an effectual but unhealthy heating device.

Life on the roof begins soon after sunset. It is very interesting to watch, from a height, roof-life springing into existence. First one and then another will bring out the family bedding, spread it on the floor of the roof or on low wooden benches, and then sit and chat till dinner-time. Very often the evening meal is eaten on the roof, and shortly after the family retires to rest. A Moslem takes great pains to have his roof well shielded from the gaze of onlookers, and if he is at all suspicious that he is overlooked he will immediately raise his wall. This being the case, the roofs in a Moslem quarter are generally very much shut in by high walls, which keep out the air and make the nights much less bearable.

The climate of Kerman is almost perfect for those who can stand it. Situated about 6500 feet above the sea, surrounded on all sides by mountains and deserts, the result is a delightful bracing air and invigorating climate. In Kerman there is no need of resting in cellars by day or sleeping on roofs by night. Indeed the climate would be hard to beat anywhere. The winters are charming, bright and cold, with snow-covered mountains always in view. For a month or two in the summer it becomes fairly hot, when flies and mosquitoes nearly drive one wild, but it is generally possible to get away for a little time, and during the remainder of the year the climate is all that could be desired. And yet it seems strange that in spite of all this Europeans have found it difficult to live there.

Our mission in its infancy had a very chequered career, owing to the breaking down in health of its missionaries. The first to open the work there was a Mr. Carless, a clergyman of the Church of England. He went there a young man in the vigour of youth, and at the end of three years, having gained the love and admiration of Moslem and Parsee alike, he was laid in a solitary grave away in the desert, in a valley surrounded by hills. After a short time his work was taken up by a Mr. and Mrs. Blackett, but the latter was able to remain only a few short months, at the end of which time she returned to England, broken down and shattered in health. Then my husband was appointed to open Medical Mission work there. Unfortunately, before the year was out, we too had to leave, this time on account of my health. During our stay there an English engineer came to seek for artesian wells. After two or three months he contracted fever and died at our house, and he too is resting in that quiet spot amongst the mountains by the side of Mr. Carless. On our leaving, another doctor was appointed to take my husband's post, but his stay in Kerman was not even as long as ours had been. And so it seemed as if the work there could not be carried on, but fortunately this chapter of accidents has now come to an end, for our missionaries have been living and working there for some three or four years. All agree, too, in saying that the climate is a very healthy one, provided the people living there have sound hearts!

CHAPTER V

HOLIDAYS IN PERSIA

How to ensure a prosperous journey — Natanz — Astonishment of natives at sight of hairpins — Pulivagoon — Mahoon — Aliabâd — Prince under canvas — Visit from a Persian princess — A Persian deer-hunt.

"If all the year were playing holidays,
To sport would be as tedious as to work."

SHAKESPEARE.

In a climate such as has been described in the foregoing chapter, it is necessary for the sake of health to get away during a part of the hot season. Fortunately there are suitable places near at hand to each of the large cities, so it is no very difficult matter to get away for a few weeks. The difficulties lie rather in reaching these places, and in transporting all one's belongings — at least all those that are absolutely necessary — to the place chosen.

After having decided upon the desirability of having a holiday, the next thing is to fix a day of departure. This sounds easy to say. Yes, it is quite a simple matter for you to say, "We will start on such and such a day," but you are perhaps reckoning without considering your muleteer. On the morning appointed you rise early, see that everything is in readiness, and then sit down to wait for the baggage animals to arrive. Time goes on, the sun begins to get hot, and no sign of the muleteer or mules, so by-and-by you send your servant to investigate matters, and he brings back with him the muleteer, who smiles sweetly and says, "Ensha'allah farda (to-morrow, God willing) we will start on our journey." His mules have gone to a village, and will be back "ensha'allah farda." We can console ourselves that very likely the same thing will occur again on the next day. It is always "farda" with these people, so we must try to possess our souls in patience, and hope for the best. Persians are never in a hurry, and cannot understand why it should make any difference whether we start "to-day" or "to-morrow." Oh, those endless "fardas"! how tired we got of them before we had been very long in the land. But it is good to learn patience, and the sooner you have mastered this lesson well, the happier will you be living in the East.

Preparing for a holiday in Persia is rather a different matter to starting off at home for the seaside or elsewhere. Everything has to be taken — pots and pans, tables, chairs, beds and bedding — in fact, everything that is necessary for four or five weeks' stay in a house where nothing is provided but the bare walls. It is wonderful what a number of things are necessary even for a short stay, in the so-called simple life.

The natives are very superstitious about many things when starting on a journey. For instance, it is very unlucky, in their eyes, to proceed if any of the party happens to sneeze on the point of starting. They would much rather postpone the start for a more propitious occasion, than disregard this bad omen. I heard of one man who insisted on continuing his journey in spite of the warning given in the form of a sneeze, and the consequence was he fell off his mule and broke his leg! The natives also are careful to have a good supply of copper coins ready when starting on a journey, to give to the beggars. Whenever we left home our servants always distributed freely to the poor who were living around, to ensure a blessing on our journey, but they never forgot to put the amount down in the daily account!

While in Persia we had some very enjoyable holidays, but as I could not endure the altitude we were never able to go to the mountains, which of course make the ideal summer resorts. However, we managed to find some very pretty and fairly cool places in the plains or on slightly elevated ground. Our first holiday in Persia was spent in a very pretty little village called Natanz. I had been taken ill on our way to Isphahan, and the lady doctor who came out to meet us suggested our going for a week or so to this little village before entering Isphahan. Spring was already well advanced, and it is difficult to recruit in the hot season.

Natanz is a picturesque little village, slightly off the general route, so that the natives had not then become very much used to Feringhis staying with them, and our coming caused no little excitement. We arrived there about twelve o'clock one night, and were conducted to our room by an admiring throng, and this throng continued to "admire" for the whole time we were there. The windows of our room were composed of lattice work only, so all interested could always have a good view of our movements. On waking in the morning there were our faithful followers to be seen with their faces flattened against the trellis work, waiting for us to wake, and see what we were going to do next! At times this interest shown on the part of the inhabitants was a trifle embarrassing, but as often as they were driven away by our servant just as often did they return again whenever his back was turned. For the first day or two I did not leave the room, but when I felt stronger I used to sit in a chair outside the window reading or writing. The moment my husband left me the women all swarmed round like bees, full of curious questions. Unfortunately at that time I was not able to talk to them, not knowing the language, but I could make out what they were saying to a great extent from their gestures. My fountain pen was a cause of great amusement and astonishment, as were also my hairpins. The delight of some of the women on being presented with a hairpin was very funny. They seemed to think I stuck them into my head, as into a pincushion. At first the women were rather shy, as they could not be quite sure whether I was a man or a woman, but one of them came and peeped under my hat and seeing I had long hair concluded I was a woman. My husband received a visit from the governor of the village, who was very delighted to see an English hakeem. We were quite sorry when our little holiday in Natanz was over, but being anxious to push on to Isphahan, did not care to prolong our stay longer than was necessary.

Our next holiday was in the summer of the same year 1900. This time we went only a few hours' drive out of Isphahan to a place called Pulivagoon. It was a very pretty little village, and a nice house, belonging to the Zil es Sultan, had been lent to us for a month. The house was built practically on the river, as our windows hung right over the water, and the sound of its rushing torrent reminded us of the lapping of the waves on the seashore in dear Old England. There were some lovely woods near by, to which we often used to take our tea, and pass the time pleasantly paddling, bathing, and fishing in the river. The following year we were at Kerman, and went for our holidays to a lovely garden about nine hours' ride from the city. Mahoon lies very high; it must be at least 6700 feet above sea-level. The climate is beautiful, but the altitude proved too high for me to enjoy it much. We had a very tiring ride from Kerman; starting one day soon after noon we rode for three or four hours, then had a refreshing cup of tea under the shadow of a large spreading tree. But we could not afford to linger, for we still had a good half of our journey before us, so once more we mounted our respective steeds, hoping to reach our destination about nine o'clock, but alas for our hopes! Nine o'clock came and went, and still we seemed no nearer; ten o'clock, and still no sign of our village. It was now pitch dark, and we were all very tired and hungry, and I was so dead beat that I could hardly sit upright on my animal. My husband rode close by my side, to be in readiness in case I should fall off in my sleep. To the oft-repeated question, "How much farther?" the answer always came, "Ensha'allah—only half-an-hour." Oh, those half-hours, how wearisome they became! I did so wish that they would say two hours or three hours for a change, for the everlasting half-hour was so tantalising. Our servants told me afterwards that they said this to keep up my spirits, as they thought, if they told the truth about the distance, "the Khanum's heart would melt within her." At last, just after midnight, we heard a very energetic coo-ing ahead of us, and knew that at last we were within sound of rest and food. It was so dark that we could not find the path leading to the garden, and our animals went floundering about over great boulders of stones or stumbling into ditches, and of course all in the wrong direction, till some one met us and conducted our tired party into the house. Here we found that our baggage animals, with Bagi and the other servants, had not yet turned up, though they had started an hour or two before us. They did not arrive till morning, so there was nothing for it but to lie down on bare boards and go to sleep supperless. The only drinking vessel to be found was a saucepan, from which we had a most refreshing drink of water and retired to our luxurious couch, sleeping as well and as soundly as if we were lying on beds of softest down. We were awakened about eight o'clock next morning by the sound of bells, and knew that our belated caravan had come in. While they were settling disputes and unpacking we strolled off into the garden to dip our faces into the cool water that was flowing through the grounds. It was, or rather had been, a magnificent garden, but, like everything else in Persia, was even then fast falling into decay. There was water in abundance, flowing on both sides, and fountains playing on the top terrace and also at the foot of the garden. The whole garden was built in a series of terraces, and steps led from one level to the next. The houses and gardens had been built by H.H. Farman Farma, at one time governor of Kerman, and must have cost a great deal of money.

We took up our quarters in the house at the top of the garden, and after a few days our consul came out from Kerman and occupied the lower one. We spent a very enjoyable month here, riding, shooting, bathing, &c. My husband opened a dispensary for the villagers, to which he went two mornings each week, and the people appreciated this very much, as I do not think they had ever had an English doctor amongst them before. We much enjoyed the use of the Persian "hammam" (bath) while there. It comprised a series of rooms built a little way off from the house; each room was built of marble and blue tiles. The first or outer room was simply for resting in, having a fountain in the centre; passing through this, you entered a large vaulted room, which was used for a dressing-room and "cooling-down" place; from this you passed to the actual hammam, which was a large tank of water about 15 feet by 10 feet, and from 1 to 6 feet deep, shelving gradually in depth from the edge. This had not been used for some years apparently, but my husband had it cleaned out and filled with fresh water, and we were very thankful for it during the hot weather. At first we tried taking our afternoon siesta in the outer or resting-room, but found it too feverish; however, we were able to sit in it during the early part of the day, and generally had our Persian lesson there, as it was easier to work in the cool. We always made our holidays a time for language study, as my husband rarely could find time for it while at work in the city, and we both longed to be able to speak Persian properly. I must say the natives were always wonderfully good and patient over our mistakes, and never laughed, however terrible and feeble our attempts at conversation might be. Unfortunately, just as we were beginning to feel our way in Persian a little, we had to start learning a new language, so to a great extent we have forgotten our Persian.

Our last holiday in Persia was spent in Aliabâd, a dear little village about ten hours' drive from Yezd. H.R.H. the Jalal el Dowleh (nephew of the late Shah) kindly lent us a house there, and as it was rather a small one, he erected a large tent in the garden for us, which did duty as dining and sitting-room combined. The Jalal also kindly lent us one of his carriages to drive from Yezd to Aliabâd. The first part of the way the road was very good. We left Yezd just before sunset, reaching our half-way place shortly before midnight. Here we had to rest the horses till morning, so we spent the night in a garden by permission of the owner. Spreading a rug on the ground, and using two of the carriage cushions as pillows, we spent a very comfortable night, and awoke in the early morning fresh and ready for the second part of our journey. We were off before sunrise, as we wished to reach our destination before the great heat of the day began. I shall never forget that drive. For the greater part of the way there was not even a semblance of a road, and the whole path was strewn with huge stones and boulders; it was a marvel to me how the carriage ever got safely over them. But oh, the jolting and the shaking! Driving up the Pyramids would be smooth and easy compared to the horrors of that road! We repented often of having accepted the kind offer of the carriage, as the saddle is much more preferable on such roads. However, all things come to an end to those who have patience; so at last this memorable drive ended, and we were very thankful, about ten o'clock, to see the trees of our village rising on the horizon. We found the little house very comfortably arranged and breakfast waiting for us in the tent, as our servants had pushed on instead of resting during the night.

Aliabâd contained, I suppose, some fifty houses, all of which were occupied by Moslems of rather a fanatical type. It was surrounded on all sides by mountains and hills, and this gave it a rather shut-in feeling at times. After sunset, too, it was very chilly and damp, as there were so many gardens lying under water at that time, this being the usual method of irrigation. I wanted to make the acquaintance of the village women, so I let it be known that I should generally be in the garden during the morning, and should welcome all who came to see me. In this way I saw most of the women, but they were not very responsive on the whole. It was here, sitting in the garden one morning, that I tried to learn from them how to "tell the beads" according to the Moslem method, but I found it too intricate and difficult. I managed, however, to master one very simple method of trying the beads for good or ill fortune. This was as follows: holding the rosary before you in both hands, you separate a certain number of the beads; then, closing your eyes, you "tell" them, repeating the mystic words "Adam, Eve, Satan," until the last bead is reached. If this happens to be "Adam," the luck is sure to be of the best; if "Eve," the result is neutral, and the beads must be counted again; while "Satan" indicates the worst of fortune, and would absolutely prevent any one from undertaking any contemplated action.

It was no uncommon sight to see the women counting their beads and mumbling to themselves, "Adam, Hava, Shaitan (Adam, Eve, Satan), Adam, Hava, Shaitan," before making up their minds as to whether they should drink their medicine or not. Or perhaps some patient has been advised an operation, and he is trying his beads to see whether the doctor's advice is to be taken or not. It is a strange thing that, when they *very* badly want to do a thing, they can generally make it come to "Adam," or else they keep on repeating the words till it does come to the lucky name, and then they are happy.

When we had been in Aliabâd some days the prince-governor of Yezd brought his "anderoon" to the same village. Of course there was no accommodation for them in the village, so they erected a town for themselves. It sprang up in one night, and looked in the morning as if a large company of soldiers had suddenly come along and fixed their camp. The ladies' quarters consisted of about twenty large tents, and were enclosed by a huge canvas wall, quite shutting them off from the outside world. The prince had his reception tents and others outside the wall, but quite near to it.

A day or two after their arrival the princess sent down her carriage for me, with a request that I would go and see her, which I gladly did, and found her surrounded by all her home comforts, and dressed, as usual, in some lovely silk costume. After this she always sent for me about three times a week, and we had walks and talks together. Whenever we came to a garden, she and her ladies always gathered the cucumbers and onions and ate them, thoroughly enjoying the impromptu picnic, and never giving a thought to the poor unfortunate owner, who dared not voice a remonstrance, however much his garden was stripped of its produce.

A eunuch or two always went before when the princess walked out, to warn off any of the dreaded menkind who happened to be about. One day the prince gave permission for his wife to come and call upon me. This was the first time she had ever been allowed to pay a visit. I was sorry we were not in our own house, as I should have liked to show her an English home. However, we made the place as tidy and home-like as possible for her reception. My husband had to be banished, and also all the men-servants. Bagi (our woman servant) prepared all the refreshments, but the princess's own servants handed them to her, as Bagi was a Parsee, and it would have meant defilement for a Moslem to take food from a despised follower of Zoroaster.

The prince spent most of his time hunting, and my husband went with him on several occasions. The sport did not seem to be very exciting, from all accounts. The Jalal would take with him about thirty to forty of his followers, and form a kind of cordon round the spot where the gazelles were known to be; they then gradually closed in, each rider knowing and keeping his own position. At last the gazelles would be sighted, and all would gallop madly towards the spot, and shoot as they got within range.

We were kept so well supplied with venison during those holidays that I felt I never wanted to taste it again!

Quite near to Aliabâd there were some large caves in which the natives had stored frozen snow, so that even in the height of summer we were able to have a large block of ice every day.

Altogether our time at this little village was very enjoyable, and we were quite sorry when our holiday was over and we had to return to the broiling heat of Yezd.

CHAPTER VI

SOCIAL LIFE IN PERSIA

Kerman—House-hunting and building—White ants—Housekeeping in Kerman—Servant question—Truth v. falsehood—Abdul Fateh—Bagi—Recreations—Some exciting rides—Persian etiquette—Dinner at the governor's.

"Society is no comfort to one not sociable."

SHAKESPEARE.

The social life of Europeans in Persia differs very much according to the town lived in. In some parts much life and gaiety are to be found, and in others this element is conspicuous by its absence. In Teheran, where we have our Legation, of course social life is at its height. At Isphahan, too, there is quite a large European community. When we were there in 1900 and 1903 there must have been at least fifty Europeans, and very happily and sociably all lived together. From Isphahan we went to Kerman, where for some five or six months we were the only foreigners, but in spite of having none of our own countrymen to call upon or visit, we were very happy. After a time a British consul was appointed, and we felt quite gay, and I at once started a European "at home" day, and every Wednesday our consul was a most regular visitor. He was always very homesick, and liked anything that helped to remind him of dear Old England.

On one occasion we actually mustered four Englishmen to dinner, as two travellers happened to be passing through at the same time, one of whom was Mr. Savage Landor, who entertained us with most harrowing accounts of his time amongst the Thibetans. Just before we left two English ladies arrived, so the social life at Kerman began to grow, and to-day it boasts of quite a number of Europeans, consisting of consuls of various nations, as well as missionaries, bank and telegraph employees.

HOUSE-BUILDING IN PERSIA

The houses are built chiefly of sun-dried bricks of earth and chopped straw, and then plastered on the outside. The bricks are generally made on the premises.

PERSIAN SHOPS

A peep into the bazaars of Isphahan. In these open shops all goods are exposed to view, and the passer-by is invited to take a seat and inspect.

When we arrived at Kerman we found great difficulty in choosing and leasing a house. Many were only too anxious to show us their houses, and to assure us that all their property belonged to us, to do what we liked with; but when it came to making definite arrangements it was quite a different matter. So long as it was only "talk" the various would-be landlords were willing to promise everything and anything, but it was quite another question when suggestions were made as to the desirability of committing those promises to paper. At last we settled on a house outside the town, which possessed a nice large garden, but the house itself only consisted of about two rooms, and these were in a very tumble-down and filthy condition.

The landlord (a Parsee) promised to build according to our plans, and to spend the whole of the first three years' rent in making improvements and additions to the house. The consequence of this delightful arrangement was that during the greater part of our time in Kerman building operations were going on, and only just as we were leaving was the work completed and the house made inhabitable. But in the end a very fairly comfortable house was built, and has been occupied ever since, I believe, by our C.M.S. missionaries.

Our garden was very large, but only half of it had been cultivated; the further end we had hoped to have made into a tennis court, but unfortunately we had to leave before it was possible to do so. All the bricks used for building were made from the earth of the garden. The process is simplicity itself. Water is mixed with the earth till it becomes a thick mud, then it is stamped into the required shape by means of a wooden block, and then left in the sun to dry. Sometimes straw is mixed with the mud, when it is necessary to have very strong bricks.

Directly we moved into our house I found to my horror that it was infested with white ants. This was my first experience of these wretched little creatures, and I hope it may be my last. They are disturbers of one's peace of mind, for once they are settled in a house it is impossible to get rid of them, and the only thing to hope for is that by continually waging war against them you may keep them slightly in subjection. I remember so well the day I first made the acquaintance of these noxious things. I had with much difficulty succeeded in finishing our drawing-room, and considering all things I may be forgiven if I confess to having felt a certain amount of pride as I looked at the result of my labours. Certainly it was not too luxurious; but it was comfortable and "homey." Alas! my pride soon had a fall. After a day or two my husband had need of some book, and upon taking it from the shelf found it eaten half through! I then began to hunt about, and found the room was swarming with these abominations, under the carpets, behind the pictures, cosily ensconced in books—everywhere they were having a right royal time. From that moment almost to the day we left, I never ceased to hunt and destroy these ubiquitous ants. We were having two new rooms built, and I said to my husband, "One comfort is that the ants cannot be in the new rooms;" but, alas, my hopes were vain! The builders had used an old piece of wood for a beam on which the ceiling rested, and this was infested with white ants, and so in a very short time they had *that* room, too, to revel in. I tried all manner of things to get rid of them, but found the most successful remedy was pouring petroleum down the holes from which they came. This drove them away from *that* hole, but they only burrowed a little further, seeking for a new outlet. Nothing could or can destroy them. As long as the queen ant remains they can never be exterminated. An English engineer who came to Kerman told me that, when he was living in India, he was building a house, and before he laid the foundations he offered large rewards for all queen ants found in the grounds near, for, said he, "This is the only way to ensure freedom from these pests." He also told me that one night he left his evening shoes out in his room, and in the morning the leather was eaten half away. I can quite believe this now, after having seen for myself their tremendous digestive powers.

One of our missionaries had to leave Kerman quite suddenly while we were there. Before leaving he packed all his most valued books into tin-lined cases and had them soldered down, thinking they would be safe against the intrusions of white ants. Shortly after his departure we suspected these wretches of being at work amongst the books, and so came to the conclusion we had better open and see. There, sure enough, they were, and busily they had been engaged too, for like "Mother Hubbard who went to the cupboard," when we went to the box we found it bare! if not quite, almost so; for, with the exception of a few stout leather covers, all trace of Mr. Blackett's valuable library was gone! Such are the literary instincts of white ants. But indeed nothing comes amiss to their tastes—books, boots, pictures, carpets, clothes, papers—all vanish under the business-like efforts of these horrible creatures. What with white ants and bad servants to contend and combat with, housekeeping in Kerman was enough to turn one's hair grey! The struggle was unequal, and I generally got the worst of it.

To begin with, the servants we had brought with us from Isphahan refused to stay in such an out-of-the-world spot as Kerman, so no sooner had we begun to unpack than first one and then another declared his intention of going, until we were left stranded. Then began the joys of servant-hunting. In some parts of Persia this is not a difficult task, but in Kerman it was practically impossible to find a decent servant, or one that knew anything about his work.

The chief drawback to Kerman domestics is the fact that they are all opium-smokers. The native saying in Kerman is, "That every fourth man out of three" is an opium-smoker. Although this may be a slight exaggeration, yet it was decidedly hard to find any one who was not addicted to this terrible habit. Awful specimens presented themselves as "cooks," but one look at them was enough! At last a veritable "Uriah Heep" offered his valuable services to us; he came armed with wonderful credentials and menu cards. These latter he claimed to have successfully negotiated when in the employ of some Frenchman, but I have grave doubts as to the veracity of this statement. On the strength of these menus we thought we could not do better than engage him; so he came, and proved himself to be a most aggravating specimen of humanity, specially formed, I believe, to try the patience and tempers of poor unsuspecting foreigners. Nothing ever put him out or ruffled his sweet amiability. How I wished it would, and that he would depart in wrath and anger at my repeated complaints against him! But no, nothing of the kind; he came to stay, and stay he did, till he bade us an affectionate and touching farewell on our departure from Kerman. His money accounts were always atrociously high, but so cleverly did he manage them that I could rarely detect him cheating, and at last I gave it up as a hopeless task, concluding the game was not worth the candle.

When we were alone his cooking was passable—at least it was generally eatable; but if ever we had friends to dinner he always managed to surpass himself with some act of stupidity or wickedness, I never could make out which it was.

KERMAN

A photo taken from the top of our house in Kerman, showing the
mountains in the distance and our garden in the foreground. The
circular roofs are those belonging to our kitchens, the round hole
at the top being the only means of ventilation.

On one occasion the English consul and one or two others were dining with us. We had safely reached the "sweet" stage, and I was just beginning to congratulate myself that this time, at any rate, our lovely cook was not going to disgrace himself or play any trick. Just then a "chocolate cream" was handed round. It looked all right. The consul took some, tasted it, and promptly laid down his fork; his example was followed by others. I hastily called the "boy" to bring me some, and on tasting it found to my horror that the chocolate cream was highly flavoured with naphthalene! We had lately received a box from home; in it was some of this useful stuff for destroying moths; doubtless the cook thought it was a nice and specially delicate flavouring for puddings! On another occasion I had been experimenting on some dessert dish, which necessitated part of the ingredients soaking for an hour or two over a slow fire. I put everything ready, and left strict injunctions with "Uriah" that he was to touch *nothing*, and so I left. Shortly after, feeling rather uneasy as to the welfare of my concoction, I returned to the kitchen, just in time to see the wretched man pouring my "Dream of Delight" down the sink! I confess to having been guilty then for the first and last time of boxing a servant's ears; but really was the provocation not great?

A STREET IN KERMAN

A corner of a street in Kerman, leading into the long, covered bazaar.

Another of our "treasures" was a man called Neamat 'allah. He was a splendid "show man," but no good for work of any kind. He shone when visitors came, as he felt the dignity of his Sahib depended in a great measure on him.

Then there was an awful boy, Rustem. I did my best to make him into a decent parlour-maid, but utterly failed. Although only about eighteen years of age, he was a confirmed slave to the opium habit. His chief *forte* was smashing crockery and telling lies. Of course we never expected our servants to speak the truth, but this boy seemed the most incorrigible of all. One day he said to me, after I had been trying to instil into his mind some idea as to why we should speak the truth, "Well, Khanum, what is the use of my speaking the truth, for if I did you would not believe me, and would only say it was a lie?" This is true, I am afraid, to a great extent, for after being deceived so often one gets sceptical about the possibility of a native speaking the truth, especially if he is an opium-smoker too. And yet sometimes they look at you so innocently, with such an air of injured righteousness, that you begin to wonder if after all they are not for once speaking the truth; but, alas, the wonder soon passes!

Shortly before leaving Kerman we were fortunate enough to secure the services of a real treasure in the person of an Indian. He came to Kerman with his master, Mr. Patrick Duncan, whose object was to sink artesian wells, but unfortunately he died before his work was completed. His man, Abdul Fateh, was heart-broken at the death of his master, as he had been with him for many years. He begged my husband to engage him, and very gladly we did so, and he proved a great comfort to us all our time in Persia, acting as "pishkhedmat" (chief servant), not only being good and honest himself, but keeping the others up to their work, and not allowing them to cheat us too much. Before leaving the subject of servants I must say just a word about our woman servant; she was such a dear little body—a Parsee. We called her Bagi, which means a female servant. She had been with Miss Sykes for a time, so knew a little about Feringhi ways. She was a picturesque figure, waddling about the house in her big baggy trousers and her gaily coloured overall reaching to her knees, while on her head she wore the usual number of coverings, in compliance with the Zoroastrian idea that a woman's head must be well covered! It is a great "shame" for a Parsee woman to be seen with her head uncovered. One day Bagi had been washing her hair, and the doctor happened to see her in passing before she had replaced her many coverings. She came to me in great distress to know what was she to do. The Sahib had seen her with her head uncovered!

The recreations of Kerman are confined almost entirely to horse riding. There are many very good picnic places near by, and an excellent stretch of desert for a canter or gallop, but not so good as the desert outside Yezd. When we first went to Kerman I was told that I must on no account ride through the bazaars, as no Englishwoman had ever been seen in them. I might ride outside the town and view the bazaars from a safe distance, but this did not fall in with my ideas at all, and as soon as we were fairly settled down in our house I asked my husband to take me to see the bazaars. So one afternoon we started off to try the experiment, taking with us two servants, one to walk in front and one behind, my husband and I riding our horses. I will not say that as we entered the dark, dreary-looking archways leading to the bazaars my heart did not beat a little faster than usual, as I thought of all the horrible things which had been told me as to what *might* happen when first an Englishwoman was seen in the open bazaar. After a few minutes, however, I saw there was nothing to fear, for beyond a good stare and a few curses from some of the people, nothing happened. I had, of course, taken the precaution of wearing a thick veil. My second ride through these same bazaars was much more exciting. It was during the time of the Passion Play in the month of Mohurram, referred to in another chapter. As we were riding quietly along we suddenly came across the whole company of excited, maddened creatures returning to their homes after the play was over. The crowd was headed by about a hundred men, whose garments were streaming with blood, their heads and faces covered with gashes of all sorts and sizes. In their hands they held and waved frantically their swords or daggers.

Our servants were fearfully alarmed, and hurriedly turned our horses' heads into a narrow passage, and hoped the crowd would not notice us. But unfortunately they did, and with a wild cry of "Feringhi! Feringhi!" they immediately formed up just in front of the opening to our passage and began their wild dance for our benefit. It was rather a gruesome sight in the dimly-lighted bazaars to see a hundred or more naked swords flashing, blood on everything and everybody, men yelling, shouting, cursing, and dancing. We were not sorry when in a few minutes they took it into their heads to move on, thinking, no doubt, that they had paid great honour to the Feringhis by this exhibition for their special benefit. After this experience I felt there certainly was no longer any need for fear, and since then we have all ridden and walked quite freely in and through the bazaars. Only once was I spat upon in Persia, and that was in Yezd.

Persians have often been called the Frenchmen of the East. They certainly are a most courteous and polite people, outwardly at all events, and are masters in the art of paying compliments to one another. But to a novice it is no light matter to know just the right amount of flattery to deal out, as it is almost as bad a mistake to give any one a great deal too much flattery as not to give him enough. The art lies in knowing just what is due to each person, according to the rank of life he occupies. When you wish to visit any one it is not polite to send word to say, "I am coming." You must couch your message in much more flowery language, such as, "I want to honour myself by coming to see your nobleness." The answer will be "Bis'millah—Please bring your tashrif (dignity)." There is great etiquette, too, over the kalian-smoking and tea-drinking, each one deprecatingly suggesting that his neighbour should partake first and the other declining the honour with a sweeping bow; but every one knows who is entitled to the first whiff of the kalian or the first cup of tea, and no one would dare to think of defrauding him of his right.

It seems such a pity that Persians of high class are gradually falling into European ways, for they do not suit these Frenchmen of the East half so well as their own manners and customs.

While we were in Kerman the governor was one who had lived in Europe a good deal, and liked everything done *à la* Feringhi; he much enjoyed English afternoon teas, home-made cakes, &c. Soon after our arrival there an invitation came from the governor for dinner the following week. On the evening appointed a carriage came for us and drove us to the "Arg," as the house of the governor is called. We found a splendid dinner waiting for us, served in French style, about twenty courses of excellently cooked dishes. After dinner we were amused by Persian musicians and singers. We were entertained by the nephew of the governor, who apologised for the absence of his uncle, who, he said, was suffering from a bad attack of fever which prevented his presiding at the table. We heard afterwards that the real reason of his non-appearance was not fever, but a fear of being laughed at. He knew how things ought to be done according to European fashion, and was afraid that he had not all the necessaries to carry out a dinner successfully, and so preferred not to show himself. However, when he saw how splendidly the first dinner-party went off he decided to give another, so in about a week's time we received a second invitation to dinner. This time the governor himself took the head of the table, and did the honours of it well, too. He certainly had nothing to be ashamed of, for everything was served in perfect French style. From the soup to the dessert, with all the intermediary courses, everything was dished up in perfect taste and on good china. The glass and table decorations would not have disgraced a European table.

The Governor of Yezd, on the other hand, preferred to hold more to his own traditions, and I have much enjoyed a meal there with his family, served and eaten in true Persian style.

CHAPTER VII

THE WOMEN OF PERSIA

Home life—Anderoon, women's quarters—Jealousy in the anderoon—Anderoon of Khan Baba Khan—Two days in an anderoon—H.R.H. Princess Hamadané Sultané—Visit to the anderoon of H.R.H. the Zil-es-Sultan.

"The more your prayers to me, the more will your wives be in Paradise."

From LIFE OF AL-JAZULI.

"Women are weak, as you say, and love of all things to be passive,
Passive, patient, receptive, yea, even of wrong and misdoing,
Even to force and misdoing, with joy and victorious feeling,
Patient, passive, receptive; for that is the strength of their being,
Like to the earth taking all things and all to good converting."

A. H. CLOUGH.

Whilst in Persia I had a good many opportunities of becoming well acquainted with some of the Moslem women, especially in Kerman, as there I was for some time the only Englishwoman, and naturally the women liked to see as much of me as possible, in order to see and hear about life amongst the Feringhis. The Persian women are much more volatile and genial than their Arab sisters, but on the whole I prefer the latter, perhaps because I have had so much more to do with them. The Persian lady is ready, the moment she sees you, to shower compliments upon you and to tell you how much she loves you, while her more austere sister of Arabia takes time to consider whether you are a person to be trusted or not; and if after a time she does give you her love, it is something worth the having.

When I first went to Persia I found the questions of the women most disconcerting, but after a time, if their conversation became too objectionable, I always told them it was not our custom to talk on such subjects, and they generally took the hint, at any rate for the time being. When in Kerman I started an "At Home" for Moslem ladies, and in this way I got to know some of them very well, and also by visiting them in their homes. They quite liked the idea of an "At Home" day, and I well remember our first one. About twenty ladies came, each one attended by a slave or two and a small boy to guard their shoes, which of course they left at the door. It was quite a business unrobing all these ladies from their black silk "chuddars," and arranging each lady in her respective place, according to the honour due to her. We had in our drawing-room a long divan, about 12 feet by 6, occupying the whole of one end of the room, and cushioned according to Eastern ideas. On this about twelve of the ladies seated themselves and looked very comfortable and at ease, while the rest sat on chairs arranged round the room, and looked most uncomfortable and uneasy. By-and-by I noticed first one foot being tucked up and then another, till most of the ladies were sitting native fashion on their chairs, and it looked so curious I could hardly keep from smiling. After all were settled, and their chuddars and veils carefully folded up and put aside by the slaves, then the kalian or water-pipe was brought in, each slave preparing the pipe for her own mistress.

I had arranged that my woman-servant, Bagi, should hand round tea, but the ladies were horrified at the idea of taking tea which had been poured out by a Parsee, as they believed it would make them unclean for I don't know how long; so my poor Bagi had to take a back seat and see others take her place. My next "At Home" day I was wiser, and secured the services of the mother of our syce, who was a Moslem, as I did not like to see a strange woman doing the honours of the tea-table.

THE MOSQUE GATE, CITY OF KERMAN

Amongst the ladies that day was the wife of one of the ex-governors of Kerman, and the good lady did not let any one forget that fact! They were always most interested in seeing and hearing all about Feringhi life, and were specially interested in photographs and pictures. One lady said to me directly she was seated, "I want to see a picture of Jesus Christ;" and on my showing her one, she most reverently kissed it and put it to her forehead. They much enjoyed listening to our little organ, and one lady was so delighted that she gave her husband no peace till he bought her one, and then nothing would satisfy her but I must go and teach her how to play. As her instrument arrived from Teheran with half its notes missing, it is easy to imagine that her musical talent (?) was somewhat put to the test. However, she was very proud of her instrument, and quite happy playing with one finger an accompaniment to some weird Persian song.

Of "home life" in Persia there is none; there is no word in their language for "home," and so it plays no part in their lives. Life in the home varies very much according to the rank of the husband. The poorer wives and village women are blessed by being obliged to work, but the better class have absolutely nothing to do, from morning till night, but smoke, drink tea, and talk scandal. The poorer wife is certainly the better off of the two, for she has to rise early in the morning to get her husband his early cup of tea before he goes off to work; then she has the house to look after and the children to think of and sew for; and last, but not least, the evening meal of pillau or kabob to cook ere her lord and master returns from his labours; while her less fortunate neighbour has nothing to do but to talk of the latest scandal of the anderoon, and then to pay a visit to another anderoon to tell and receive the latest news there.

The anderoon is that part of the house which is given up to the women, and is as a rule the best part of the house, for there the men of the house retire when their work is done, to be waited on and fussed over by the womenfolk.

When a man is well off and has more than one wife, he generally keeps them in separate compounds; but often two will be living together in the same anderoon, and as a rule they do not love each other very much.

The great and chief causes of jealousy in the anderoon are the children, or rather lack of children. For instance, a young bride is brought to her husband's house, and for a time she is the pet and favourite of her husband, and all is well; but if as time passes no child comes to cheer her heart, then the husband soon tires of his new plaything and looks about for a new and prettier one, till one sad day the poor young wife hears that her husband is about to bring home another to share her life and home. We can imagine what rage and jealousy will burn in her heart, and how she will hate the new inmate of the anderoon, and especially if after a time her enemy becomes the mother of a boy. Then her hatred reaches a climax, and it is by no means uncommon for her to have recourse to the "cup of coffee" either for herself or her enemy. That "cup of coffee" is a most useful (?) institution in Persia, as it is often very difficult to detect the poison hidden therein.

It is impossible for us even to think of the miseries through which some of these poor women pass; and if we see how unhappiness and wretchedness is fostered in an anderoon containing two wives, how much more miserable and awful must be the life when the number of wives is multiplied by two or even more.

But while there are many unhappy anderoons, yet as "the exception proves the rule" in most cases so it does here. For I remember one home in which two wives were living in apparent peace and happiness; but here, again, there was reason for their unity, as neither of them had any children, and so there was no cause for jealousy. Their husband was an aristocratic old man of about seventy years of age, and he had taken these two young wives to cheer his old age. He had a little son by one of his many former wives, of whom he was passionately fond, and this boy was very ill for some months, suffering from heart disease. His two young wives nursed this boy day and night in a most devoted manner, and apparently really loved the boy, and were very sorry when he died. It was owing to this boy's illness that we had the opportunity of spending two days in the anderoon of Khan Baba Khan, and very pleasant and interesting days they were too. It was the year that we were in Kerman, and we had just gone away for our summer holiday to that lovely garden of Mahoon, when one day a very urgent messenger came to my husband from Khan Baba Khan begging him to go and see his boy, who was very ill. The old man had sent his carriage for us, with instructions to his man to drive the doctor straight to his garden, situated some sixteen miles on the other side of Kerman, where the boy had been taken ill. As soon as we were ready we started off, but could only reach Kerman that night, where we rested, and the next day arrived at the garden of the Khan.

It was a very pretty garden, with plenty of trees and running water. On our arrival we were ushered into the room prepared for us, and in a few minutes the poor little invalid was brought in, and even then he seemed to have the mark of death on his face; but he was a very self-willed boy, and every one had to humour him in everything, as the fits of temper which he indulged in were very dangerous for him in his weak state of health. While the doctor was examining and prescribing for the invalid in another room the two ladies came to see me, and brought a very appetising dinner; chickens cooked to perfection and pillaus formed the staple part of the meal. The ladies then retired, and my husband and I thoroughly enjoyed our first meal taken together in a Persian anderoon.

After dinner my husband again visited the patient, and the ladies came to prepare our room for the night. This was quite an elaborate undertaking. First of all, a huge mosquito net was fixed up by attaching the four corners to tapes and nailing them to the wall. The underneath part of the net rested on the floor; on this the mattresses were placed, so that once you were inside the net you were in what seemed like a good-sized room. In fact, during the next two days we used to sit inside the net reading or writing, as outside there was no respite from the plague of mosquitoes and sandflies. Sleeping on the floor is very comfortable; in fact, I don't quite see the need of bedsteads, unless the room is infested with rats or other creeping creatures! The next two days passed very pleasantly; whenever my husband went out of the room, almost simultaneously I would hear a voice at the window asking permission to enter, and the ladies would come in for a chat. We became great friends, and this friendship lasted till we left Kerman some months later, and then the Khan lent us his carriage to drive to Yezd, as he wished to express his gratitude for all my husband had done for his boy. Unfortunately the boy even then was past human aid, and after two or three months of suffering he died.

I have always been glad of these two days actually spent in a Persian home, as it enabled me to see what their everyday life really was; but as I have said, this was quite an exceptionally happy anderoon, with none of the wrangling and quarrelling generally connected with the homes of Persian women.

While in Yezd I met and soon became very friendly with a most charming Persian lady. She was a daughter of one of the late Shahs, and thus was a princess in her own right; her husband was a nephew of the late Shah, so she was doubly connected with Persian royalty.

H.R.H. Princess Hamadané Sultané was in many ways quite unlike the majority of Persian ladies. She was a strong-minded, clever woman, and was very anxious that her children should be brought up in European fashion. These children certainly had a very good time compared with other Persian children, as their mother refused to let them become little women before they had passed out of childhood's days, and although they were then nine and ten years old were generally playing with their dolls or other toys brought from Paris for their amusement. The princess very much wished her children to learn English, but I suggested that she should learn it herself first and then teach it to her children. To this she gladly consented, and so twice a week I used to go up and give her lessons. She quickly got over the A B C stage, as she had some slight knowledge of French, and took a great delight in picking out the words of an easy English reader, and in a very short time she greeted me in very quaint broken English: "Good morning; I hope you are well." Unfortunately, I had to leave my interesting pupil at this stage, as we were leaving Persia for England, and I never saw her again; but I have heard that she continued her English lessons for some time. I do not think I ever knew any one with so many dresses as this princess had; every time I saw her she appeared in a different costume, and always in rich silks, satins, or brocades. I asked her once if she knew how many gowns she possessed, and she confessed that she had no idea, and added that it would not be at all right for me to see her more than once in the same dress! And I certainly never did, although I was visiting her twice weekly for some months.

This good lady exercised a very great influence over her husband (a most unusual thing in Persia), partly, perhaps, on account of her social position and also because she possessed a large amount of property in her own right. Before she came to live with her husband in Yezd she said she would only come with the understanding that she was to be the only wife, and I believe the prince kept to the agreement as long as she was with him. But he must have found it very hard, for I have heard that before his wife came no girl dared be out after dusk, so afraid were they of the prince and his courtiers.

One day I was visiting in the anderoon in company with the lady doctor who was attending one of the children, and lunch was announced; so the prince made us sit down with them and partake of the mid-day meal. After lunch the prince amused himself by vaccinating all the children he could lay hands on (not his own, but those of the servants). The children did not seem to see the joke quite so much as the prince did! They were much too frightened to run away, and stood trembling in their shoes waiting for their turn to come. At that time, too, no one in the anderoon dared say they had toothache, for if they did immediately the prince would call for his forceps, and out would come a tooth. Perhaps it might happen to be the offender, but just as likely it would be an innocent tooth which had never given its owner a moment's pain!

I shall never forget the delicious coffee which was always served when visiting at this house. It was a mixture, I believe, of coffee and chocolate; and I have never tasted anywhere such coffee. I asked the princess to give me the recipe, but my make never came up to the original, and I think perhaps they did not mean it to!

The princess was very fond of sending to Paris for boxes of goods on approval, and it was rather amusing to be there when the things arrived. Sometimes most beautiful Parisian blouses would come, quite unsuitable for her; but she loved to try them on and then put them away, never, perhaps, to be looked at again. I have very pleasant memories of my friendship with Princess Hamadané, and have as a *yâd gari* (remembrance) a lovely silver tray of Persian work, which she presented to me on our leaving Yezd; also the photographs of her three children—two girls and a boy.

It is quite impossible to tell of all the interesting visits paid to different anderoons; but I should like to mention some visits paid to the anderoon of the Zil-es-Sultan, a brother of the late Shah. He was then Governor of Isphahan, and my husband at that time was taking charge of the medical work there for a year.

The governor one day sent his carriage, with the request that the English doctor would go to see one of his wives, and also bring his wife with him; so we went, and had a very pleasant three-mile drive from Julfa to Isphahan. Arriving at the palace, we were met by the chief eunuch and conducted to the anderoon, into a large room surrounded by glass mirrors. Here in a far corner, seated on the ground, was "something" covered with what looked like a large white sheet. This "something" turned out to be one of the ladies of the anderoon, who was suffering from dimness of sight. She was one of the prince's favourite wives, and so he had taken the trouble to allow her to see the doctor. After a great deal of palaver she consented to lift a corner of her chuddar, and, while shielding the other part of her face, to uncover her eyes. Her husband was very anxious for her eyes to be thoroughly examined, and he ordered a dark room to be speedily prepared, so that the examination should be as complete as possible. While we were waiting for the room and lamp to be ready the prince took out a little pocket-mirror from his waistcoat and carefully looked to see if his hair was in perfect order, and then, having satisfied himself that all was as it should be, he entered into conversation with my husband over the state of his wife's eyes.

Another day I paid quite an informal friendly visit to two or three of his wives. Each wife had a separate compound to herself, and her own set of servants and slaves, and no wife was allowed to visit another without special permission from the chief eunuch or from the prince himself.

That afternoon two or three had asked for and received permission to drink tea in the house to which we had been invited, so we had quite a nice little tea-party, and a very gay one too so far as the costumes were concerned; but the subject of dress being so stupendous, we will leave it for another chapter.

CHAPTER VIII

MORE ABOUT PERSIAN WOMEN

Costumes — Wedding festivities — Wedding dinner — Kindness of Persian husbands — Story of brutality — Divorce — Aids to beauty — Degradation and cruelty of women.

"Women are made by men:
The nations fade that hold their women slaves:
The souls of men that pave their hell-ward path
With women's souls lose immortality."

JOHN DAVIDSON.

The indoor costume of the Persian women is not at all pretty or graceful. It consists of a short, loose jacket, generally made of some gaily coloured material, and in the case of rich women of bright brocaded silk or velvet, and a very short skirt, just the length of a ballet dancer's. In fact their dress is an exact copy of the Parisian ballet dancer. Many years ago all the women wore those picturesque baggy trousers, with long flowing garments over them, but while one of the late Shahs was visiting Europe he saw the ballet dancer, and his fancy was so taken by the costume, that on his return he ordered all the inmates of the royal harem to adopt the same dress; and as royalty always sets the fashion for the country, in a short time all the Moslem women of Persia had adopted this hideous fashion.

I remember so well the first time I saw this costume; it was the evening of the day on which we first arrived in Isphahan. After dinner Miss Stuart (the bishop's daughter) and I were walking on the roof of their house, when suddenly a woman appeared on the other side of a wall and began chattering with Miss Stuart. I felt inclined to look the other way, thinking the good lady had forgotten to complete her toilet, but seeing that Miss Stuart did not seem surprised, I supposed it was all right, and so began to feel more at ease; but certainly the first sight of these costumes is rather alarming, especially if the woman is not wearing the long stockings, as they generally do, but often leave off in very hot weather. On their heads they wear a square of white muslin, and flowing down their backs, and attached by a pin to their hair, is a long, graceful chuddar, generally made of a pretty muslin or silk; and as the women walk about the house, these chuddars flow behind, and look very graceful indeed. The ladies do not like the fashion of the short skirts, and many were the requests made to me to cut out dresses such as I was wearing, and if I had wished, I could have had my time in Kerman fully occupied in cutting out dresses according to European fashion; but with the exception of pleasing two or three of my special friends, I always told them I had no time for dressmaking, but would always be pleased to lend them patterns. So ashamed were some of the women of their short skirts, that they would often take their long, flowing chuddars from their heads and wrap them round their waists, giving the appearance of a draped skirt.

The outdoor costume of the Persian women is much more becoming than the indoor, though it is decidedly hot in the warm weather. It is made up of three pieces; the big voluminous trousers which slip over the feet and cling closely to the shape of the foot, but above the ankle fall full and baggy; over these are worn the large black chuddar, the poor wearing black calico and the rich silk; and then, covering the face, is the veil. This veil is a long strip of white calico with open work for the part covering the eyes, and fastened together at the back of the head by brass, silver, or gold and jewelled clasps, according to the rank of the wearer. Through the open work part of the veil the woman is able to find her way about, and see all that there is to be seen, while no one can see the face behind the veil.

To see a group of Persian ladies decked out in their silks and satins is a sight not easily forgotten. There is nothing these women love more than some festivity at their own or a friend's house, which gives them an opportunity of showing off their finery, and also of meeting all their acquaintances, and having a good "gufti goo" (chat). I was often invited when in Kerman upon these occasions, but found, if I accepted all invitations, my time would be taken up with going to betrothal feasts, weddings, &c., and so I used to look in for a few minutes and then excuse myself. On one occasion I went to a wedding at the house of one of the chief mullahs of the town. I was asked to go at sunrise, but did not put in an appearance till about nine o'clock. When I arrived, all the guests had been there already some hours; it was certainly a very pretty sight. Two large compounds were given up to the entertainment of the bride's party, while the bridegroom was holding his reception in another house.

As I entered the door leading into the anderoon, I could but stand and admire the scene before me. Quite two hundred ladies were present, each one dressed in gorgeous silks and satins, and all wearing the graceful chuddar falling from the head. The majority of these chuddars were of silk—Indian, Japanese, or Persian silks, all vying with each other in their brilliancy and beauty. Some were rainbow silks, all colours merging into each other; then again, others were gaily flowered, and others "shot" or lustre silks—the whole forming a wonderfully harmonious and striking picture, and I longed for a camera that might give a true representation, both in colour and vivacity, of this butterfly scene before me. To add to the gayness of their attire, each married lady was wearing a spray or wreath of flowers in her hair, and many carried or wore bouquets of roses. The whole effect was charming, and formed a marvellous study of colour, gracefulness, and Eastern beauty.

We have kept our hostess waiting quite a long time while we have been admiring her guests, but now we must hasten to pay our respects to her, and take our seat amongst this gay throng. I was alone that day, being the only European woman in the town; but it will be much more pleasant if my readers will come with me in imagination to that wedding feast.

We are ushered into a large room full of gay ladies, who immediately all rise from the ground as we enter, and salaam us. It is rather difficult to know which is our hostess amongst so many, so we must be impartial in our salutations, and pray God that "their kindnesses may never grow less," or "their hands never pain them," &c. Then we all take our seats, and conversation is resumed. The ladies will begin with a series of questions, such as—

"How old are you?" "Have you a mother?" "Why do you not black your eye-brows?" "Are you happy?" "Is your husband kind to you?" "Do you like him?" "How much did your dress cost?" and so on, like a group of children—and when you think they have finished, they will begin again. After a short interval tea is handed round. Tea, did I say? well, it is dignified by that name, but in reality Persian tea is not much more than sweetened water coloured with a drop of tea. To begin with, the cups are very tiny, generally made of glass. They are first filled up with three or four lumps of sugar, then a teaspoonful of tea is poured over these, and water added until the cup is full, and the result is—Persian tea! However, it is rather pleasant to drink, and helps to pass the time. After a short interval more tea is handed round, and then glasses of sherbet, made from juices of different fruits, and then, for a change, coffee is served.

About noon, just as I am afraid we are all feeling very tired and sleepy, a welcome change comes; a stirring and commotion begins in the courtyard, women rush about with enormous trays on their heads and carrying all kinds of dishes: this is but a prelude to dinner being announced. Two large rooms are laid out for dinner; in each room about one hundred guests sit down. I was taken in by the mother of the bridegroom, so we will all pass in under her protection. (The mother of the bride is not in evidence on these occasions, being supposed to be overwhelmed with grief at losing her daughter.) The "table" is the ground, so we must gracefully (?) sit on our heels. On the "table" are over two hundred different dishes—pillaus, chillaus, chicken, kabobs, vegetables, fruits—all laid out in tempting array. The hostess having pronounced the Moslem benediction, "Bismi'llah" (In the name of God), all the guests fall to work in real earnest: very little talking is done, eating being the business of the moment. Spoons and forks were provided for me, but I preferred to do as they did, and so ate with my fingers, though it requires a good deal of practice to do it neatly and gracefully. As a mark of respect and honour, the hostess from time to time breaks off pieces of meat from her portion and places them on my plate, and once as a special mark of favour placed a dainty morsel of chicken in my mouth. I hope my readers have enjoyed their dinner as much as I have, for to my mind a Persian feast is a most delectable entertainment.

After dinner we all washed our hands in a basin brought round for the purpose, the water being poured from an ewer on to our hands by a servant. Then we all retired to our reception-room of the morning, and again tea and sherbet were handed round, and the kalian or water-pipe was much in request, each lady taking a whiff and passing the long tube to her neighbour.

But where is the poor little bride all this time? We have neither seen nor heard her all day long, and yet the feast is supposed to be in her honour. All through the long, hot June day she has been cooped up in a tiny room, and as sunset approaches her friends and relations go to dress her and to decorate her from head to foot with jewellery and finery. Into her hair is woven a quantity of golden thread, so that in the distance it looks like a mass of gold, and must be very heavy on the poor tired little head. She is brought out into a large room, and seated on a chair in the middle of it; then every one goes up to her, and after kissing her, says, "May you be blessed." The poor little mite (she might be thirteen years old, but hardly looks it) seems absolutely wretched and miserable, and when food is brought to her refuses to eat. Just at sunset she is taken to her husband's house in a closed carriage, and our hearts must ache as we think of what is in store for her. Even if her husband is kind to her at first, yet she has nothing much to look forward to but misery and degradation, and if by chance she goes to an anderoon already containing two or three wives, then may God take pity on her, for her fate will be a sad one. As soon as a man marries a girl she is absolutely his property, and he may do exactly as he pleases with her; there is no redress for the poor unfortunate girl. If the man is a brute and half kills his wife no one dare say a word to him, or if perchance there is one brave enough, he will only be told that "the girl is his wife, and he can do as he likes with his own," and so it is no wonder if the shadow of the future lies darkly on the faces of those poor little children, as they leave their mother's home as brides to go out into the unknown which lies before them.

I remember a poor little girl who was brought to the hospital in Julfa, while we were there. She had been married to a brutal man, when about eleven years old. Being very unhappy with him, she often used to run away and take refuge with her mother, who lived in a village a mile or two away from her husband's house. On many occasions he had beaten her severely for some childish fault, and each time she had fled to her mother, and stayed with her till her husband came and carried her off again by force. This went on for some time, till the poor child's life was nothing but wretchedness and misery.

One day she displeased her husband by not cooking the dinner to his liking, and he was so enraged with her that he behaved in the following abominable manner.

First of all he saw that the windows of his house were barricaded and the door locked: then he stripped the trembling, frightened child, and deliberately poured paraffin oil all over her body, and finally set a light to her and left her to her fate, taking care to lock the door after him, as he went out. The neighbours, hearing the girl's screams, rushed to the house, but the doors being locked and the windows fastened much precious time was wasted. When they finally smashed open the window it was only to find the child a mass of flames. They picked her up and rushed wildly with her into the street, and dropped her into the nearest stream to quench the flames! It was a marvellous thing to think that after all this there was any life left in the poor child. The neighbours took her to her mother, who plastered all her wounds with red earth and left her lying in the corner of the room for some ten days. Then, taking the advice of some friends, they procured a cradle and lifted the poor wee child into it, and hoisted the cradle and its occupant on the back of a donkey, and took her some five days' journey to Julfa. They had heard of the Mission Hospital through some of their villagers, who had been treated there, and so they brought this little victim of Persian cruelty to the lady doctor, who took her in, dressed her wounds, and laid her in a clean, comfortable bed. All that human love and kindness could do was done to alleviate her sufferings, but nothing could save her life, and after three days she passed away—a martyr indeed to the creed of Islam, which enables and allows men to treat their women as something lower than the beasts of the field.

Ought not the cries of distress and agony from the poor women of Persia so to rouse us, their sisters in England, that we shall determine to do all that lies in our power to lighten their burdens and to bring some rays of light into the dark lives of our Eastern sisters?

One thing which adds greatly to the misery of these women is the ease with which their husbands can divorce them. A wife never knows from day to day whether or no her lord may not divorce her. Often for most trivial matters a man will cast away his wife. This being the case, the woman will lie and deceive her husband in order to escape divorcement. If the wives of Persia could only be raised to the level of true womanhood I believe they would become good wives and mothers, but while they are what they are, how can there be any hope for them? There is nothing but utter darkness till the true Light shines into their lives, and then and then only will the day break for these downtrodden, degraded beings.

The Persian ladies are great beauty specialists, and bestow a good deal of attention upon their complexion and general make-up. They do not believe in beauty unadorned, for even when quite young they use the rouge-pot very freely, and often use it to great advantage too! I have often known a girl who was quite ordinary-looking, sallow and dark in complexion, but when dressed for her wedding I hardly recognised her, so changed was she by all the numerous "aids" to beauty. Her cheeks were now a lovely rose tint, and her eyebrows darkened and lengthened till they almost met in the middle, and the edges of her eyelids were also blackened with "kola," and really the effect was very good.

They also spend much time and trouble in dyeing their hair with henna, not only from a fear of grey hair, but also because the dull red tint produced by henna is the fashionable colour.

The Persian lady has very little in her life to elevate or refine her mind, and so we cannot wonder if at times we see in her many revolting characteristics. When we think of all she has to endure, and how little happiness comes to her lot, our wonder is that she retains even a semblance of womanhood. Should we be any better under like circumstances?

If a woman is treated continually as if she was nothing but a beast of burden, is it to be wondered at that in some cases her nature becomes almost as the beasts of the field? Weird stories are told of the extremities to which women have been driven, and the cruelties which they have perpetrated.

The following is one which I heard when in Persia. It was in the days when famine was rampant throughout the land. There was a certain man of high position who collected and stored all the corn he could gather, and then refused to sell at anything but famine prices; finally he was arrested and sent to Teheran, where he was tried and condemned to death. The Shah could not determine on the manner of death to be ordered for this rascal, but at last decided to hand the unfortunate man over to the mercies of the royal anderoon to be put to death by them. The ladies and women servants consulted together, and decided to keep the wretch in their quarters and kill him by inches, day by day. The method they chose was to cut him to pieces with scissors till he died!

I cannot vouch for the truth of this story, and I trust it is not true, but I give it to you as I heard it. But one thing I know to be true, and that is, when a Persian woman is once roused to anger, jealousy, and passion, there is hardly anything too dreadful for her to contemplate doing, in her longing for revenge.

CHAPTER IX

SOME POINTS IN THE MOSLEM FAITH

Fasts and Feasts—Seyyids, dervishes, mullahs—Legends of the drowning mullah, and the yard square hole.

"Religion's all or nothing."

R. Browning.

There are five things which every true Mohammedan must either believe or do. The first is the declaration of their faith or "Kalimat." "I declare that there is no God but God, and Mohammed is His Apostle;" "La Allaha il Allah wa Mohammed rasool Allah," this is the all-important witness, and must be continually recited by all true believers. Secondly, Moslems are bound to repeat prayers five times a day—at daybreak, noon, shortly before sunset, during twilight, and an hour after dark. I do not say all Moslems do repeat prayers at each of these times, but that is their rule, and those who consider themselves *good* Moslems adhere most righteously to these set times for prayers. Needless to say, it is but a form of words and position, any slight error in posture taking away all the benefit to be derived from the prayer. Often in Persia women have said their prayers in our drawing-room, if the call to prayer sounded while they were visiting me.

Living in the East, one gets very fond of the call to prayer, heard from some neighbouring minaret. The first sound that catches the ear at daybreak is "Allah, Allaho Akhbar" (God is most great), repeated four times. "La Allaha il Allah wa Mohammed rasool Allah"—this is said twice, and then other calls and invocations, always finishing up with the final declaration of "Allah, Allaho Akhbar."

There is a great difference in the way this call to prayer is chanted, some men having most melodious voices, others harsh and grating; but wherever a true Moslem may be when he hears this call, he lays aside his work at once and begins to repeat his prayers, bowing, prostrating, touching the ground with his forehead, &c., till the duty is finished, when he returns to his work, perhaps to his cheating and his lying, for this repetition of prayers has no effect on his life or manner of living.

Thirdly, all good Moslems are supposed to give voluntarily to the mullahs a tithe of all they possess, also alms to the poor. In the Koran we read, "Prayer carries us half way to God, fasting brings us to the door of His palace, but giving of alms procures admission." In many cases the mullahs are provided for entirely by the freewill offerings of the people, all gifts being sent anonymously.

Fourthly, every true believer is expected to undertake, if at all possible, a pilgrimage, preferably to Mecca, but if that is out of the question then to Kerbela or Meshed. The former, of course, brings the greatest merit, and men and women will do all they can to perform this pilgrimage. On their return they are treated with great respect, and looked up to as little gods. They generally think so much of themselves after having performed this wonderful act of self-denial that they become quite unbearable to their friends. There is an Arabic proverb which shows the effect this pilgrimage to Mecca is supposed to have on the pilgrim. It is as follows: "If your friend has been to Mecca, trust him not. If he has been there twice, avoid him. But if he has made the pilgrimage three times, then flee from him as you would from Satan himself."

Women often undertake these pilgrimages, spending weeks or months it may be over the journey, but resting for ever afterwards in the great glory and honour resulting from it.

The fifth point to be observed by Moslems is that of fasting during the month of Ramadan. This lasts for thirty days, and is a real hardship for the poorer people when the fast falls during the summer, as from sunrise to sunset not a morsel of food or drop of water may pass their lips — or, as the Koran expresses it, from "the time you can distinguish between a white thread and a black, then keep the fast until night." For the rich and idle it is no great effort, for they simply feast and revel all night and sleep by day, but for the servants and labouring class it comes harder, as they must work by day and cannot sleep properly at night. Children are always very anxious to begin fasting, and often little mites of five or six will tell you with great pride that they are keeping the fast. They generally start by fasting for half days, and how proud they are, and how they gloat over other children who have not yet begun this work of devotion! Perhaps what the people who fast miss more than anything else during Ramadan is their smoking: they are such slaves to this habit, both men and women, that it is almost life to some of them, and they find it very hard to go without. When the cannon booms forth the hour of sunset, giving the Prophet's permission to his faithful ones to break their fast, generally the first thought, after moistening their lips with water, is that now they may enjoy their smoke, either of a cigarette or kalian.

Mohurram is the month of mourning, when all the country mourns for Hassain and Hussein, the martyred sons of Ali, who are looked upon by the Shiahs as the rightful successors of the Prophet. During this season the majority of the people go into deep mourning, and the bazaars are sometimes draped in black. It is in this month that the great Passion Play of Persia is enacted, and while in Kerman we were fortunate enough to have an opportunity of witnessing this "tazieh," as the Passion Play is called. It certainly was a sight worth seeing at least once in a lifetime.

The tenth day of this month of Mohurram is the one set aside for this festival, and is kept as a general holiday, so that all might go to see the great spectacle enacted on that day in memory of the death of Hassain and Hussein, the two grandsons of Mohammed.

The Governor of Kerman had kindly invited us to view the performance from his house, and accordingly that morning at about eight o'clock he sent his carriage for us, and we were driven through the packed bazaars till we arrived at his house, or "Arg," as the governor's residence is called in Kerman. We were at once admitted by a private entrance, and ushered into a large verandah, which had been set apart for the use of Feringhis. As my husband and I were the only Europeans in the city at that time, we had it to ourselves. Here, before the commencement of the Play, we were regaled with tea, coffee, jam, bread, cheese, and cakes. Looking out, the sight was a wonderful one. In front of us was a large garden in which I suppose some 10,000 people were gathered. At one end of the garden was a large "hoze" or tank of water, over which was spread a huge awning, and near by a large pulpit from which the mullahs preached to the people, and tried to rouse their feelings to a high pitch of excitement. One man was specially successful in doing this, causing the women to wail wildly and beat their breasts frantically, and the men to smite their heads. After a delay of about an hour, the performance began with a long procession, which entered the garden at the far end and wound in and out till it had traversed the whole garden. This procession represented the family travelling as captives after the death of Hassain and his brother.

First of all came six gaily decorated camels, with men riding upon them, beating drums and making a tremendous noise. Then came more camels carrying the tent furniture and other goods, followed by horses and mules laden with heavy loads. After these came four stretchers borne by men, on which lay four dead bodies (figures stuffed) representing Hassain and his three brothers, who perished from want of water, which had been cut off from them by their enemies. On each dead body sat a dove, supposed to be mourning. Then came a horrible sight, one which I never wish to see again. About a hundred madly excited men dressed in long white robes, armed with swords, were slashing their heads until the blood was streaming down their faces on to the robes, white, alas, no longer! As they reached the tank of water they formed into a line all round it, and kept up for some length of time a horrible kind of war dance. It was a ghastly sight. The dancers looked more like demons than men. One poor man fainted from loss of blood, and had to be carried away, and a little boy of about eight years of age also collapsed. It was bad enough to see grown men cutting themselves, but to see the little children being wounded in this way was terrible. This is, of course, looked upon as a work of great merit. The more numerous and deeper the gashes, the greater the merit they accrue to themselves. The wild dance was continued till a sign was given to the dancers by the governor, that he had seen enough to satisfy him. Then they all lined up in front of the verandah where the governor was sitting, and demanded that five notorious prisoners should be released from the prison close by. He at once acceded to their request, as it was the custom at this festival for the governor to release from the prison any prisoners who are interceded for by these wild, fanatical dancers.

After this ghastly sight came a motley crowd of men and children on horses, all beating their breasts or heads. Some of the riders were so tiny that they had to be held on to their steeds by men-servants.

Then came another body on a bier, with a man dressed in a lion's skin, embracing and fondling the dead body. It looked so weird to see the pseudo-lion kissing and hugging the remains of its late friend and master, and expressing in various ways great sorrow and anguish over its loss.

After this came several batches of boys stripped to the waist, all beating their breasts. It was really a very pretty sight, for the boys kept such perfect time, one boy acting as leader, like a group of children performing gymnastic exercises. As their hands simultaneously clapped their breasts, there was a sharp report, at which they all shouted "Hassain! Hussein! Hassain! Hussein!" The whole proceeding was an interesting but sad spectacle, which I shall never forget. The clash of swords, the beating of drums, the weird wailing of the women, accompanied by their spasmodic shrieks, the shouting and yelling of the fanatical mob, all contributed to the making up of one of the most notable scenes of Eastern life. And yet it made one's heart ache to watch this crowd of human beings for whom Christ died, and who as yet know nothing of Him, but are only anxious to obtain merit for themselves by taking part in these gruesome religious performances.

All over Persia "religious men" are much looked up to and respected. Of these the dervish is one very much to the fore. He is a religious mendicant, having taken a vow either for a certain time or permanently. The vow is not a very strict one, only consisting of poverty and obedience to a chief, to whom a portion of the alms received must be paid.

These dervishes wander from place to place, chanting, singing, and begging. The natives do not like to refuse them anything, from fear more than love, perhaps, as it is considered meritorious to give alms to these religious people.

They generally dress in dirty white, wear their hair long, and carry an axe or club, more often than not beautifully chased and inlaid, also the well-known dervish bowl, which is made from a huge nut, carved and decorated. Often these dervishes will come and seat themselves in the courtyard and begin their monotonous chant, and it is very difficult to get them to move, as the servants will never use force, and their reiterated requests to "move on" meet with no success whatever till the dervish is satisfied that he has extracted all the "backsheesh" likely to be forthcoming.

The Seyyids are another class of people much respected in the country. They claim to be the direct descendants of the prophet Mohammed, and are allowed many privileges on account of this. They wear a green turban or waistband, to be known of all men. Looked upon as a religious body, the natives are afraid to offend them in any way.

Then there are the "mullahs," or priests of the Islamic faith. They exercise a great deal of power over the people, but are not, as a rule, loved by them over much.

The Persians are Shiah Mohammedans, whilst the Arabs and Turks are Sunnis. As the former know very little Arabic, the reading of the Koran is to them an unknown tongue, and they regard their "mullahs" as "sacred men," able to interpret the "Holy Book." Thus the Shiah priest gains great influence, not to say considerable wealth, in Persia, and the Shah himself fears the influence of the priesthood. The Sunnis, on the other hand, know Arabic, as a general rule, and many of them are able to consult the Koran for themselves, the result being that the "mullah" gains but little influence compared to the "Shiah" priest, and is often quite poor. Briefly, the Shiah priesthood is comparable with that of the Roman Catholic Church of Christendom, while "Sunni" mullahs do not claim, or would claim in vain, any such authority, thus more nearly resembling the "status" of Church of England clergy. The result is obvious: Persia is a priest-ridden country; in "Sunni" lands the people are freer, and dare think for themselves. It is a well-known fact that a Persian mullah will exact the uttermost farthing from his followers, but will never lend a helping hand to them in their need. For instance, if a man dies without an heir, his property according to law goes to the poor, but unfortunately it has to be done through a medium, and that medium is the mullah. He promptly pockets the property and gives its *supposed* value (valued, mark you, by himself) to the poor. We can imagine what a large percentage the poor receive of that property.

Here is a story which was told us in Kerman, illustrating how loath the mullahs are to give anything away. The scene is a large pool of water, in it a mullah struggling to reach the bank, and in danger of drowning. A passer-by, seeing his distress, runs to his aid and cries, "Give me your hand, oh my lord, and I will pull you out." "No, indeed," answers the mullah, "I have never yet given anything to any one, and I certainly will not begin now." The kindly passer-by, not liking to leave the mullah in his sad condition, tries to think of another way out of the difficulty. Suddenly a bright idea strikes him, and running to the priest, he calls out, "Will you *take* my hand, then, oh my lord?" "Gladly," says the mullah, and allows himself to be drawn out of his perilous position.

Another rather good story is told, showing the meanness of the priests. A man had agreed to pay a workman eight krans (2s. 8d.) for digging a hole one yard square. At the end of the day the workman had only dug a hole half a yard square, so the master went to a mullah to ask him how much he ought to pay the workman. "Why, of course," says the mullah, "half the sum agreed upon, that is, four krans." After deliberating awhile he said, "No, two krans is enough," and this decision he gave as final, although he impressed upon the man that one kran was all he could legally claim, as he had scientifically only done one-eighth of his work!

In the next chapter we shall see a little of another religious sect, which is fast becoming a power in Persia.

CHAPTER X

OTHER RELIGIOUS SECTS

Other religious sects—The Báb and Babism—Short sketch of life of the Báb—His imprisonment and execution—Parsees, or Zoroastrians—Persecutions of Parsees in seventh century—Sacred writings of Parsees, Zendavesta—Fire-worshipping—Fire temples—Holy fire—Parsee wedding—Costume of women—Death customs—Burial customs.

"How many crimes have in religion's name been wrought."

Lucretius.

"Too oft religion has the mother been
Of impious act and criminal."

Lucretius.

The founder of Babism was a native of Shiraz, by name Mirza Ali Muhammed, born in 1820; it was not till 1844 that he publicly proclaimed himself to be The Báb or Gate, through which all who wished for peace and happiness might pass into the inner chambers of mysticism and sacred mysteries. He soon gathered a large following around him, and in an astonishingly short time the fame of the Báb was noised abroad throughout the length and breadth of Persia. At first the Government and mullahs paid little attention to this new religion, thinking and believing it to be only a passing fancy of the people, but in its second year it took such rapid strides that they began to be alarmed, and to look about for means of checking its progress. The Báb was placed in prison, and his followers were forbidden, on pain of death, to teach or discuss their new religion. Soon afterwards, however, the Báb escaped, and fled to Isphahan, where the governor of that city protected him for some months, but on the death of the governor the Báb was again cast into prison. During his imprisonment he was not idle, for he wrote many books, setting forth his doctrines, and exhorting his followers to remain firm to their new faith in the face of all opposition and persecution.

While the Báb was busy in prison, his followers were also busy, preaching and teaching, and by all means trying to extend the doctrines of their leader, and so great was the opposition and strife raised that the Government decided that the Báb must forfeit his life as a means of putting a stop once and for all to this new and dangerous sect. Accordingly the Báb was brought from Tabriz, where he had been imprisoned, and after a mock trial was sentenced to death. On the day appointed for his execution an enormous crowd gathered to witness his end—many from curiosity, and also many from love and pity for the youthful martyr, who to the last maintained the calmness and courage which had characterised his whole term of imprisonment.

To make the lesson more emphatic, it was decided that two of the Báb's chief disciples were to be executed with him. One of these at the last moment recanted, and so was allowed to go free. It was said that his recantation arose not from cowardice or fear of death, but from a special revelation given to him, whereby he was commanded to recant in order to be able to carry away all books and papers belonging to the Báb, and deposit them in a safe place: however that may be, it is known that after an interval of two years he too became a martyr. Efforts were made to entice the other disciple to recant, but all proved unavailing, and he and his master the Báb were suspended, by ropes placed under their arms, to a beam placed a few feet from the ground. As they hung thus the disciple was heard to say, "Master, art thou satisfied with me?" and then the order was given to fire. When the smoke cleared away the body of the disciple was found to be riddled with bullets, but no Báb was visible. What had happened? Had a miracle been performed, and an angel been sent to rescue him from the hand of his persecutors? This was the thought of some, and, indeed, a miracle had been performed, for in spite of the many bullets which had been aimed at him not one had touched the Báb, but had only brought him deliverance by severing the ropes which bound him, so that he fell to the ground unhurt. At first it seemed as if the multitude would have pity on the unfortunate man, and spare him a second attempt, but these feelings were only of short duration, and the Báb was again dragged forth from his hiding-place, where he had taken refuge, and was a second time suspended. A fresh batch of soldiers had to be told off for the execution, as the first company absolutely refused to fire again. This time there was no intervention, and in a second or two the body of the young martyr of Shiraz was pierced with bullets. The bodies were cast out to the jackals, but were afterwards recovered and buried in Teheran by the order of the new Báb, Mirza Yahya.

This event took place in 1850, and in spite of persecutions, oppositions, and cruelties, the Babis continued to grow in number and strength, and to-day they form a very large and important community throughout Persia. In fact, by the very barbarity of the persecutors their own end was defeated, for all the people were astonished at the heroism and fortitude displayed by the martyrs. Professor Brown[1] says, "Often have I heard Persians who did not themselves belong to the proscribed sect tell with admiration how Suleymán Khan, his body pierced with well-nigh a score of wounds, in each of which was inserted a lighted candle, went to his execution singing with exultation." The effect of such courage and heroism was only to stir up more people to be disciples of the Báb, as the following story shows.

During the persecutions in Yezd, a young man went to scoff and jeer, but when he saw with what courage the martyrs endured torture, and met death, he called out, "I am a Babi, kill me too." While we were in Yezd the Babis were keeping very

---

[1] "A Year amongst the Persians."

quiet, but, nevertheless, a great work was going on amongst them, but none dared say, "I am a Babi." A year or two after our departure from Persia we heard of terrible cruelties and persecutions enacted against these suffering people, but in spite of all, their number continues to grow and increase throughout the whole land of Persia, and to-day the Babis are stronger and more numerous than ever before.

The Parsees of Persia are another most interesting and important sect: they live chiefly in Yezd and Kerman. They are a people within a people, living in Persia, and with the Persians, yet keeping quite distinct from the present inhabitants of the land. Only a few thousand of this large and influential body of people, who up till the seventh century were the inhabitants of the land, now remain in Persia. When the armies of Mohammed conquered Persia, most of these people fled to India; others preferred to adhere to the new religion, while a few remained faithful to their old belief, and refused either to flee to a new and strange country, or to change their creed, and so they remain till this day a distinct people, following their own customs, and holding to their own religion amidst a new and domineering nation.

The founder of the Parsee religion was one called Zoroaster. Very little is known of his life; his birthplace is uncertain, though it is known he lived for many years in Bactria of Eastern Persia, and it is probable that it was in this place that he thought out the idea, from which in later years he constructed his religious system. The priests of this religion were the "magi" of the Old and New Testament, and it is very likely that at least one of the "wise men of the East" who went to offer their adoration to the new-born King was from these Parsees of Persia.

The date of Zoroaster is very uncertain too. It is known, however, that in the sixth century B.C., when Cyrus was king, the Zoroastrian religion was firmly established in Western Persia. Some historians give him a date between 1000 and 1400 B.C.

The sacred writings of the Parsees are called the Zendavesta, and are said to be inspired by God through one of their priests. This priest, having cleansed and bathed himself in the most careful manner, lay down to sleep clothed in pure white linen. He is said to have fallen into a deep sleep, from which he did not awake for seven days; at the end of which time he awoke and recited the faith of the Zoroastrians, while priests in waiting committed the whole to writing. In this way was the Zendavesta reduced to the form of a book.

While fire-worshipping forms a large part of their religion, it is quite a mistake to suppose it comprises the whole, for Zoroaster laid down many laws concerning morality and the duties and destiny of man.

The Parsees of to-day, as seen in Kerman and Yezd, are a fine race; their commercial ability is very much above that of the ordinary Persian, and they are a much cleaner and more moral set of people than their conquerors. They regard fire as something sacred, as being the symbol of their god, and nothing will induce them to treat fire lightly. For instance, we could never persuade our Parsee servants to blow out a candle; and smoking is prohibited on account of their religious principles, though nowadays many do smoke in secret. Their habits of cleanliness and continual personal ablutions have perhaps contributed to make them the healthy race they are to-day. A good Parsee will wash many times a day, always before and after praying, as well as on many other occasions.

All Parsees wear a girdle round their waists, twisted into three knots in a most complicated and intricate way. Whenever they wash they must take this off, and after their ablutions are over they replace the girdle, repeating certain prayers for each knot. These three knots represent the threefold cord, which is not easily broken, of good thoughts, good words, good deeds.

There are said to be some thirty or forty fire temples still existing in Yezd, and in these the holy fire is always burning; the light is never allowed to go out, it being the work of the priests to keep it continually bright and trimmed.

The office of priesthood descends from father to son, and besides attending to the religious needs of the people, the priest is also supposed to look after their temporal necessities, especially in the case of poverty-stricken families.

Parsee women have a much freer life than their Persian sisters; they go about the streets quite openly, never veiling their faces, and altogether enjoy a much better position than the Mohammedan women. In some cases the women are even allowed to eat with the men of the house—a great concession indeed! The children are bright, and in many cases clever. When seven days old an astrologer is consulted as to the future of the infant; and when seven years old a boy is blessed by the priest, who invests him with the sacred girdle, at the same time throwing upon the child's head portions of fruit, spices, and drops of perfume.

Girls are married when quite young, and the astrologer is again consulted on this important matter. When in Yezd we were invited to a Parsee wedding, and a very interesting sight it was. The invitation—which was written in letters of gold, and arrived some days before the date fixed for the ceremony—was acknowledged and accepted by us with much pleasure, as we were anxious to see something of the customs of these interesting people.

When the day arrived we arrayed ourselves in gala attire, and set out to the house of the bride. It was just midnight when we arrived, and already the guests, some hundreds of them, had been feasting for hours—in fact, I might say "days," for this was the seventh and last day of the wedding festivities, and many of the guests had been present each day. They all looked thoroughly worn-out and tired. A room had been set apart for the Europeans to dine in, and just after midnight a most sumptuous dinner was served, consisting of about a dozen courses. When this had been satisfactorily disposed of we dispersed to visit the different rooms occupied by the guests, my husband remaining with the men, while I and another English lady sought out the bride to give her our salaams and good wishes. The confusion was terrible—drums beating, cymbals clashing, women dancing and singing, children yelling and crying, and amid it all, seated upon the ground, sat the poor little bride-elect. No one seemed to be taking much notice of her, every one apparently aiming to amuse herself in the most noisy way possible.

By-and-by a large, silk-covered cushion was brought out from a back room, and on this the bride was placed, and covered entirely with a large silk shawl. I wondered what was going to happen next, when suddenly a group of men appeared at the door. These were the representatives of the bridegroom, who came to ask formally for the hand of the bride. They came and stood in front of the covered-up bride, and called in a loud voice, "Oh, my daughter, will you consent to be the bride of this man?" (naming the bridegroom). This was repeated six times amidst a silence which could be felt, all listening for the answer of the bride. On their repeating the question the seventh time, a very timid "Balli" (Yes) was heard coming from the region of the shawl, upon which the commotion started again with redoubled vigour, in the excitement caused by the acceptance on the part of the bride of her bridegroom. Of course this was a mere form, as everything had been arranged long beforehand. I shocked one good old lady by asking what would happen if the bride had said "No" instead of "Yes" to the oft-repeated question!

After receiving this very satisfactory answer to their inquiries the men went off, and the women began to prepare the bride for the last and most important part of the programme—viz. that of taking her to the home of the bridegroom. They covered her with a large silk chuddar, and over her head threw a thick shawl, so that the poor girl could see nothing, and had to be led and supported on each side by her proud relatives. The distance between the two houses might perhaps have taken five minutes to walk in an ordinary way, but that night we took quite an hour. The procession was headed by two "vakeels" (agents), who were bargaining the whole way as to the dowry of the bride. Every now and then they would come to a standstill, and the bride's vakeel would refuse to go a step further till more money had been paid, and after a great deal of shouting, gesticulating, and wrangling, the bridegroom's vakeel would end by throwing some coins into the other's hand, and then the procession would proceed for a few steps till blocked once more, while the whole process of bargaining was gone through again. Fireworks were going off the whole time, and were apparently laid along the route, for every now and then we were startled by having a rocket fly up from beneath our feet. About every twenty yards or so we came across huge bonfires of dried faggots right in our path, and the whole procession had to wait till these had died down before they could pass on. Arriving at the door of the bridegroom's house, a final and most exciting scene took place between the two vakeels, the one threatening even then to take the bride away, and the other, getting more wildly angry every minute, declaring he did not want the bride, and would not pay a "para" (½d.) more for her, and ending up by giving the sum bargained for. If we had not known it was all part of the ceremony, we might have expected the two men to come to blows; but it all ended happily, and we trooped into the new home of the bride. Then came a long time of weary waiting, during which my sympathies went out to the tired, frightened bride; but just as we thought there was nothing more to wait for, three interesting scenes took place. The first was the actual marriage ceremony, in which a priest read many long prayers from a book, and then tied the couple together with a silk thread and pronounced a blessing upon them.

The second scene took place in the open courtyard, in the centre of which was burning the sacred fire placed on a pedestal. The priest and parents of the bride and bridegroom now joined hands with the happy couple and walked in solemn single file round and round the fire, the priest chanting the whole time; this was done seven times, and then all retired quietly, leaving the fire burning in the court.

To the third and final scene only a favoured few were admitted; fortunately I was amongst that number. Into the room prepared for the newly-married couple the little wife was now led, and for the first time the coverings were taken from her head and face. She was placed on a huge silk-covered mattress, then the husband came and took his seat by her side: both of them were looking thoroughly miserable! One of the women then brought a copper basin and ewer filled with milk, and the bridegroom proceeded to wash his wife's feet in milk, and she in her turn washed his hands. This done, we all bade farewell to the newly-married couple and the wedding ceremony was at an end. Hastily saying good-bye to our host and hostess, and expressing our good wishes for the welfare and happiness of the young people, we made our way homewards, to find it was not very far off dawn, but having thoroughly enjoyed our first experience of a Parsee wedding ceremony.

The costume of the Parsee women is rather quaint and pretty; it consists of very baggy trousers gathered in at the ankle. These trousers are often made of very pretty pieces of embroidery joined together. As soon almost as a girl can sew she begins to embroider strips of brightly-coloured materials in order to have them ready for her wedding trousseau. Over these garments they wear a loose shirt reaching to just below the knees; this is also made of strips of different coloured materials, or in the case of a bride is also embroidered. Then comes the head-dress: it is far beyond my powers to say of how many pieces this is composed, or as to how they are arranged. The number of coverings on their heads is legion! First comes a little tight cap fitting closely over the head and ears. Over this is arranged in a most marvellous way some six or seven different pieces of calico or linen, the top one of all generally being a very bright calico, a mixture of red and yellow being the favourite pattern. The men are obliged to wear dowdy colours as a mark of submission to the powers that be. For the same reason also they are not allowed to ride through the bazaars, and if a Parsee is riding outside the city and meets a Moslem he promptly has to dismount and walk till he has passed his more fortunate neighbour; *then* he may resume his riding. This is, I believe, the case even if the Moslem be a poor man and the Parsee a flourishing merchant.

To pass from life to death. A Parsee when he is dying sends for the priest, who anoints him with sacred juice, repeats some verses from the "Avesta," and prays for a safe crossing of the "bridge" and admission into Paradise. As soon as the breath has left the body, a dog is brought in from the street to ascertain if life is really extinct. This idea originated evidently from the old Zoroastrian idea that the evil spirit is expelled from a dead body by means of a "four-eyed dog" being brought in and made to look at the dead, the extra "two" eyes being represented by two black spots over the brow of the dog. The body is then placed on a bier and carried to the Towers of Silence, or "dakhmehs," by men specially set apart for that purpose. These men are looked upon as unclean from their contact with the dead, therefore only those whose work it is to do so will touch the body, the cleansing necessary after defilement from contact with the dead being so exacting and laborious.

On arriving at the dakhmeh, prayers are recited by the priests and the body laid on an iron grating, so that when the vultures and other birds of prey have done their horrible work, the bones fall down and are safe from molestation by dogs and jackals.

The dakhmehs, always some distance from the town, are built in a circular shape, some of the largest being 200 or so feet in diameter. They are generally built on rising ground, and form a landmark for many miles around.

Prayers for the dead are said for three or four days after the death, and holy fire is kept burning in the house of the deceased during the whole of that time, as the soul is not supposed to leave the body till the fourth day after death.

The better-class Parsees "mourn" for a year after the death of a near relative; that is, they keep up certain ceremonials for that length of time, and offer flowers and fruits on behalf of their dead.

The Parsees have a governing body called the Anjiman. This consists of a number of leading men, representatives of each class of society. The Persian Government acknowledges the Anjiman, and accepts one of its number to act as its representative.

CHAPTER XI

DESERT DELIGHTS

*Songs of the desert—Sunsets, sunrises, mirages—Illness in the desert—
Mehman khanehs, caravanserais—Chappa khanehs—Lost in the desert—Its cruelties, and sadness.*

"The desert wide
Lies round thee like a trackless tide
In waves of sand forlornly multiplied."

F. W. FABER.

To a lover of the desert a journey across its boundless tracts is always full of
interest and delight. It is strange what an attraction the desert has for some people,
and stranger still is the fact that this magnetic power increases as time passes, and
instead of wearying of the wilderness, they love it more and more. And any one
who has once heard the call of the desert is always longing to answer that call, and
to fly once more, as a needle to its magnet, to that great, wondrous world. For it *is* a
world of its own, this great, boundless ocean of sand—a world altogether different
from any other part of God's earth.

I once heard an address on "The Desert," and the speaker said that he did not
think it possible for any one with an uneasy conscience to bear the solitariness of
the desert. Be this as it may, one thing is sure: no one can live and travel in the
desert without feeling the majestic Presence of God. Everything speaks of Him,
the great sea of sand, the flowers springing into blossom at His word, the tiny
lizard darting across your path, and other countless creatures, all finding life and
sustenance in the desert, each telling of the wonderful Creator who watches over
and cares for all.

The songs of the desert, too, are fascinating; songs which, heard elsewhere,
would seem incongruous and lacking in harmony. The camel or mule bells, boom-
ing out in the silence of the night, remind one of home and loved ones. Often have
I been awakened in the night by the sound of the caravan bells, and for a moment
thought they were the bells of the dear old church in Devonshire. Then, again,
the crooning songs of the muleteer, as he trudges along hour after hour, have a
peculiar charm, which grows on one wondrously after a while. And what can be
said of the marvellous mirages—visions which come as messengers of hope and
leave us victims of despair? For who has not experienced relief and joy at the sight
of some beautiful mirage, resembling the welcome sight of a village with trees

and water, all apparently within easy reach of the weary traveller, but which in a moment of time vanish, leaving blank disappointment behind. And where can be seen such glorious sunset effects as in the desert? especially when, as is so often the case in Persia, the desert is surrounded by mountains and hills, which catch the after glow, and reflect all those indescribable shades of crimson, gold, and blue, all merging into a beatific and not easily forgotten vision.

But to come to the more practical side of desert life. Travelling in the desert is not all a path of roses, but, given good health, fine weather, and pleasant company, it is a very enjoyable way of passing two or three weeks. On the other hand, I know of nothing more wretched than being overtaken by illness when far away in the desert. *Then* you feel how utterly alone and helpless you are, for it is impossible to travel on, and at the same time well-nigh impossible to stay where you are! We have had this experience more than once during our many travels, and found it not at all pleasant. Once I was taken ill in this way, and the only place to be found as shelter was a filthy stable, full of rats, cockroaches, and other horrible creatures.

A MOUNTAIN PASS

The traveller from Resht to Teheran passes through very varied scenery. Beginning with beautiful forests of walnuts, planes, willow, and olives, he soon loses this wealth of vegetation as he ascends the Elburz, and once these mountains are crossed, the track lies chiefly through the desert, with its ranges of mountains away in the distance.

A CARAVANSERAI

A specimen of one of the "hotels" of Persia. These caravanserais
are built in the form of an open square. The rooms are situated
round the quadrangle, while the courtyard is the resting-place of
camels, mules, horses, and donkeys.

If you wish thoroughly to enjoy a journey across the desert, you must choose
your time well and wisely. The best time is the early spring, before the great heat
begins. If it is essential to travel during the summer, all the stages have to be done
by night, and this is much more tiring, as it is seldom possible to sleep during the
day owing to the pest of flies, mosquitoes, and other lively companions.

The rest-houses of Persia are of three grades or kinds, viz. "mehman khanehs,"
"chappa khanehs," and caravanserais. The first of these three are found between
Resht and Teheran. They are supposed to be run after the plan of a European hotel!
Beds are supplied, and sometimes a tooth-brush and comb! The traveller is shown
into a room in which the beds are kept ready for all passers-by: it is not thought
necessary to change the bedding too often! The furniture consists of a washstand,
table, and couple of chairs, and everything is as dirty as can be. I much prefer the
ordinary caravanserai, which is found all over Persia. These are generally built by
a wealthy man who wishes to do some "good deed," to make a name for himself,
and gain merit in Paradise. A caravanserai is not the cleanest spot on earth! But
after travelling a little you get used to a certain amount of dirt, and are very much
surprised if by chance you come across a fairly clean rest-house. These caravanserais are built, as a rule, in the form of a square, the sides of which are occupied

by rooms leading off the courtyard, the centre being the resting-place of mules, donkeys, horses, and all other kinds of animals. At the end of the stage you fix on the cleanest of these rooms, and your servant sweeps all the accumulated dirt and dust of ages into one corner, thus raising a cloud of dust and disturbing the peace of myriads of "pilgrims of the desert." After waiting a few minutes to allow the dust to settle a little, you then furnish your room for the night by spreading a rug on the filthy floor, and setting up your travelling beds, chair, tables, &c. As likely as not, there will be no door to the room, so you knock in a couple of nails and fasten a curtain over the doorway to keep out the prying eyes of your too near and inquisitive neighbours. Then you begin to think about your evening meal, and your servant goes off to bargain and wrangle over some unfortunate fowl, the result being that in about an hour's time your dinner is ready, and shortly after you very thankfully retire to rest, hoping for the best.

The chappa khanehs, or post-houses, are often a trifle cleaner than the caravanserai. Here the animals are kept for the post, and any one travelling "chappa" is supposed to find fresh relays of horses at each of these places, but very often the number is short, and the poor, wretched, underfed animal has to do duty for a second stage: a "stage" is anything from fifteen to thirty miles. My husband once rode "chappa" from Yezd to Kerman, a distance of 250 miles, in 2½ days, to attend an English doctor who was very ill with typhoid fever. It was very hard and rough riding; the roads were bad, the horses worse, some of the animals being blind, others lame, while the majority of them were so over-worked and badly fed that it seemed impossible that they could ever do the stage. A doctor once riding in this way to visit a European, is said to have arrived at one of these post-houses, and finding no horse, demanded a mule. On this beast he made the next stage, to be told on arrival that there was only a donkey available. Nothing better presenting itself, he accepted this mount, and in time reached the next stage, where he was met with the comforting announcement that the only animal at liberty was a cow! History seems uncertain after this point, so we will draw a veil over it!

Sometimes these caravanserais and chappa khanehs are the only signs of life to be seen at the end of a stage. There they stand, alone, surrounded on all hands by vast stretches of desert, and form a landmark for miles around. One such I remember very well, as each time we passed that way it seemed to have become more lonely and desolate. Visible from a distance of 5 farsakhs (18 miles), it made the stage seem very long! The atmosphere is so rarefied that distant objects appear near, and the buildings, which were in reality 15 miles away, looked quite close at hand. In this chappa khaneh we were once guilty of inscribing our names on its already well-filled walls. Some years after a lady was visiting us in Mosul, and told us she had read our names in that far-distant chappa khaneh.

It is not a very pleasant sensation to be lost in a desert. Only once did this experience befall us, and then we were glad when it was over.

We were on our way from Yezd to Kerman, and had reached the second stage out. We had arranged with our muleteer to start at a certain hour that morning, but when we came down from the "bala khaneh" (upstairs room) where we had been sleeping, we found no signs of our caravan being ready to start. After loitering about for some time, we decided not to wait any longer, but to ride on ahead. This was quite contrary to our usual custom, as we always found it wiser to see the caravan off first, otherwise the muleteers dawdled half the morning away. However, we thought this once we would alter our plans, as the dawn was even then breaking, and we knew that in a very short time the sun would be scorchingly hot. So off we went, telling our servant to follow as soon as possible. We received minute instructions as to which direction we were to take, and thought we could not possibly mistake our road.

Outside the town, on the edge of the desert, we came to two roads, one leading straight ahead, the other branching to the left. We decided to take the former, thinking it looked more trodden, thereby showing more signs of traffic. So we went gaily on. My husband occasionally remarked, "I hope we are on the right road," and I always lightly answered, "Oh yes, I am sure we are," as I pointed out to him the fact that we were following the same path along which another caravan had evidently passed a few hours before. Howbeit we were *not* on the right road, as we very soon found to our cost. By this time the sun was blazing down upon us, and we began to wonder why our servants and caravan had not caught us up. Time went on, and not a sign of life was to be seen. Standing in our stirrups, we scanned the horizon, but nothing could we see but the scorching sand. We then began seriously to think that we had taken the wrong turning and were lost. Lost in the desert, without a drop of water or a scrap of food! Pleasant thoughts these were as companions! We could not go back: to go forward was worse than useless. After considering a little as to the best thing to be done, we decided to gallop on till we came to a small hill to be seen in the distance. This we accordingly did, and as we neared the summit saw to our great thankfulness a tiny speck on the horizon in the direction from which we had come. This "speck" soon developed into a moving object, and by-and-by we could see the figure of a man and horse galloping hard. As the horse and rider came nearer, our thankfulness was indeed great to see that the rider was our own servant, George. If ever we had cause for thankfulness it was then, and we certainly said, and felt from our very hearts, "Alhamd' llillah" (Praise be to God!), and vowed we would never stray away again from our caravan unless we were quite sure of our road.

Our man was so delighted to see us safe and sound that he wept for joy. After a long delay the caravan had at last started from the chappa khaneh just as the sun was rising, and set out upon its way. They were all surprised to think we had gone so far, but concluded at first that we had galloped on in order to reach the lunching-place before the great heat. On arriving at the spot, however, great was their dismay to find we had not yet arrived. Our servant immediately rode back to the village to make inquiries. On his way he met a man who told him he had seen us riding off in the opposite direction. George immediately took the path indicated, with the result already told. By the time we regained our caravan we were well-nigh worn out with heat and thirst, having been under the blazing sun without food or water for most of the hottest hours of the day, but very thankful to be on the right track once more.

One thing that saddens a European traveller during a journey in Persia is to see the cruel way in which the muleteer often treats his animals. The sufferings of these poor beasts are terrible. I often longed to be able to thrash the muleteer for his cruelty to a poor, long-suffering little donkey. Bowed down, maybe, under a load twice his own size, the poor ass does his best to keep up with the other animals, but only receives kicks and hard knocks for his pains. The wretched creature is urged on and on by having a steel or iron instrument run into some horribly sore place by his kind and compassionate owner. Often have I seen a mule or donkey stumble and fall beneath its enormous load, unable to raise itself, till its master with blows and curses comes to lend a hand. Again and again will this happen, till at last the poor beast can go no further, and is left to its fate. Death is the kindest master some of these suffering creatures possess.

I remember once seeing a mule unloaded, and the sight under the pack-saddle was enough to make one's heart ache. A deep wound about twelve inches long was exposed to view, just under the arch of the saddle, where all the heaviest pressure and friction came. The owner then heated till red hot a long wire rod, passing it through and through this wound till the poor creature was nearly mad with pain and agony. The next day a boy was ordered to ride this wretched beast, but the stench from the wound was so great, and the flies attracted by it so numerous, that he could not endure it, and asked to be given another animal. This request was granted, but the poor brute of a mule had to pay the penalty by receiving an extra load upon his poor wounded back. At the first town we came to, the muleteer sold this mule, doubtless to some one who would work the last particle of strength out of him. Poor burdened beasts of the desert! one can only hope for them a speedy end to their troubles, and rest hereafter.

Another sad sight to be seen in the desert sometimes, are brick pillars in which some unfortunate victim has been walled up alive. This is a horrible method of inflicting capital punishment. The victim is put into the pillar, which is half built up in readiness; then if the executioner is merciful he will cement quickly up to the face, and death comes speedily. But sometimes a small amount of air is allowed to permeate through the bricks, and in this case the torture is cruel and the agony prolonged. Men bricked up in this way have been heard groaning and calling for water at the end of three days. At other times the victim is placed in the pillar head first, and in this way he is walled up.

The first time I saw these pillars was in the desert outside Yezd, and I could hardly believe the awful tales which were told me of the cruelties perpetrated; but alas, they were all too true! It is sad that the beauty of the desert should be desecrated by such things.

CHAPTER XII

PERSIAN MEDICAL MISSIONS[2]

The need of them—Work in Isphahan—The "little devil" transformed into a boy—Amputation—Brothers in adversity—H.R.H. Zil-es-Sultan as a patient—Fanaticism overcome.

"What restless forms to-day are lying, bound
On sick beds, waiting till the hour come round
That brings thy foot upon the chamber stair,
Impatient, fevered, faint, till thou art there,
The one short smile of sunshine to make light
The long remembrance of another night."

H. E. HAMILTON KING.

"Medical Missions" need no apology or excuse. Even in the comparatively few years that have elapsed since their commencement, they have abundantly justified their existence, both from the missionary standpoint, and also as philanthropic agencies. If this be true for purely pagan lands, it applies even more accurately to work in Mohammedan countries. Medical missionary work is, without doubt, the golden key that unlocks the door of the heart of the most fanatical Moslem, be he Persian, Arab, Kurd, or Yezidee (devil worshipper). I write this deliberately, after eight years' experience in Persia, Palestine, and Mesopotamia. But in this book it is not meant specially to emphasise the missionary aspect of our life in these distant lands, but more to give a slight glimpse of native life as we found it, and the following, therefore, must be taken as notes from a doctor's diary, covering a period of eight years' work in Persia and Mesopotamia.

The year 1900 found us at Isphahan. We were living in Julfa, the Armenian suburb of that great city, and I had temporary charge of the C.M.S. Medical Mission. The hospital at that period was simply a native house that had been adapted, more or less, for the requirements of a dispensary and hospital. There was no lack of work, patients coming from Isphahan itself, and from all the country round about. Soon after settling down to the routine work, a little Persian boy was brought to me from an outlying village by his father. He was about twelve years of age, and his face was badly disfigured from a "hare-lip." The Persians believe that this congenital malformation is the mark left by the foot of the Evil One, so this poor boy was known in his village by the unenviable title "little devil," and

[2] By Dr. A. Hume-Griffith.

had been a good deal tormented by his playfellows. He was admitted to hospital, operated upon successfully, and after some ten days' careful treatment the dressing was finally removed, and I handed the boy a mirror that he might look for the first time upon his "new" face. As I watched his countenance while he regarded himself steadfastly in the glass, I was amply repaid for the time and trouble spent, by his look of joy, incredulity, and amazement. Tears of joy rolled down his face as he kissed my hand, and murmured brokenly, "I am no longer a little devil, I am no longer a little devil!" He could go back to his village now gladly, no longer fearing to join in the games of his comrades, and I feel sure he afterwards often posed as a hero in his little village, as, the centre of an admiring throng, he recounted the details of his visit, treatment, and cure at the Mission Hospital.

A VERY ANCIENT BRIDGE

Built over the river which divides the city of Isphahan from its
Christian suburb of Julfa.

In all Mohammedan lands, doctors always find it extremely difficult to persuade their patients to submit to amputation. However hopeless a condition the injured limb may be in, many would rather die than enter Paradise maimed. Some perhaps fancy that after death, when the prophet Mohammed comes to conduct them over that fragile bridge that leads to the "realm of the blest," he would indignantly repudiate the claims of an armless or legless disciple! However that may be, the fact remains that many a poor patient dies who might, by timely amputation, have recovered and lived for many years. But curiously enough, soon after our arrival in Julfa, I admitted, within a few days of each other, two Persians suffering from diseases of the legs necessitating amputation, and both, after much persuasion, agreed to the operation being performed. Both were men, and had been admitted to different wards, but as after-events proved, neither knew of the other's presence in the hospital: both thus believed that *he* was the only Mohammedan doomed to pass the rest of his life bereft of one leg, with the possible risk of non-admittance hereafter to the Moslem Paradise.

A TYPICAL STREET IN BAGHDAD

The two amputations were duly performed, on different days; the amputated limbs being at once handed to the relatives for decent interment. Both patients made good recoveries, their progress being somewhat retarded by their continual lamentation over their irreparable loss. In due course of time, crutches were provided, and the two men were encouraged to practise walking with their aid. A day or two later I was standing at the door of the operation theatre, which opened into a corridor, with which both the men's wards communicated. Suddenly the doors of each ward opened simultaneously, and on the threshold stood these two men, leaning on their crutches, their faces a perfect picture as they beheld each other. Remember that, in some curious manner, neither had heard of the presence of the other in the hospital, and both firmly believed that *he* was the only Mohammedan that had ever submitted to the indignity of losing a limb, and lo and behold, here was a brother in affliction! Crutches were hurled on one side, and the two men, hopping across the corridor, excitement lending them the needed strength, fell into each other's arms, rolling over and over on the floor, weeping, condoling, exclaiming, while we watched the scene, highly amused, but also feeling inclined to weep in sympathy.

The Governor of Isphahan was H.R.H. Zil-es-Sultan (Shadow of the King), elder brother of the late Shah. In former years he had been much more powerful, and practically ruled over Southern Persia, but his enemies in Teheran roused the suspicions of the Shah against him. He was summoned to the capital, and there kept a prisoner in his house, but ultimately allowed to return to Isphahan shorn of his former power.

The Zil-es-Sultan had his own private physician, but would often call in the English doctor either for himself or his household; in this way I made his acquaintance, and, like most Europeans who have come in contact with him, admired both his shrewdness and ability. He always proved himself a good friend to the English mission, and later I got to know much more intimately his eldest son, H.H. Jalal-el-Dowleh, who was the able governor of Yezd, a city some three hundred miles eastward of Isphahan.

Soon after reaching Julfa, I was sent for by the governor to examine his eyes. I found him in a garden outside the city, which he had just had constructed for a summer residence. He received me cordially, and, after the business part of the interview was over, chatted freely, telling me of all he had undergone at the hands of other physicians. A few years before, he had become alarmed about the state of his eyesight, and became possessed with the idea that he was gradually going blind. He believed himself to be suffering from a very hopeless eye disease, very prevalent in Persia, known as "black cataract" (glaucoma), and despite the assurance to the contrary given by Dr. Carr (the English doctor) and others, he persisted in sending for two eye specialists, one from Paris, the other from London. Both had thoroughly examined his sight, and had confirmed Dr. Carr's assurances that there was no disease, but his fears had put him to considerable expense, as both the specialists were treated right royally. Laughingly he told me how much he had dreaded the interview with the London specialist, and how the fateful day had at last come. The doctor had merely lightly placed his fingers on the eye, felt the tension, and then had smilingly assured His Royal Highness that there was no fear of glaucoma, a subsequent careful examination confirming this verdict. "And to think," pathetically added the governor, "that I had spent all those thousands of pounds for nothing!" Of course I at once suggested that to have had all his fears of blindness so happily set at rest more than compensated for any expense that he might have incurred, but he remained unconvinced.

During the year we remained in Isphahan I had many opportunities of being received by the governor. He always treated me with the same kindness, and upon our departure for Kerman, presented me with a large signed photograph of himself.

Isphahan is a great city that has passed through many vicissitudes: at one time it was the capital of Persia. Its population to-day is probably about 150,000. As in all Shiah (Mohammedan) lands, the priests (mullahs) possess great power. The Moslem archbishops are termed "mujtiheds." In each Persian city there are generally two mujtiheds, one official (Sheikh-es-Islam), the other elected by the people, and the latter, as a rule, possessed the greater influence.

In 1900 the popular mujtihed was the eldest of three brothers, all mullahs. His power was very great—too great for the taste of the Shah, if one may credit rumour. Only a few days after our arrival, a carriage was sent for me, from the second brother of this mujtihed, who for many weeks had been anxiously looking forward to the arrival of an English "hakim," as he was suffering from a troublesome disease which might at any time develop serious symptoms. All these Isphahan mullahs had proved themselves hostile to the presence of foreigners, and on more than one occasion they had endeavoured, by preaching against them in the mosques, to inflame the populace and cause a riot.

At the patient's house I was joined by another doctor (Dr. Aganoor), who was also the English Vice-Consul, and to whom we were indebted for many acts of kindness during our stay in Isphahan. The mullah was really his patient, and I was called in for consultation as to the advisability of operating. We were ushered into a large room with a fountain playing in the centre, and there we found the patient, supported by both his brothers, besides innumerable friends.

We sat in solemn conclave for over an hour, discussing the pros and cons of the case, and then, having decided upon the course of treatment, we took our departure. Some days later we were again sent for, and found our patient in great pain, and the whole house crowded with his innumerable friends, who had hurriedly come together at the rumour of his approaching death.

Our patient was in a very excited state, angrily refusing the consolation offered by his disciples and friends, and violently shouting, "A thousand tomans (£200) to any one who can take away this pain." Then, as he felt an extra bad twinge, "Ten thousand tomans to any one who will cure this pain" (about £2000).

However, we soothed him, injected a little morphia, assured him there was no immediate danger, and as the sedative commenced to work, and the pain disappeared, with it went all thought of rewarding his benefactors: on the contrary, he took extra trouble to explain how poor a man he really was, and that it was due to the malice of his enemies that rumour reputed him wealthy. However, to cut a long story short, by means of a simple operation, and much patient care and attention on the part of Dr. Aganoor, he ultimately made a good recovery, and was really grateful, using his influence afterwards rather to restrain than augment the anti-European fanaticism of his other two brethren. Later a nephew of the chief mujtihed, himself a mullah, actually consented to come into hospital to undergo an urgently needed operation, and this proving successful, gained for us another staunch friend from priestly quarters, whose friendship stood us in good stead on another occasion which might have ended rather differently, but for his intervention. A few months had elapsed: rumours still reached us from the city of occasional attempts made to stir up the fanaticism of the people against us, the chief offender being the third and youngest brother of the mujtihed before mentioned.

USING THE X-RAYS IN JULFA HOSPITAL

The two assistants are both Armenians. The girls make very good nurses, and the boys as a rule quickly become very efficient helpers in the mission hospitals.

A WARD IN THE JULFA HOSPITAL

This was a corner of the men's ward in the old hospital at Julfa. Now a large new hospital has been built in Isphahan with accommodation for one hundred patients.

One day Dr. Aganoor and I were both sent for in a great hurry. We heard that the whole city was in an uproar, that this fanatical mullah had been poisoned, some said "by order of the Shah," others that the governor had asked him to a feast, and as he returned, ere reaching home, the symptoms had started; others that the women of his "anderoon" (quarter of the house in which no man but the husband may enter) had given him "oil of bitter almonds" by mistake. On approaching the house we found a crowd round the door, and the house itself packed with disciples and friends of the great man. We were hurriedly shown into a large hall, with marble pillars and floor, densely crowded with a mass of human beings, all engaged in watching the last gasps of the poor mullah, who was lying on a pile of carpets stretched on the marble floor. We learnt to our dismay that he had been unconscious for four hours, and apparently precautions had been taken that the English doctors should not be called in until that amount of time had elapsed. Before that intent, silent, fanatical crowd, we did all that could be done to save the life of the man who had been our bitter enemy, taking turns to perform artificial respiration, &c., but all in vain, for, as in my turn I worked the dying man's arms, he took his last breath, and I whispered Dr. Aganoor that all was over. It was getting towards midnight. Julfa was three miles distant, and we were alone in the midst of that fanatical crowd. Well did my colleague know that once the intimation was given that the end had come, the scene would baffle description; the whole city would be roused, and our lives might even be in danger; knowing these things, he whispered me to go on performing artificial respiration while he got ready to go. So I went on with my task, working the dead man's arms until all was ready for our instant departure. Then reverently folding his hands on his breast, I drew over his face the coverlet, as an intimation that all was over. I never again wish to hear such a yell as then arose from the throats of that great throng. Doors were flung open, the mob from without rushed into the room, women poured in belonging to the dead man's household, shrieking, wailing, tearing their clothes and hair. Some of them made a wild rush at us as they passed, and it really looked a bit serious, for already amidst the uproar we could detect occasional cries of "The Feringhis have poisoned him." To my relief, amidst the excited throng I noticed the face of my old friend the mujtihed's nephew, who had been an in-patient in the hospital, and when he noticed that I had observed him, he beckoned us to follow him. We obeyed gladly, and he led us away by a private passage, which finally emerged into a public square a long distance from the dead man's house. There our good Samaritan left us, promising to send us our horses and servants, whom we had left waiting outside the patient's house. As we waited for them to come, we could hear the sound of cries from all parts of the city, followed by wailing of women, and the scurrying of many feet, as all flocked to the quarter where the holy man's body lay. At last our servants and animals arrived, and we made haste to escape, reaching home after midnight, thankful to God for preserving us from what might have proved a very dangerous position. Next day we heard that the whole city had gone into mourning; all the bazaars were shut, and the shops draped with black, and this mourning was kept up five whole days. Rumours were persistently circulated that the English doctors had poisoned the mullah, but no one really believed it, and I was able to attend the city dispensary as usual, even during the funeral ceremonies, and patients rather increased than diminished, some of the dead man's relatives even coming for treatment.

So ended priestly opposition; the chief mujtihed himself was frightened at the mode of his brother's death, and kept very quiet, for fear, perhaps, that a similar accident might happen to him. His surviving brother and relatives were now quite friendly, and a few years later Dr. Carr was able to obtain ground and build an excellent hospital in Isphahan itself, welcomed alike by officials and priests. There is also an excellent Women's Hospital (C.M.S.), in charge of Dr. Emmeline Stuart, who has for many years given her life to work amongst Moslem women, and whose name is held dear by many a poor Persian village woman, who has found relief and loving care at her hands, and those of her staff.

CHAPTER XIII

PIONEER MEDICAL MISSION WORK IN KERMAN[3]

Pioneer Medical Mission work in Kerman — Waiting for drugs and instruments — Native assistant proves a broken reed — First operation in Kerman — An anxious moment — Success — Doctrine of "savab" convenient to the Moslem — Fanaticism tempered with prudence — Opium slaves — Persian therapeutics — Persian quacks and their methods — Sure way of curing cancer — Hysteria.

"Charms for lovers, charms to break,
Charms to bind them to you wholly,
Medicines fit for every ache,
Fever and fanciful melancholy."

R. Bridges.

We had been appointed to open a Medical Mission in this city, and as soon as our temporary residence in Isphahan was finished, proceeded to our original destination. We arrived at Kerman early in 1901, and received a hearty welcome from the only other European there — the Rev. A. R. Blackett, also of the Church Missionary Society. Two houses were secured, both outside the city wall; in one we took up our residence, while the other was made into a dispensary, and small temporary hospital. Unfortunately we arrived before our supply of drugs and surgical instruments, so we had to do our best with the very small stock of medicines borrowed from our stations in Isphahan and Yezd. However, patients began to come in large numbers, and the out-patient department was soon in full swing. We had brought with us from Isphahan two Armenians to act as assistants, one for dispensing, the other (a man who had been employed in the Mission for many years) to interpret and help generally in the work. I had hoped much from this last-named assistant, and had relied upon him greatly for advice and help, as he had been in Kerman before, and knew the people; but I soon found him a "broken reed." He was married and had a large family, which he had been obliged to leave behind in Isphahan, and very soon he began to show signs of home-sickness. Then he commenced to imagine himself ill, and developed symptoms of different ailments. In the first place he one day came to me with a woeful face, and besought me to carefully examine his chest, for he was convinced he was developing phthisis. After being reassured on this point, he became absolutely sure that he had heart disease; next

---

[3] By Dr. A. Hume-Griffith.

his kidneys troubled him, and so on, until he became a confirmed hypochondriac, and completely useless for work. One day I remember his coming to me imploring that I would inject morphia to relieve him of the intense pain from which he was suffering. I gravely took the hypodermic syringe, and carefully injected distilled water, and the pain disappeared with lightning rapidity!

However, I had to send him home, and I believe that, once safely reunited to his family, he at once lost all his symptoms, and was able to resume his old work at the hospital.

In the meanwhile my surgical patients were clamouring for operations, more especially those afflicted with cataract. I had opened another dispensary in the city itself, and many poor blind people had come for treatment. It went to one's heart to have to send them away day after day with the same disheartening story. "The instruments have not yet come; until they arrive, nothing can be done." I fear that many commenced to think that the English doctor was a fraud, and that his excuses concerning the instruments resembled those framed by their own "hakims" to hide their own ignorance. At last the boxes actually arrived. They had to be brought by caravan from Bushire (the port in the Persian Gulf) to Kerman, *viâ* Shiraz and Yezd, a distance of some eight hundred miles, taking a couple of months.

We admitted our first in-patient, a well-known merchant in the city, who had been blind for three years with cataract. The Persian surgeons also operate for this disease, using the old Eastern operation known as "couching." An incision is made into the white of the eyeball (without any anæsthetic), then a thick, blunt probe is worked into the interior of the eye, directed so as to dislocate the lens. If successful, the lens drops back into the posterior chamber of the eye, and the patient "sees," but alas, the vision obtained is, in ninety-eight cases out of a hundred, only temporary! Twenty-four hours later, inflammation of the eye supervenes, and the sight is gone, and the eye lost. Needless to say, the operator obtains his fee either before the operation is done, or during the few hours that his patient is rejoicing in his newly found vision; then if he is wise he disappears from the town, and resumes his practice elsewhere. However, during eight years' practice in the East, and having had the opportunity of examining thousands of eyes, I can remember *two* cases only where this operation had been done and there had been no subsequent inflammation, but the great majority of eyes are lost.

Well, we had our first Kerman cataract patient, and it seemed to us as though the whole future of the little pioneer Medical Mission depended upon the success or failure of that operation.

The day fixed for the operation arrived: a Persian doctor practising in the city had requested leave to be present, no doubt on behalf of the many friends of the patient, to report particulars and see fair play. The patient was brought in, looking exceedingly nervous. After a short prayer (a practice almost invariably adopted in medical missionary hospitals, and much appreciated by the patient, even though he be a fanatical Moslem), the operation was started. I am afraid we were all unduly nervous, the possible consequences for good or ill to the Mission assuming undue proportions. At any rate everything went wrong; the cocaine (used as the anæsthetic) would not work, the old man *could* not keep his eye still, and *would* look up when he was told to look down. I was only able to complete the incision, and that with the greatest difficulty; and fearing to proceed further, the patient getting more and more excited, I had reluctantly to postpone the operation for a couple of days. We all felt very depressed, except, perhaps, the Persian "hakim," who doubtless greatly relished the failure of the English doctor. However, two days later we tried again, the Persian hakim once more being amongst the spectators. Much prayer had been offered up that *this* time there might be no hitch. Everything at first went well; the patient lay quite quietly, moved his eye exactly as he was told, the cocaine proved satisfactory, the incision was remade, and other preliminary steps in the operation disposed of: then came the hitch. In the European method of operating for cataract, the opaque lens is extruded from the eye by gentle pressure, through the incision first made. Well, when the time came for the lens to be extruded, it would not budge! I tried all possible means of extraction without success (afterwards I discovered that adhesions had formed between the lens and the curtain of the eye, as a result of the first operation). The perspiration ran down my face, as I realised what this second failure meant, not so much for my own reputation, but the hindrance it would prove to the success of the work I loved. I glanced at my wife: she was looking very anxious. I looked at my assistants: their faces were pictures of dismay. They had seen me before in Isphahan do many a cataract, and could not imagine what had gone wrong. The Persian doctor looked particularly happy: he smiled as he politely expressed his sorrow that I was experiencing any difficulty in bringing the operation to a successful issue. It certainly was an awkward fix—perhaps the most awkward that I have ever been in; but as I lifted up my heart in silent prayer to God, asking for guidance, the thought flashed into my mind, "The man has both eyes blind: you have failed with the one; do the other at once, and it *will* prove successful."

Gently covering the eye that had proved a failure, I explained matters to the patient, obtained his permission, thoroughly cleansed his other eye, and proceeded to operate, meeting with no difficulty and easily extracting the lens, to the palpable disappointment of my Persian medical friend, and was overjoyed to find that the patient old man had obtained exceedingly good vision. After a week the patient went back to his friends, seeing well, and full of gratitude for all the kindness and care he had received. I saw him some months later, and inquired whether he cared to let me have another try at the eye that had proved unsuccessful; but he refused, saying he was an old man, and had obtained good sight with the one, and did not need to see with the other. Of course the result of this first operation had been anxiously awaited by many, and since it proved successful, we soon had our little temporary hospital full, and had no further trouble in getting in-patients. I have described this case rather fully, avoiding technical terms as far as possible, as it illustrates fairly well the difficulties and responsibilities met with and tackled by pioneer workers, be they missionary or official.

The Persians (especially the Kermanis) have a great idea of doing "savabs" (good works), hoping to reap their reward hereafter. This is common to the West as well as the East; but the Kermanis in addition hold a convenient doctrine, namely, the appropriation of the savabs of infidels for themselves! At least one of the chief mullahs in Kerman surprised me somewhat by the cordial reception he accorded me; but later said, "How glad he was that I had come to Kerman and was doing such 'good works' amongst the sick and poor, as hereafter God would credit the true Moslems with all the savabs done by infidels, who of course could derive no benefit at all from their performance."

As Kerman is a city proverbial amongst the Persians for its great wickedness, I could understand the old mullah's satisfaction, as doubtless he felt that many of their savab accounts were rather low and needed a trifle of "credit," which might with advantage be obtained from the savabs of an infidel doctor!

Once yearly the Persians celebrate the death of the martyrs Hassain and Hussein, as has already been described in a previous chapter. We had a good opportunity of witnessing this Persian Passion Play while in Kerman. The sword-dancers, clad in white garments, work themselves up into a frenzy, gashing their heads with the swords and sometimes inflicting severe wounds. A true believer is supposed to have his self-inflicted wounds healed spontaneously through the agency of Hazrati Ali (grandson of the prophet Mohammed); but I was a little amused by the appearance of several of these devotees at my out-patient clinique some days previous to the "celebration," all of them begging for a little English ointment to keep by them for use in case miraculous healing should be delayed.

As has been already mentioned, the curse of Kerman is opium; everybody smokes or eats it—generally the former. The native doctors are partly responsible, as they recommend the drug as a "cure-all"; but even the cultured Kermani smokes opium, possibly to relieve the monotony of his life! Cases of poisoning repeatedly occur, and some of these we were called upon to treat. Our dispensary had a small garden attached to it, and when the Mission had gained the confidence of the people it was no uncommon sight to see several opium patients being treated at the same time in this garden. The treatment used, though somewhat vigorous, proved very effective. A man would arrive at the dispensary, escorted by an excited throng of relatives. On inquiry we would find that he had taken a big dose of opium to end his life: afterwards repenting, he had confessed to his relatives, and they had at once brought him to the English doctor. The treatment began with the administration of a strong emetic followed by repeated doses of strong coffee; then he would be handed over to the care of an attendant, with instructions to walk him round and round the garden and prevent his going to sleep. The native assistants and the patient's friends, armed with sticks, carried out these instructions, and at the first signs of languor exhibited by the unfortunate man he would be beaten and kept effectually awake!

OPIUM-MAKING

An enormous quantity of opium is grown and exported from Persia every year. The juice is extracted from the poppy head by scratching it with a small iron instrument, and as it oozes out it is gathered, and when dry rolled into cakes ready either for use in the country or for export.

THE RICH BEGGAR

This old man is said to be very rich. By day be dons his rags and goes forth on his lucrative profession of begging; at sunset he returns to his home and, exchanging his rags for more respectable garments, spends his earnings in luxury and feasting.

One day I was summoned in haste to the house of an influential Kermani; his only son, a child of two years, had been poisoned with opium. It is a common practice in Kerman for mothers to keep their babies from crying by giving them a little opium to suck. This boy's mother had given him a big lump by mistake, and grew alarmed when she found that all her attempts to wake him were ineffectual! On arriving at the house with my assistant, we had considerable difficulty in making our way into the courtyard, as it was thronged with all the relatives and friends; the neighbouring houses were crowded, a great multitude thronging the flat roofs, which commanded a good view of the courtyard belonging to the patient's father. On examining my little patient I found him nearly dead, exhibiting all the symptoms of an overdose of opium. However, for over an hour we worked away, washing out the child's stomach, injecting strong coffee, &c., all in the open air before the excited multitude, and gradually the little patient showed signs of recovery. When he had come completely round and was crying vigorously, there was great rejoicing. Thinking the opportunity too good a one to be lost, I asked my assistant to tell the father that God had heard prayer and restored him his child, and that we would now like him to join with us and thank God for answering our prayers, if he would tell the crowd what we intended doing. Although the father was a mullah, and had the reputation of being very fanatical in his hatred of Christians, he at once consented to our proposition, announcing to the crowd our intention. During the short thanksgiving prayer every head was bowed and not a sound of protest heard, while Christian and Moslem alike returned thanks to the great God who had heard and answered prayer. Medical Missions had once again won a triumph over Moslem fanaticism, and the scowls and threatening looks which had greeted our arrival were replaced by cordial thanks and vehement expressions of gratitude!

Persian therapeutics are very simple, dating back to the time of Hippocrates. All diseases are divided into two classes—hot and cold—to be treated accordingly with hot or cold remedies. All foods are similarly classified. With this knowledge, plus a few Persian medical books and an appropriate turban, the native quack sets up as a doctor. His impudence and native wit are inexhaustible; he will cheer his patients with extracts from Hafiz or Ferdosi (the great Persian poets), talk learnedly of vapours, and have a specific for every mortal ailment. The quack physician is amusing, and probably confines himself to fairly harmless compounds; but the Persian surgeon is a man to be avoided at all costs. Of course, I am only here speaking of quacks; in Teheran there is a good medical school, and many of the graduates from that school proceed to Paris or Berlin, and return fully qualified to exercise their profession; but they also have to compete with these native quacks.

I remember one case of a poor man brought to the dispensary with a big swelling on the left knee, which prevented his straightening the leg. Careful examination convinced me that the case was one of malignant cancer of the thigh bone, and that nothing could be done but amputation. This was explained to the patient and his father, who indignantly rejected the proposed operation. I lost sight of the man, but some weeks later one of my assistants asked me if I remembered the case; on my replying in the affirmative, he informed me that the patient had since died. It seems after leaving the dispensary the father had taken his son (a young man twenty years old) to a native surgeon (who combined the exercise of his profession most appropriately with the trade of a butcher) and asked his advice, saying the English doctor had advised amputation of the leg; but he had refused, as the swelling caused little pain, and all his son wanted was to be able to straighten his leg so that he might once again walk. "Oh," replied the butcher, "that's easily done; that English doctor knows nothing; I will cure him." So he got the father and other men to hold the unfortunate youth firmly and some other helper to seize the leg; then seizing a huge slab of stone in both his hands, he brought it down with all his force on the bent knee. The leg was straightened ... and needless to add, the poor patient only survived a few days.

My wife has written quite sufficient about the Persian women to enable her readers to appreciate the monotony of their lives behind the veil. This is more especially true of the upper classes, who have no need to work for their living. In Kerman the usual result is that many of these poor women suffer from hysteria. I have often been called in to treat some of these patients, and have found them develop almost all the varying types of that curious disease; but one of the most interesting cases I ever remember occurred in Kerman.

I had been treating the unmarried daughter of one of the wealthiest men in the city, and had prescribed for her some simple bismuth mixture, as she had complained of indigestion. Two days later her brother came galloping his horse to the dispensary, and demanded to see me immediately. He was greatly excited, and said that his sister had been taking the medicine I had prescribed for her and had suddenly gone blind. This was in the early days of the Medical Mission, and I was especially anxious to win the confidence of the people, so did not at all appreciate this complication. I assured the brother that I would return with him at once, and informed him that the medicine could not possibly have caused the blindness; but he was not at all appeased. Upon reaching the house I found all the family distracted with grief, and not at all inclined to be cordial. Moreover, they had called in a native eye-doctor, who had gravely announced that the blindness was most certainly due to the patient having taken the infidel's medicine! In order to reassure the parents I bade them bring the bottle of medicine, and, finding there were still two or three doses left, called for a glass, poured out the remainder, and drank it. This seemed to reassure them partially, so they allowed me to examine the girl. She was a nervous, highly-strung patient, and I had expected to find that she had been malingering; but to my surprise, upon thorough examination I convinced myself that she had really gone blind. Examination of the interior of the eyes showed no disease, and upon inquiry, finding that she was the subject of periodical hysterical attacks, I ventured to predict to the parents that with suitable care and supervision the girl would regain her sight. They were still inclined to be sceptical, but ten days later I heard that my prediction had come true and that she was quite cured. Similar cases of hysterical loss of vision are on record, but are exceedingly rare.

Barely had we managed to get the little Medical Mission well started when circumstances connected with my wife's health arose that forced us to leave at a moment's notice the people we had learnt to love. Fortunately the work was not given up; another doctor succeeded me, and now there is a flourishing Medical Mission with two hospitals, one for men and the other for women patients, with a lady doctor and nurse; while the influence exerted by that Mission is felt throughout the whole of the great Kerman province, which stretches eastwards to the border of Beloochistan, and is bounded on the south by the Persian Gulf.

CHAPTER XIV

MEDICAL MISSION WORK IN YEZD[4]

A hospital — A friendly governor — A suspicious case — Superstition — The opium habit — A case of cataract — We return to England.

"By medicine life may be prolonged....
With the help of a surgeon he may yet recover."

SHAKESPEARE.

The last of our three years' sojourn in Persia was spent in Yezd. Here there was already a small Mission Hospital, all the pioneer work having been done by Dr. White of the C.M.S. A wealthy Parsee merchant had presented the site for a hospital in the form of an old caravanserai (an Eastern inn). This had been gutted and made into a nice little hospital, with an out-patient department. Dr. White being on furlough, the doctor taking his place in Yezd exchanged with me, as it was hoped that my wife would be able better to stand the lower altitude of Yezd than the heights of Kerman. Yezd is an island city in a sea of sand. The waves, driven by the winds, surge against the city walls and threaten to engulf the whole place. At some parts of the wall, the drifted sand reaches almost to the level of the wall itself.

The Governor of Yezd during the time we lived there was H.R.H. Jalal-el-Dowleh, the eldest son of the Prince-Governor of Isphahan (the Zil-es-Sultan). The Jalal-el-Dowleh had the reputation, like his father, of being a strong man, and ruled with a firm hand. He had already proved a good friend to the Mission, and was accustomed to pay a state visit once yearly to the hospital, where, after being entertained at the doctor's house, he would proceed to make a very thorough tour of inspection, and before leaving would hand the English doctor a sealed envelope containing the munificent sum of £40 as a donation. During our stay in Yezd we saw a good deal of the governor, and I had to add to my duties those of court physician.

In Yezd, as in other Persian cities, there are many quacks, who not unnaturally resent the presence of a European doctor. I had not been long in the city before I made the acquaintance of some of these gentry, in a somewhat dramatic manner.

Early one morning I was hurriedly called to the house of the chief native doctor, as his brother had been taken seriously ill.

On entering the patient's room, I found it crowded with his friends, the pa-

[4] By Dr. A. Hume-Griffith.

tient himself lying upon a mattress placed on the ground. One glance at the patient sufficed: he was dead, and had apparently been so for some hours. When I announced the fact to the brother, he became very angry, and assured me that I was mistaken. He begged me to pour some medicine down the man's throat, or to do something to rouse him, as he had only fainted!

Upon further inquiry, I found that he had been poorly for some days, and his brother had been treating him. My suspicions were aroused, as the brother and his friends crowded round me, imploring that English medicines should be tried, and after further careful examination only served to confirm my first opinion, I refused absolutely to comply with their entreaties, and left the house with my assistant. The brother and some of his friends pursued us, offering large fees if only we would give some medicine, absolutely refusing to accept my verdict. It is a necessary custom in Persia and the East generally, to bury a dead body within a few hours of death, but we heard that the brother refused to allow this corpse to be buried for three whole days, alleging that the English doctor was mistaken: however, in the end they were obliged to bury him. The native doctor was strongly suspected of having poisoned his brother, and this doubtless accounted for the urgent manner in which he begged me to pour something down the dead man's throat, so that he could accuse me of being responsible for his death.

TYPES OF PERSIAN JEWS

The Chief Rabbi at Yezd (sitting in the centre). This photo was
taken in the author's garden at Yezd.

THE WATER SQUARE

The "Maidawi ob," or water square, is a favourite gathering-place
of the inhabitants. They love to linger round the edges of the water, drinking their coffee, striking bargains, and exchanging news.
The water is none too clean, nor the odour too sweet which greets
the senses as we ride by.

All Persians are superstitious, and are great believers in goblins and 'jinns.'
One day a young man was brought to me suffering from an acute attack of chorea
(St. Vitus' dance). He was well educated, and had been employed as a clerk in a
merchant's office: now he was unable to hold a pen in his hand, and exhibited all
the symptoms of the disease in a very marked degree. He was promptly admitted
to hospital, and discharged cured in a few weeks. According to his own statement
the cause of the attack was as follows. He had gone for a walk in the desert outside
the city after his day's work was over, and had wandered on further than usual.
Suddenly he came across an old well, and round the well were numbers of hideous dwarf-like goblins pelting each other with stones. When they saw him they
crowded round laughing, jeering, pulling his clothes, and then began to pelt him
with stones. He turned and fled, running the whole way back to the city, and to
this shock he attributed the commencement of his symptoms.

In my last chapter I referred to the prevalence of the opium habit in Kerman,
but we found many addicted to it also in Yezd. So much was this the case, that I
started admitting some of those who expressed a desire to give up the habit into
the hospital, submitting them to a special treatment, with very good results. It was

a curious sight to see these patients grouped together in the ward, smoking their carefully weighed out amount of opium, which was gradually reduced day by day, until they could go without altogether.

The opium habit is in truth a curse, but upon one occasion I really believe it greatly helped to save a man's life. It happened in this way. A well-known merchant in Yezd was found in his house apparently sleeping. His women-folk, unable to rouse him, became alarmed, and sent for me. I found the patient unconscious, exhibiting every symptom of belladonna poisoning. An excited crowd, as usual, collected, watching us as we tried every possible means of saving the poor fellow's life. Strychnine and morphia had been injected, cold water poured on his face, all without avail: there was no sign of returning consciousness. A happy thought struck me. Turning to some of the men in the crowd, I asked whether they were opium-smokers. Three or four somewhat shamefacedly acknowledged that they did a little, so I ordered them to bring a pipe and a little of the drug. Then I made them sit round the patient's body, take the pipe in turn, and as they smoked, puff out the smoke into the patient's face, occasionally blowing it into his nostrils, and down his throat. I confess that I had but little hope of any good result, but what was my delight and surprise, after about a quarter of an hour's perseverance in the treatment, to see unmistakable signs of recovery in the patient's face. His widely dilated pupils began to contract, and soon he returned to consciousness and was able to sit up. On the following day I found him quite well, and thoroughly enjoying the sensation that his marvellous recovery had made in the city. Hundreds of people had been to see him, and I am a little afraid that the value of the opium as a "cure-all" was not diminished by the incident!

We had quite a number of cataract patients in the hospital, many coming several days' journey for operation. A small hospital for women had been started, and a lady doctor had been sent to take charge. The first case admitted was an old lady with cataract. When the day arrived for the operation, everything went well at first, but in the middle of the operation the patient started up screaming. She said she had seen a snake, and she thought it was going to bite her. Her vision cost her dearly, the operation necessarily being spoilt, and the eye lost, but unfortunately it also kept away other patients suffering from the same disease, but only for a short time, the lady doctor soon winning their confidence, and finding more work on her hands than she could comfortably get through.

After a very happy year in Yezd, my wife's health still remaining unsatisfactory, we were obliged to leave Persia, and return to England for a short rest. Both of us were grieved at having to leave a country and people that we had learnt to love, and amongst whom we had hoped to spend our lives.

Medical Missions in Persia have already worked wonders, breaking down opposition, winning friends even amongst the most fanatical. Here is not the place to speak of results, neither would it be wise to do so, but I would like once for all definitely and decisively to repudiate the oft-quoted statement, often made, unfortunately, by Christians who should be better informed, "that it is impossible for a Mohammedan to become a Christian." With God *all* things are possible!

PART II

CHAPTER I

THE CITY OF NINEVEH

*The city of Nineveh — The fast of Jonah — The bridge of boats — Traditions as
to ancient history of Mosul — Alkosh, birthplace of Nahum the prophet —
Shurgât — Climate of Mosul — Cultivation and industries — Importance
of Mosul.*

"A ruin, yet what ruin! from its mass
Walls, palaces, half cities have been reared.
Heroes have trod this spot — 'tis on their dust ye tread."

Byron.

"Nineveh, an exceeding great city of three days' journey."

The ancient city of Nineveh, the former capital of the Assyrian Empire, is situated on the eastern bank of the river Tigris. Little is to be seen to-day of the once famous city but huge mounds of earth which cover the site of this historical and interesting place. There are two principal mounds, separated from each other by a small rivulet. The larger of these is called Kouyunjik, the smaller Nabbi Eunice. The former contains the ruins of the palace of Sennacherib, before whom Jonah stood and delivered his message; but nothing now remains to tell of its former glory and wealth. When we first visited the spot over three years ago, there was one huge man-headed lion remaining, and a few pieces of sculpture representing fish swimming in water, &c. But now even these have disappeared, for about eighteen months ago the Turkish Government sold *all* the visible remains of Nineveh for the enormous sum of two Turkish liras (36s.)! the buyer grinding everything to powder, including the huge statue, for purposes of building!

Nineveh is best seen to-day at the British Museum or the Louvre, Paris, as both of these places contain many interesting and valuable remains of that city. Nineveh was closed to excavators about four years ago, but it is hoped that investigations will be renewed again in the near future, as there still remain thirteen rooms of the palace to be examined.

The other and smaller mound, known as Nabbi Eunice (Prophet Jonah), was once the site of a church named after the prophet, on account of the tradition that he preached upon that spot. The church stands to this day, but is used as a mosque, as it now belongs to the Moslems, who venerate the place as being the tomb of the prophet.

OUR HOME IN NINEVEH

The houses of Mosul generally consist of two compounds. The inner one is used as the "hareem" or women's quarters, while the outer one is the men's reception rooms, stables, etc. The above picture shows the "hareem." The pillars are made of marble, which abounds in the neighbourhood of Mosul.

They accept the whole story of Jonah's mission to Nineveh and the adventures he encountered *en route*, as we have it recorded in Holy Scripture. It is an interesting fact, too, that year by year the inhabitants of Mosul, Christians and Moslems alike, keep in remembrance the three days of fasting and repentance mentioned in the Book of Jonah. The fast is still kept for three days, by some very strictly, while others keep it from sunset to sunset, only eating once a day. Every one may please herself as to the severity of her fasting, but almost all join in the remembrance of those three memorable days in the history of Nineveh. "Herself" is used advisedly, as it is especially kept by women who are seeking some particular gift from God, and they will often fast absolutely for the three days, not even allowing a drop of water to touch their lips. They hope by so doing that God will hear their prayers, even as He answered the petitions of the Ninevites of old. The memory of Jonah is perpetuated, too, in Mosul by parents naming their boys after the prophet, Eunice being quite a favourite name amongst Christians, Moslems, and Jews.

The tomb of Jonah is guarded very zealously by the Mohammedans against the Christians, and it is very difficult for the latter to gain admission to the interior of the building. A friend staying with us in Mosul was very anxious to see the tomb, so we rode over to Nabbi Eunice one day, but the mullah in charge politely but firmly refused us permission to enter beyond the portal!

Kouyunjik is now a favourite place for picnics from Mosul, and in the early spring a day spent amongst the old ruins of Nineveh is very delightful. It is too hot in summer, as there is no shade. From the top of the mounds we have a beautiful view of Mosul, with the Tigris in the foreground and the mountains stretching away on either side. It is not considered safe for any one to wander about alone on the mounds; the natives will never go there alone after dusk. Some years ago two Europeans who were passing through Mosul visited Nineveh by themselves. As they were rambling over the old remains, one said to his companion, "I am going round there," indicating a projecting piece of marble. His companion waited and waited, and as his friend did not return went in search of him, but not a sign of him could be seen. After seeking in every possible place without success, he returned to Mosul to institute a search party, but all efforts proved fruitless, and to this day nothing has been discovered as to the fate of this man. Whether he fell down some disused shaft or was carried off by Arabs is not known, and probably will always remain a mystery.

Mosul is connected with Nineveh by an old bridge of boats, which probably existed in the days of Jonah. There are twenty-one or twenty-two of these old-fashioned flat-bottomed boats, fastened together by heavy chains, a platform of wood being laid from boat to boat and the whole covered with earth. This part of the bridge is movable, and is connected at one end with the mainland by a permanent stone bridge consisting of thirty-three arches. In the spring, when the rush of water is very strong consequent upon the snow melting in the mountains, it is loosened at one end and allowed to swing with the current. Sometimes, however, the river rises suddenly, carrying the bridge away and playing havoc with the banks. When this takes place it is very difficult to replace the bridge. Often for weeks together the bridge is not open, and all traffic across the river has to be conveyed by boats, the owner of the ferries reaping a golden harvest. The toll of the bridge is taken by a man who rents it from the Government. He is said to be one of the richest men in

Mosul. Foot passengers are allowed to pass freely, but all four-footed beasts have a small charge levied on them ranging from a halfpenny to twopence, and carriages are charged half a mejideh (1s. 8d.). As some thousands of camels, mules, and donkeys are continually passing to and fro, it is no wonder that the toll-collector is a rich man.

A BRIDGE OF BOATS

This bridge over the Tigris connects Nineveh with Mosul. When the rush of water is very great the bridge swings open, and is sometimes only closed with great difficulty. In the right-hand corner of the background may be seen the village of "Nabbi Eunice," where the prophet Jonah is said to be buried.

I am not at all fond of riding across this bridge; it is not very wide, and camels jostle you on one side with their huge burdens, donkeys and mules vie with each other in trying to pass on the other, quite oblivious of the fact that there is no room; while underneath the river rushes madly on. Altogether, I always heave a sigh of relief when the opposite bank is safely reached.

There are many traditions as to the probable origin of Mosul, but its true early history is involved in obscurity. The following has been gleaned from some of the many traditions circulated amongst its inhabitants.

Mosul is said to have been built some four thousand years ago, and was then a small village consisting of a few houses built of mud. This village was believed to be the fourth village built after the Flood. About four days' journey from Mosul there is a mountain called Judy, on which the ark is supposed to have rested after the Flood. The natives living near this mountain say it *must* be Mount Ararat, because close by grows the only olive tree for miles around! and also they have in their possession enormous wooden nails *said* to have been used in the construction of the ark! These nails were found on the mountain many years ago. At the foot of this mountain lies a village which claims to have the honour of being the *first* built after the Flood. Quite near by is another small town called Jezirah, which is said to have been the second village to spring into existence, while some village in Egypt takes the third place, and Mosul the fourth! If these traditions are to be trusted, then Mosul has indeed a right to be termed ancient.

Some 1260 years ago Omar el Khattab the Calipha conquered Jerusalem and Damascus, and then turned his attention to Mosul. He sent down one of his chiefs named Eyath, son of Ghoonum, to besiege Mosul, with orders to convert the city to Mohammedanism at all costs, if necessary at the point of the sword. Many of the inhabitants at that time were Parsees, belonging to the old fire-worshipping religion; others were called "Charamika," but no trace of their belief has been found. These and many others were converted to Mohammedanism by the strong argument of the sword.

In the twelfth century Mosul had a sovereignty of its own, a brother of the Sultan of Damascus then reigning over this province. In 1180 it withstood the armies of the famous Saladin, who was a native of a town some five days' ride from Mosul. In the thirteenth and fourteenth centuries it suffered defeat from the hands of its enemies, and in 1743 Nadir Shah of Persia bombarded the town for forty days. Since then Mosul has suffered much from time to time through various causes—from the cruelties of some of its governors, from a famine caused by the crops being utterly destroyed by locusts, and also from the plague which visited it in 1831 and left the town almost a desert. It is stated that 100,000 people perished at that time from this terrible scourge.

The walls surrounding Mosul are very old. They were built, in the first instance, about 2000 years ago by a man named Marvan, one of the kings of a tribe called "Umayya." They were repaired 170 years ago by Hadji Hussein Pasha, one of the Abdul Jaleel family. They are now in many places fast falling into ruin, and are in great need of restoration. These walls are pierced by about twelve gates, which are shut at sunset or soon after.

About five hours' journey from Mosul is the little village of Elkosh, believed by many to have been the birthplace of the prophet Nahum, and also the scene of his life-work and burial. This village, now inhabited by Chaldeans, is reverenced by Moslems and Christians alike, but more especially is it looked upon as a holy place by the Jews. There is a synagogue in which is supposed to lie the tomb of the prophet; to this the Jews flock for the yearly pilgrimage, having done so from time immemorial.

Kalah Shurgât is another interesting place, situated two days' journey from Mosul. It consists of an old Assyrian ruin, said to be the remains of the ancient city of Asshur. The Germans have been excavating there for some years, and are doing it very thoroughly. The whole ground floor of the palace and temple are laid bare, and are in a wonderful state of preservation. One of the excavators pointed out to us the "bathroom" of the palace, running through which was a mono-rail, evidently having been constructed for the purpose of conveying water from the reservoir to the bath. This tram-line must have been one of the first ever invented! It was simply a groove cut in the marble floor, on which probably a one-wheeled trolley ran.

The climate of Mosul is a very variable one, the summers being excessively hot and the winters cold.

During the hot months all the inhabitants sleep at night on their roofs, starting about the 1st of June, and continuing to do so for five months, or till the first rains come. Many of the houses are provided with "sirdâbs" or underground rooms, for use during the middle part of the day. The marble from which most of the houses are built retains the heat of the sun so long that they do not cool down in the evenings; on account of this, as the summer wears on, the houses become almost unbearable with accumulated heat. For this reason we generally try to go away somewhere for a month's holiday in August or September. There are no cool places near Mosul, and to find a suitable summer retreat it is necessary to go three or four days' journey. For two years we only went to a large house about three miles from Mosul, kindly lent us by a patient of my husband's. Here the heat was intense during the day, but the evenings were delightfully cool as a rule, for the river ran at the foot of the garden.

The winters in Mosul are often very cold. Two years ago the Tigris was nearly frozen over, and for three days the only water we could obtain was from melted snow. The cold was so severe that men died as they sat at their work. While such cold weather lasted it was impossible to keep the patients in the hospital, as having no stoves in the wards we were not able to warm them sufficiently. But this was a record winter, there having been no such frost for one hundred and fifty years.

Spring and autumn are beautiful seasons in Mosul, especially, perhaps, the former. During March, April, and part of May the land for many miles around Mosul is green with waving corn—a refreshing sight for weary eyes. When the grass is about a foot in height, all the inhabitants pitch tents outside the town and spend their days there. Those who have horses tether them in front of their tents, and allow them to eat grass to their hearts' content. A friend lent us a tent last year, and for a month or six weeks we enjoyed the luxury of green scenery! Every day some of our congregation were able to get out, each of us taking our turn at providing afternoon tea. It was such a relief to get away from the heat of the city walls, and to enjoy, if only for a short time, the lovely fresh air of the corn-fields!

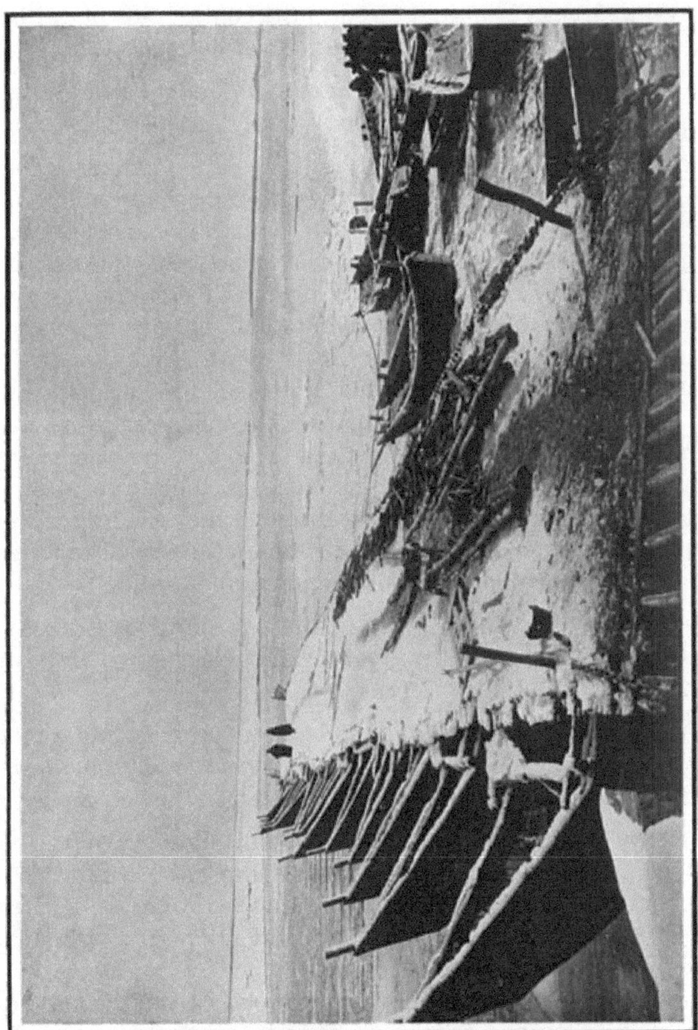

THE BRIDGE OF BOATS OVER THE FROZEN TIGRIS

Such an occurrence is very unusual. It is 150 years since the river was frozen over before.

The autumn days are very pleasant too, but as a rule this season is only too short. The summers last till the rains begin, and then almost at once cold weather sets in. The most trying part of the whole year comes towards the end of summer, when the clouds "come up." It is very marvellous the way the natives can tell, almost to a day, when to expect the first clouds. They generally last from ten to twelve days, and the relief is great when they depart. On the whole the climate of Mosul seems to be a healthy one. At certain times of the year malarial fever is very prevalent, but, "alhamd'llillah!" neither of us have ever contracted it.

The highest degree of heat registered in the coolest part of our house is 110°, but the average heat of the three hottest months is about 98° to 105°.

Three to four months of this kind of heat is generally quite enough!

The land round Mosul is cultivated to a great extent, corn being the chief product. The success of the crops, however, is entirely dependent upon the winter and spring rains. Should the rainfall be great, the harvest is abundant; but if the season is a dry one, then the result is disastrous. Mr. Layard speaks of one such occasion when, during the whole of the winter and spring, no rain fell. As a consequence of this, the crop failed and famine ravaged the land. This famine is still spoken of in Mosul as something never to be forgotten, and many events are marked as dating from "the famine." Some are not ashamed to own that they made their fortunes during that awful time, by storing corn and then selling it at famine prices; while others, who had been prosperous merchants till that year, were then rendered penniless, and have never been able to retrieve their fortunes. There are a few rude wheels constructed along the banks of the Tigris for the purpose of irrigation; but as these are highly taxed by the local government, they are by no means general. This mode of raising water is very simple but expensive, as it requires the labour of several men and at least two animals, either oxen or mules.

Gardens near the town are irrigated in this way, either by drawing water from the river or from deep wells, but the great stretch of land sown with corn is dependent for its nourishment on the rainfall.

Cotton is also grown and exported. Melons, cucumbers, and tomatoes are cultivated very largely, and as the river recedes in the summer, the moist bed is sown with water-melon seeds, which flourish splendidly in the damp soil.

Fruit is largely grown in the mountains, and brought down on donkeys. Apricots are very abundant; cherries, plums, peaches are less plentiful. The best apples are brought from Damascus; they *look* good, but are flavourless. Grapes are very largely cultivated, and are brought to great perfection. The large black kind are very delicious; there is also a white grape which has a very sweet flavour. Vegetables of all kinds are grown in the gardens near Mosul: beans, peas, spinach, carrots (red), beetroot, onions, artichokes, as well as many other varieties. Potatoes are brought from Persia, and sometimes suffer so much from the long journey that they are only fit to be thrown away when they reach Mosul. Last winter several hundreds of sacks of potatoes were thrown into the river at Mosul, as they had been frostbitten on the journey from Persia, and so were useless.

"Manna" is found in the mountains, and is collected and sent to Mosul, where it is made into a sweetmeat called "halawwi."

The industries of Mosul are chiefly spinning and weaving. A very strong kind of cotton cloth is woven, also calico and woollen goods. Many years ago this industry was much larger than it is at present, and in those days Mosul gave its name to muslin, a fabric exported by the French from that town in the last century. Weaving is done by men, while the women do the spinning and dyeing of the cotton or wool. Weaving is a very favourite occupation, as the weaver can do just as much or as little as he likes, being paid accordingly. For this reason a man who is inclined to be lazy would much rather be a weaver than a servant.

Furs are largely exported from Mosul. The skin of the fox is most common, but there is another fur much resembling the sable which is highly prized amongst the natives, a coat lined with this fur costing something like £50. Some years ago furs could be bought quite cheaply in Mosul, but the merchants finding a good market for their goods in Europe, the prices soon went up, and now even fox is becoming expensive.

The industries of Mosul are not what they were, but we trust better days are coming, when the old prosperity of the town will be renewed and increased.

The three great questions now under consideration with regard to the land of Mesopotamia will have great influence on the future of Mosul. The first is the navigation of the Tigris from Baghdad to Mosul. This, when an accomplished fact, will make a great difference in the export and import trade of the city. The Baghdad railway will also greatly increase the importance of Mosul, for the line running through it will bring the East in close touch with the near West. Perhaps the most important subject of all in connection with the future of Mosul is that of the irrigation of Mesopotamia, which, once accomplished, will turn the whole of that vast desert into a garden. The means to be employed for this end are simply the reviving of the old Assyrian method of irrigation. This method consisted in the digging of canals to intersect the land between the rivers Tigris and Euphrates. Maps of these same canals are still to be seen in the British Museum and other places, and are of great interest. These great canals, made in the prosperous days of the Assyrian Empire, are now choked up, after having been in use for many centuries by the inhabitants of the country. Layard, in his "Discoveries at Nineveh," says, "Herodotus describes the extreme fertility of Assyria and its abundant harvests of corn, the seed producing two and three hundred-fold"; and adds later, "But in his day the Assyrians depended as much upon artificial irrigation as upon the winter rains. They were skilful in constructing machines for raising water, and their system of canals was as remarkable for its ingenuity as for the knowledge of hydraulics it displayed." Since the result of irrigation in those ancient days was two to three hundred-fold, surely if carried out to-day with the additional knowledge of modern science and experience the ground would yield an even larger return. It has been estimated that £8,000,000 would be sufficient to reopen all the old canals of Mesopotamia, with the certainty that the land thus irrigated would yield an abundant profit.

"Ensha'allah," this much-talked-of scheme will soon be carried out, and Mesopotamia become once more "a land of corn and wine, a land of bread and vineyards, a land of olive oil and of honey."

CHAPTER II

THE PEOPLE OF MOSUL

*Population—Moslems—Christians—Chaldeans—Nestorians—Jacobites—
Arabs—Kurds—Jews—Yezidees— Recreations—Warfare of the slingers—Hammam Ali—The recreation ground of Mosul men and women.*

"... The world is great,
But each has but his own land in the world."

A. C. SWINBURNE.

The population of Mosul has been estimated to be anything between sixty
and eighty thousand people. If the whole "vilayet" is included the number will be
something like a million and a half. These people are made up of many different
nationalities and tribes, each retaining its own leading characteristics, whilst many
have a language peculiar to themselves.

The inhabitants of Mosul are chiefly Arabs, of whom by far the larger part are
Mohammedans. These of course form the strong religious element in the city, as
they are the conquerors of the land. This is a fact, too, which they take care never
to lose sight of. In the market, the mosque, and the street, the Mohammedan is always proclaiming by look, word, and deed that *he* is the master. A Christian finds
himself at a great disadvantage in the market, for when buying from a Moslem he
is not allowed to handle the food, and must purchase his goods to a great extent
on trust.

In all mosques, which once were Christian churches, it is customary for the
mullah to preach with a naked sword in his hand. This is done in order to remind the people that the Mohammedan religion was propagated by the sword,
and must, if necessary, be retained by the same means. In the streets the difference
is very marked between the two, the Mohammedan behaving as if the whole place
belonged to him, while the Christians, and more especially the Jews, always appear as if they were apologising for their very existence.

The Moslems are the rulers, and they make their power felt. An amusing instance illustrating this feeling occurred a short time ago. A little Moslem boy was
walking through the street on his way to our house when, apparently without any
provocation, a Christian girl began to revile him as he passed. The boy instantly
turned on the girl and gave her a thrashing. I did not hear anything of this for
some days, and then only in an indirect way. Some one told me that the boy had

received a severe beating from the master of the school which he was attending, and on asking the reason of the punishment was told the foregoing story. I am very fond of the boy, he is such a dear, bright little chap, with great wondering eyes. Upon hearing the history of his encounter with the girl, I sent for the boy, and tried to tell him how wrong it was for a man to strike a woman. "But," said the boy, quite innocently, "she was a Christian!" Thus early in life is instilled into the young mind of the Moslem his inherent right to act the tyrant.

On the other hand, it is a strange truth that Moslems very often prefer to have Christian servants in their houses, as they find they are more faithful. In many hareems the "slaves," or girls who have been bought for life, are very often children of Christian parents, who have been willing for a few pounds to sell their girls. The reverse of this is also true, that Christian families often find that a Moslem servant is more trustworthy than one of their own religion. A few months ago I heard of a little black boy in Mosul, whose mother, a Moslem negress, was anxious to find him a home. We offered to take the boy and bring him up, but the mother absolutely refused our offer, as we were Christians, and she was afraid her boy might become the same, as he was then only one year old, and had not yet learnt to hate the Christians!

There are some 15,000 to 20,000 Christians in Mosul, who are said to date their conversion back to the time of St. Adday, who was a disciple of St. Thomas; others migrated from Baghdad to Mosul at the time of the Caliphas. These Christians have remained firm to the religion of their forefathers in spite of much persecution and many trials. To-day in Mosul there are many different sects of Christians to be found, viz. the Chaldean, Syrian, Nestorian, Jacobite, Armenian, and Greek. The Chaldeans in Mosul now entirely belong to the Romish Church, having been admitted to that body about a hundred years ago by means of the Dominican Mission who started work amongst these ancient Christians. They have their own bishop and archbishop, the Patriarch making Mosul his headquarters since 1256.

The Nestorians are the true Chaldeans, and repudiate the name Nestorian. They live amongst the mountains, have resisted all efforts of the Romish Church, and remain true to the faith of their fathers. They, in common with the other Christians, date their Christianity from the time of the Apostles as the converts of St. Thomas. They refuse to accept Nestorius, the Patriarch of Constantinople, as their founder, saying that he was a Greek, while they were Syrians. They assert that "he did not even know our language, and so how could he have propagated his doctrines among us?" and they also declare that their religion was an established fact long before Nestorius was born. They have their own Patriarch, who resides near Van, a distance of ten days from Mosul. They regard the Pope and his followers with feelings of great hatred, and are said to curse him and his forefathers regularly every day. In answer to a message from the Pope urging reconciliation with Rome, the Patriarch sent the following answer: "I shall never become a Roman Catholic, and should you ever induce my people to do so, I would sooner become a dervish or a mullah than degrade myself by an alliance with the Pope."

A PICNIC PARTY

The women of Mosul thoroughly enjoy a day spent in the country.
On the day on which this photo was taken about forty Christian
women had come to spend the day with us in a lovely garden,
kindly lent to us for the occasion. Lunch was served in the verandah of the house, and afterwards games were played till tea-time.

The Patriarch of the Nestorians is not allowed to marry; he is also compelled to be a strict vegetarian. When it is thought advisable to nominate a successor to the archbishopric, the wife of a near relative (if possible, a brother) of the then Patriarch is chosen as the possible mother of the future dignitary. She is set apart as holy till the birth of her child, her diet meanwhile being strictly vegetarian. If the child proves to be a boy, he is solemnly dedicated to God from his birth, and is never allowed to touch meat or flesh of any kind. Should the child unfortunately be a girl, the choice has to be made again, and great is the disappointment of the mother, the honour of being the mother of a Patriarch being much coveted and prized.

In 1843 these people suffered a terrible massacre at the hands of the Kurds; 10,000 of them are said to have perished, and after being hunted from place to place the Patriarch finally fled for refuge to the English Consulate at Mosul.

The Jacobite section of the Christian Church in Mosul is a small one, and so far remains firm to its old faith, resisting all attempts by the Church of Rome to effect a union. It, too, has its own bishop in Mosul, but the Patriarch resides in Mardin, where he has many thousands of adherents. He pays periodical visits to his scattered flock in Mosul and the surrounding country. They trace the origin of their name to one Jacob Baradæus, a Reformer who arose in the sixth century, and refusing to follow the lead of the other Syrians in joining the Romish Church, continued in the old faith, which has since been called by his name (an alternative name being the Old Syrian Church).

The population of Mosul also consists of Arabs, Kurds, Yezidees, and Jews.

The Arabs are the original inhabitants of the desert, who date their descent back to the time of Shem, the son of Noah. They are divided into many tribes, of which the most important in Mesopotamia is that of the great Shammar clan, who are to be found in all parts. There are three classes of Arabs, namely, those who have settled down in one place and become town Arabs, such as the inhabitants of Mosul: the wandering tribes of the desert or Bedouins, who live in tents and whose occupation is sheep farming: a third class of Arabs are the robbers of the desert, who subsist solely by plunder, and roam the desert seeking for a livelihood by any means that may come to their hand. The wandering tribes find it very hard to settle down to a fixed abode after the free life of the desert, and they prefer often to suffer pain and inconvenience rather than spend a few days or weeks beneath a roof and within the walls of a hospital.

A story is told of a Bedouin lady of the seventh century, whose husband rose afterwards to be one of the Caliphs. When taken to Damascus to live in luxury and state, she pined for the freedom of the desert, and gave utterance to her loneliness in the following verses: —

> "A tent with rustling breezes cool
> Delights me more than palace high,
> And more the cloak of simple wool
> Than robes in which I learned to sigh.
>
> The crust I ate beside my tent

Was more than this fine bread to me;
The wind's voice where the hill-path went
Was more than tambourine can be."[5]

Arab women have come to the hospital from time to time, but they always long to return to their desert life, and are impatient at the restraints of town life.

The Kurds are a warlike people inhabiting the mountains round Mosul. They are the descendants of the wild people of the mountains mentioned by Xenophon as the Karduchi, who so severely harassed the Greeks during their retreat. In later years they were known as the Parthians, who opposed the Romans. From this people came the celebrated Saladin, the opponent of Richard Cœur de Lion in the crusading days. The Kurds have been compared to the old Scottish Highlanders, who were noted for their devotion to their chiefs. A well-known writer, in speaking of this trait in the character of these people, says that once he heard the following story: "A chieftain having died, one of his followers, who was standing on the roof of his house when the news of his master's death was brought to him, exclaimed, 'What! is the Beg dead? Then I will not live another moment,' and immediately threw himself from the roof and was dashed to pieces."

A few of these Kurds are Nestorians, but the majority of them are Moslems, and are a very fierce-looking set of people. They carry as a rule large daggers in the waistband, and are quite capable of using them when necessary. We once had a servant who was a Kurd, and although as a rule a peaceable man, he often longed to be off when he heard of any fighting going on in his country. He used to boast to the other servants of the many people he had robbed and murdered! but said of course he would never harm us, as we were in the place of father and mother to him. We are quite hoping to secure his services again on our return to Mosul.

There are about two thousand Jews in Mosul, who date their descent from the time of the Captivity. When Cyrus issued his decree allowing all Jews to return to their native land, about fifty thousand of those living in Mesopotamia joyfully availed themselves of this permission, but a few preferred to remain in their adopted land, and their descendants are there to this day. In spite of much persecution, they have remained firm in their belief. Mohammed quite hoped at first that the Jews would easily be converted to Mohammedanism. He therefore instructed all his followers to turn their faces towards the temple at Jerusalem when praying, but before many months he saw that his hopes in this direction were doomed to disappointment. He therefore withdrew his former instructions, and ordained that in future all Mohammedans should turn to the Ka'aba at Mecca when engaged in prayer.

The Jews in Mosul are looked down upon and despised by Christian and Moslem alike. In the dispensary it is sad to see with what loathing the Jews are treated. The scornful way in which the word "Yahudi" (Jew) is hurled at these people is enough to make one's heart ache for them. If there is anything degrading to be done, a Jew is the only one to be found willing to do it. The Jews are the shoeblacks of Mosul. It being considered very degrading to clean boots and shoes, the

---

[5] Extract from "The Literary History of the Arabs," by R. A. Nicholson, M.A.

Jew undertakes this task, receiving payment at the rate of about ¼d. a pair.

MUTRÂV PAULUS

Bishop of the Syrian Roman Catholic Church in Mosul.

It is a wonderful sight to see all these different nationalities—Moslems, Christians, Jews, Kurds, Arabs, Devil Worshippers—all sitting down together in the waiting-room of the dispensary while waiting their turn to see the doctor.

It reminds one of the picture of Peace, in which the artist depicts the lion, the leopard, and the wolf living in harmony with the lamb. I am afraid the resemblance is only superficial, for in the hearts of that rude miscellaneous throng there is little of peace, and much of anger, wrath, jealousy, hatred, and murder.

The dwellers in the desert and mountain would scorn the idea of passing the time in recreations of any kind, but the town gentlemen much enjoy a little relaxation from their arduous (?) labours. Riding and racing are much in vogue in Mosul. Just outside one of the gates is a long, level stretch of land, uncultivated, which is used by the sporting part of the population for racing. Betting is not a part of the programme. Any one who possesses a horse is at liberty to enter it for the races; and every Thursday afternoon a large conclave of people may be seen watching the performance with great interest. Horse dealers who have horses for sale race their animals with the hope that they will carry off the palm, in which case the value of the horse is considerably raised.

A few of the Mosul men go in for hunting, but it is not a favourite pastime. My husband sometimes goes with some of the Begs, who are fond of hawking. The boys much enjoy slinging, and some of them are quite experts at it, at times their aim being rather too accurate. The spring is the season for slinging, and hundreds of boys may be seen outside the town on a fine day armed with these instruments of torture. They line up along the walls of the city, and take aim at every passer-by. This is somewhat disconcerting, especially when some little boy takes a shot at your horse's head or tail, a game of which the animal does not at all approve. Or sometimes the boys form armies, each opposing side being composed of an equal number of slingers. They stand at a distance of about fifty yards apart and commence warfare in real earnest. It is rather a terrible ordeal to have to run the gauntlet of these two opposing armies. The stones seem to whizz round one's head in a most alarming manner; but although my mare has received a few stray shots of which she much disapproved, yet I have fortunately never actually been hit. Occasionally boys become so vicious in their excitement that the Government here has to put a stop to their "wars" for a time, as they do so much injury to one another.

A form of recreation which is indulged in by all the Mosul people is that of paying a yearly visit to a hot sulphur spring. This spring is situated about twelve miles from Mosul on the Baghdad road, and is called Hammam Ali.

A small village has grown up around the spring, but cannot furnish anything like the accommodation needed for the thousands of visitors who flock there in the early summer. To meet this need, small booths are built of dried grass, each family renting one for the time of their visit. Two years ago it was estimated that ten thousand people from Mosul were there at one time, all congregated together without any proper accommodation, or any sanitary arrangements; the consequence was that disease and sickness were very prevalent amongst them, and many went seeking health, and found death.

Last year a similar number were as usual gathered at Hammam Ali, when one evening a lighted match was carelessly thrown down, with the result that in a few minutes many of these booths were a mass of flames. Several children were burnt to death and two women.

The next day the exodus from the place was universal. We were staying then at a house midway between Mosul and Hammam Ali, and watched the procession of people returning, a steady stream from morning till night. After a day or two, however, the sad episode was forgotten, and visitors began to flock back again.

We once saw this celebrated place. It was on our way to Mosul, and we arrived late one night at Hammam Ali, minus our tent. The villagers kindly offered us the use of the Hammam (bath) for the night, so we made a tour of inspection, but decided to decline their offer with thanks.

The place was damp, dirty, and malodorous. We preferred to pass the night in a stable, which looked a trifle more inviting, although full of rat-holes. In the morning I paid a visit to the Hammam, as it was a ladies' bathing day, and found the bath crowded with women and children, packed in like sardines in a box! The water was very hot, and I wondered the women could stand so long in it. Some of them looked rather as if they had been boiled. Here were women and children, apparently healthy, bathing in the same water as others suffering from all manner of skin diseases and other horrible things. However, they all looked perfectly happy and contented; and I would not grudge these poor creatures any little pleasure which might help to brighten their lives.

We shall see in the following chapters how little brightness they possess, and, on the other hand, how much of sadness and sorrow.

CHAPTER III

THE RIVER TIGRIS

The river Tigris—Ancient historical interest—Garden of Eden—Origin of name   unknown—Swiftness—Sources—Navigation—Keleqs—Bathing, fishing, washing—Crossing rivers.

"The softly lapsing river,
It whispers in its flow,
Of dear days gone for ever,
Those days of long ago."

P. B. MARSTON.

The river Tigris, on the banks of which Mosul is situated, is a noble stream. Though inferior in length to its sister the Euphrates, yet it is no mean rival, either in antiquity or historical fame. They share together the distinction of having on their banks the romantic spot reputed to be the Paradise of Adam and Eve. The Garden of Eden is situated, according to the tradition of the country, near the junction of the Euphrates and Tigris. When we passed that way on our journey from Busrah to Baghdad, the land was flooded by the spring rains, so we saw nothing of the beauties of Paradise.

The Tigris can also claim, in common with the Euphrates, an interesting connection with some of the ancient kingdoms of the world, extending back to early post-diluvian times. Near by, the Assyrian Empire built its towns of splendour and strength. Daniel records visions seen upon its banks, Cyrus is said to have marched his troops along its shores, Alexander overthrew the armies of the Medes and Persians near its basin, while in the plain of Nineveh the dynasty of the Ommiade caliphs was destroyed and supplanted by that of the Abassides. The origin of its name is unknown, but it is thought that the swiftly-flowing character of the river gave rise to its name. Hence the old Scriptural name Hiddekel, signifying "swift or quick." Owing to its wealth of fertilising power, it is sometimes called by the Arabs "Nahar-as-Salam," the River of Peace. At all times the Tigris is a swift river, but the velocity with which it travels differs according to the season of the year, the swiftest time of all being in the spring, when the snows from all the surrounding mountains melt and rush down to the river, causing it often to overflow its banks, and increasing its impetuosity to a great extent. At this time it is possible to travel on the river from Mosul to Baghdad in forty-eight hours, while in the late summer or autumn it takes at least ten or twelve days. When flowing at its fastest rate, the Tigris is said to be swifter than the Danube. The course of the river is a very winding one, extending for about 1040 miles. Its breadth varies very much. At Mosul it is a little less than 400 feet, at Baghdad about 600, while in one place where another river flows into it, the width amounts to over 1000 feet.

The sources of the Tigris are at an altitude about 5000 feet above sea-level, but the greater part of its fall is accomplished at its commencement, by the time it reaches Mosul the elevation above sea-level is only 353 feet, the remainder of its course, a distance of about 650 miles, being made by easy descent.

With a very little trouble the river could easily be made navigable as far up as Mosul, the chief hindrance to this being obstructions in the river which could be removed by dynamite or other explosives. A day's journey from Mosul by water there is a large dam stretching right across the river, believed to have been built by Darius with the intent to prevent Alexander from penetrating his dominions by means of the river. When the Tigris is full this is not an insurmountable barrier even as it exists now. During the summer and autumn the water is very shallow, and steamers would find it difficult to reach Mosul, but a little engineering could render the river navigable at all seasons. Once or twice steamers have reached Mosul, thereby causing great excitement amongst the natives. For the last thirty years it has been the talk of Mosul that "steamers are coming," but they have not yet started. We heard a year ago that two steamers had been chartered for plying between Mosul and Baghdad, and were only awaiting a firman from the Sultan, but so far nothing has been seen of them.

Pending the inauguration of steamers, the natives still continue to use the same method of river transport as existed in the days of Abraham and Jonah. This consists of a raft-like construction, and is employed for both passenger and goods traffic. It is composed of a number of sheep or goat skins inflated and fastened close together, upon which cross-bars of wood are laid and bound firmly in place. The skins are examined daily and when necessary reinflated; great care must be taken to keep them moist, for if they become dry they are liable to burst. The raft is manned by one or two natives, whose only work is to guide the "keleq," as the raft is called, to keep it in the middle of the stream, away from all dangerous rocks and shoals. For this purpose a rough kind of oar is used, made from the branch of a tree, with palm branches at the end forming the blade. The keleq floats down the river with the current, the passengers amusing themselves with singing and reciting stories.

When a European travels, a little hut is built for his convenience. A light framework of lath is run up, just large enough to hold a travelling bedstead and chair; this is covered with felt or water-proof sheeting and placed upon the raft. On arrival at Baghdad the whole is sold for about half its original price. The owner of the keleq sells the planks of wood forming the floor of the raft, packs up carefully his skins, and returns by land to Mosul, as the current is too strong to allow of his return the same way as he came. He is then ready to be hired for another journey. In good weather a journey on a raft is a very pleasant mode of travelling. It has many advantages over caravaning by land. There is no need of the early morning or midnight scramble preparatory to the start. The owner simply ties up after sunset, and as soon as dawn appears he quietly slips the rope, and off the raft glides, while the passenger is still sweetly slumbering, unconscious of any movement.

In summer, however, the river is the happy hunting-ground of flies and mosquitoes, the result being that rest and sleep are impossible either by day or night. In a storm, too, the keleq is not a very secure place of refuge. An English lady travelling from Mosul to Baghdad was once caught in a hurricane and her keleq blown about in such a way that she expected every minute to find herself precipitated into the river, while her little hut and all its contents were saturated through and through with water.

A raft is a good target for the Arabs whose villages lie along the banks of the river. An Englishman once placed his bicycle, which he was taking home, on the top of his hut, thinking to keep it out of harm's way. The Arabs, seeing this extraordinary-looking machine, at once came to the conclusion that it was a Maxim gun or some such deadly weapon. They immediately opened fire, and continued shooting till the raft was out of sight—fortunately with no serious result.

The French Consul at Mosul was also attacked by Arabs when travelling on a keleq. For seven hours they kept up an active fusilade, both parties making good use of their guns.

The merchants of Mosul use these rafts for exporting their goods to Baghdad and other places. After the harvest enormous keleqs may daily be seen leaving Mosul, loaded heavily with wheat and corn. All goods for the south are exported in this way. For these large commercial rafts, about three to four hundred skins are used, while others contain from fifty to two hundred, according to the size of raft and number of passengers. A European travelling alone would need about one hundred and fifty to two hundred skins to make a fairly comfortable raft.

Natives often use a single inflated skin for travelling down the river, sometimes even going as far as Baghdad on one. This latter feat a man has been known to accomplish in twenty-four hours. It is by no means as easy as it looks, to balance yourself on a skin; when bathing we have often tried, but found it very difficult. The Arabs use these skins as ferry-boats when the river is unfordable. They take off their garments and tie them round their head as a turban, so that when they reach the opposite side their clothes are quite dry.

In a village near Mosul I have seen women crossing the river in this way, many of them carrying a child on her back in addition to a large bundle of clothes which she has been washing in the river. The Arabs, both men, women, and children, are quite at home in the river—swimming as easily as ducks, and playing all manner of games in the water; it is quite interesting to watch them from a distance. The women do not take off their long loose garment, but just hold the skirt of it in their teeth if it impedes their swimming. Last summer we were staying for a time at a castle quite near the river, about an hour's ride from Mosul; while there we bathed almost every day, a small wood running to the edge of the water acting as a convenient dressing-place. The owner of the castle gave notice to all the villagers that the wood was "hareem" each afternoon, so we were always quite private. I engaged the services of an Arab woman to teach me to swim whenever my husband could not be there. She could swim like a fish herself, but had no idea of teaching any one else; however, before our holidays were over I had mastered the art. She would make me put one hand on her shoulder and then call out: "Now, kick"—that was the sum total of her instructions, "kick"! The river is considered very dangerous for bathing unless you know it well. Shortly before we were there last year, an Arab woman had been drowned. She was a good swimmer, and was swimming in deep water, when suddenly she called out that she was drowning, and before any one could go to her rescue she sank, and was quickly carried down the stream by the current; when the body was recovered life was quite extinct. For a few days the women were too frightened to bathe in that place, thinking that death was due to something in the water; but when we arrived a fortnight later they had apparently quite recovered from their fright, and were bathing as usual.

Another day we were watching the men playing in the water, when suddenly a black object appeared in the distance floating down the stream; it looked like the head of a baby. As it approached the place where the men were bathing, one of our servants swam out to see what it was, and found to his horror it was the body of a man. He brought it to the bank, and every one rushed to view the corpse. Then came the question as to who would bury it; no one was willing to do this, although the body was that of an Arab, and all the onlookers were also Arab villagers. We offered backsheesh to any one who would dig the grave, but no one volunteered, and suggested pushing the body out into the current again to be carried to Baghdad, as the easiest way of settling the matter. Finally a mullah passed by, and seeing the body, ordered some men to bury it at once. We were very thankful, as we could not bear to think of the poor body floating down the stream, or being left exposed on the banks of the river.

We watched some men dig a very shallow grave, and the body was laid to rest, the mullah reciting some Moslem prayers ere it was covered with earth and stones.

As one sees such scenes as this taking place, it is not pleasant to think that this same river forms our sole water supply for drinking and all domestic purposes! If we take a walk down the river to the place where the water-carriers fetch the water, we shall have all the more reason thoroughly to enjoy our water! There hundreds of women are to be seen washing their clothes, men and boys enjoying a swim, horses, mules, and donkeys revelling in the mud; while not at all unlikely a few dead dogs or cats may be seen floating around! All congregate in this favourite spot. This being the case, it is not surprising that often our water resembles *mud* much more than water when brought to the house. Needless to say, all our drinking-water is filtered and boiled before using. The water is brought from the river in skins on the back of donkeys or mules, at the rate of 3s. 4d. a hundred skins. It seems so absurd to be paying in this way for water when, with a comparatively speaking small outlay, it could easily be conveyed to each house by means of pipes from the river running close by. This has been done by an energetic Vali in Damascus, and the result is enviable.

The Tigris cannot be said to contain a great or varied supply of fish, but there are two or three kinds to be found, which help to vary the housekeeping monotony of everlasting mutton and chicken. A very large fish called "bis" is the best kind, as the meat is tender and mild, while the bones are few; the others seem to be all bones, and are hardly worth eating, besides being absolutely flavourless.

Fishing is carried on from the bridge by the fish-sellers. A line is generally used, baited with melon or pieces of flesh. Sometimes poison is thrown into the river in order to kill the fish, which then float on the top of the water and are easily caught. In the summer it is very risky buying fish in the bazaar, as it so soon becomes stale; so if I want to be quite sure of having fresh fish, I send a servant down to the bridge to *see* a fish caught and then bring it home. As a matter of fact, I fancy he does not at all like sitting in the sun waiting, so often beguiles the time by sitting in the coffee-house situated on the banks of the river; and then, having allowed an hour or two to elapse, returns empty-handed, saying: "There are no fish in the river to-day."

Rivers without bridges are a great trial of patience when journeying; it takes such a long time to transport everything, and the crossing generally takes place at the end of a stage when every one is tired, and—shall I confess it?—often cross too. The waiting in the burning sun while the boats are fetched, the weary bargaining, and all the usual trials of patience become exaggerated out of their due proportions when you know that just across the water is the resting-place for the night—so near and yet so far! And as you sit on the *wrong* side of the river waiting, waiting, it is difficult to feel restful and at peace with all men. I long often to be able to do as the animals do, *i.e.* swim over. A small charge is made for the transport of each animal, so the muleteer often prefers to swim over himself, taking his animals with him. There is as a rule only one ferry-boat, so that you have to take your turn; and as each passage takes about an hour, a great deal of patience is often needed.

The ferry-boat is a large flat-bottomed, antediluvian-looking construction, and you wonder how ever it can bear the weight of all that is put upon it. When a carriage is to be transported the horses are first unharnessed, then the vehicle is lifted bodily on to the boat, with all its contents, the passengers and horses finding standing-room as best they can.

When you get to the other side your troubles are not over, for on starting to put up the tent you find one of the poles has been left behind on the other side; so there is nothing to do but to sit still and continue the waiting process. Or perhaps you think a cup of tea would help while away the time, only to find that the charcoal has not yet arrived! So there is only one thing to do, and that is to wait till everything is safely landed; then you can begin to prepare for the long-delayed rest.

CHAPTER IV

THE CHILDREN OF MOSUL

*Spoiling process—Despair of the parents—The "god" of the hareem—
Death by burning—Festivities at birth of boy—Cradles and cradle
songs—School life—Feast in honour of a boy having read the Koran
through—"Only a girl"—Girl life—Girl victims of Naseeb—Marriage.*

"The household must weep for forty days on the birth of a girl."

ARABIC PROVERB.

"Is it all forgot? All schooldays' friendship,
Childhood's innocence?"

SHAKESPEARE.

"Where children are not, heaven is not."

A. SWINBURNE.

The children of Mosul have on the whole a very good time. From their earliest
days they are allowed to do pretty much as they like, and only when the process
of spoiling is completed, and the child has become a terror to all, do the parents
realise that it is far easier to spoil a child than to "unspoil" him, once the deed is
done. This method, or rather lack of method, of bringing up the children, is a great
cause of trouble and sorrow in after years both to the parents and to the children
themselves, but yet they never seem to profit by their experiences, for they still
continue to say that it is a great "aib" or shame to deny a child anything he may
want. Although this spoiling process is carried on with both boys and girls in the
earlier years of their lives, it is brought to perfection in their treatment of the boys.

I remember a pretty little child called Jamila (beautiful); she was so fair and
pretty that she was known by many as "the English child." When she was about
three years old she became very ill, and the mother brought her to my husband,
who prescribed for her, but said that the chief part of the treatment lay in the diet.
On no account was solid food to be given for at least three or four days. The mother looked in despair when she heard this, as she said, "Jamila will cry if she cannot
have her meat and bread and pillau!" A day or two later I was calling at the house,
and saw that Jamila was looking very ill, and asked the mother what the child had
been eating. "Oh," she said, "poor little child, I had to give her meat and bread, for
she tore her hair and clothes in her anger, on my refusing to give them to her, and

so, how could I deny them to her?" And sure enough, while I was there, Jamila began to cry for bread, and on her mother refusing, threw herself on the ground in a paroxysm of anger, beating her head and face with her clenched fist, till she was quite blue and black in the face. The mother ran at once and brought bread and meat, and gave to the child, who immediately recovered her equanimity of mind and temper.

Then again, I have seen a room full of people all in despair over a child of perhaps two or three years old, who refuses to drink his medicine ordered by the doctor. The father begins the performance by solemnly taking the glass containing the medicine up to the child, and saying to him, "Oh, my beloved, *will* you take this medicine?" "No," says the child, and pushes it away. The father looks round on the audience for signs of wonder and astonishment at the marvellous doings of the child. Then perhaps the uncle has a try, and meets with like success; then the mother, the aunts, and a few friends all beseech the child to take the medicine, saying, "For my sake, for the sake of your father, your mother, &c., take this," but, of course, all are unsuccessful, and they all shake their heads and say, "I told you so, he will *not* take it," and it being a "khatiya" (sin) to force a child to do anything against his will, the child, of course, gains the victory in this as in everything else. If you suggest pouring the medicine down the child's throat by force, the parents and friends will put you down as being a monster of cruelty.

DR. HUME-GRIFFITH'S STUDY IN MOSUL

OUR DRAWING-ROOM IN JULFA

If there happens to be only one boy in the hareem, he becomes almost like a little god to all the women folk. A small friend of mine was in this position, and although a very jolly little boy, was fast becoming unbearable in his actions towards his grandmother, mother, and aunts. He was only about eight years old, but one day he was calling on me with his aunt, whom I loved very much, when, without the smallest provocation, he suddenly took up a stick and gave his aunt two or three hard cuts across her shoulders with it, and then ran laughing out of the room. I did not say anything to the boy, but presently my husband came in to lunch, and I asked him to give the boy a beating, and told him what he had done. So we went to hunt for the boy, and found him hiding behind his grandmother, who besought us not to touch the darling boy. My husband gave the boy a very slight whipping, and told him if ever he did such a thing again, he would give him something to remember! The boy was so astonished at being chastised, that to this day he has been a changed boy, and much more bearable in his home life.

Another instance of the way the boys are spoilt. A woman and her daughter, a little girl of about eight years, were sitting in their verandah one day behind a pile of cotton which had just been "fluffed" by the man whose work it is to fluff cotton. The son of the woman, a boy of seven, thought it would be great fun to set a light to this cotton, which he promptly did by throwing a lighted match into the midst of it, with the result that his mother and sister were burnt to death. I called at the house some days after, and found the boy who had done this deed quite a hero in the eyes of the women folk, and far from being blamed and punished, on the contrary they were fondling and caressing him more than ever. I told them I thought the boy was so pleased with all the attention he was receiving, that very likely he would do the same thing again if he had the opportunity.

Let me give you a short sketch of a child's life, in order that you may see for yourself something of their everyday life.

As we are talking of Eastern children, we must begin with the boy, as he is so much more important a personage than a mere girl.

A boy's birth is celebrated by great rejoicings and feastings, and if the family is a well-to-do one, at least two sheep will be slain and cooked and given to the poor. Our next-door neighbours were rejoicing over the birth of a boy a short time ago, and they thought it necessary to sacrifice three sheep, and for two days the poor were coming with their little dishes and pots to carry away portions of the meat. I went to see this ceremony, and it was very interesting. Apparently no questions were asked, the only recommendations necessary being poverty and need. Also hundreds of loaves of bread were given away at this time. If we go to the hareem to admire and pay our homage to the little king, we must be careful not to praise him too much, or, if we do, we must qualify our praise by saying "Mash'allah," which will counteract any evil influence. We shall find the baby boy swathed up tightly in his swaddling clothes, his eyebrows and eyelids pencilled with native cosmetics, and very likely a beauty spot on his forehead; his little head will be covered with a little silk cap, over which a handkerchief will be wrapped, and on the cap will be seen some coins and blue beads, to avert the dreaded evil eye. We shall find him very probably strapped tightly into a cradle made of brightly-painted wood; the baby is laid on the top of the little mattress, which is level with the sides of the cradle, and then strapped down. As he grows out of his first cradle he will be given another and larger one, and much more comfortable, in which he need not be strapped, as the sides are high enough to prevent his falling out; a cord is attached to the cradle, so that his mother can swing him gently while she sits and spins or does anything she has to do. It is very quaint to listen to their monotonous chant as they rock the cradle, and very often they sing to the swing of the cradle, "Allah ho, Allah hi, Allah ho, Allah hi," "He is God, He is living, He is God, He is living."

The first time of shaving a boy's head is looked upon as a very important day, and the barber must be careful to leave a little tuft of hair on the top of the head, by which he can be pulled up into heaven, otherwise he might get left behind.

When the boy is about five, he will probably be sent to school. He is then dressed as a miniature man, in white knickerbockers, shirt, coloured vest, and silk or cloth "zeboon," a loose garment reaching to the ankles; on his head, of course, will be the inevitable red fez, adorned with charms to bring him good luck and keep off evil. Arrived at the school, our little friend will seat himself on the ground, and his education will begin by learning the ‫ا ب ت‬ (*alef, bey, tey*), the A, B, C, of the Arabic language. After he has mastered the alphabet, and can write a few words, then the Koran will be started, and the boy will be kept hard at this, each day learning a short portion till a chapter is known perfectly by heart. All the boys in the school may be reciting different portions of the Koran at the same time, and in a sing-song tone, so that, as you pass up and down the streets, it is easy to recognise these seats of learning for the young. I have often peeped into some of these schools, and watched the boys, all seated on the ground, swaying themselves backwards and forwards, repeating the Koran in a loud, monotonous voice. When a boy has been through the Koran once, a great feast is made in his honour. He is decked out in grand new garments, generally of silk and embroidery, and men dancers are engaged for a day or more, according to the means of the parents.

The son of a friend of mine in Mosul had just completed this part of his education, and his mother sent word to know if the dancers might come and dance before us in our compound. We thought this might be rather trying, as they would probably have stayed all day, so I sent a message thanking her for the honour, but saying I would prefer to come to her house to see the "tamash" (sight), as I only had a limited time to give to it. So at the time appointed I went, accompanied by a woman servant and a man, as I thought there would probably be a great commotion. On arriving at the door of the house, it seemed hopeless even to think of getting in, as the courtyard was full of men, dancing, shouting, yelling, whirling and slashing naked swords and daggers. The court was a very small one, and my first thought was to turn and fly, but the hostess was a very dear friend of mine, and I did not like to disappoint her, so I sent the man-servant in front to open a passage in the crowd and followed hard after him, and felt very thankful when we reached a room safely. The women were gathered there looking out of the windows at the fun. But this did not seem to please the dancers, for they called repeatedly for the "khatoun" (lady) to come and watch them, and some even followed me into the room, thereby throwing the women into a state of panic and fright. The men were so wildly excited that they hardly knew what they were doing. Stripped to the waist, they flourished their swords and yelled, then jumped high into the air, then crouched on the ground and again leapt into the air, all the time pointing the daggers or swords either at their own hearts or some one else's. To add to the general excitement, other men were beating drums and playing on a weird kind of stringed instrument. After receiving their "backsheesh" they departed, for which I was not sorry. The boy in whose honour all this is taking place is very happy and delighted, and thinks *now* he is a man, and so, as he is leaving his childhood behind him, we too will leave him and pass on to the much less important subject (from an Eastern standpoint) of the childhood of a girl.

"Only a girl" — "Only a girl." These are the words which generally follow the announcement of the birth of a girl. Poor little mite, her entrance into the world is not a cause of great joy or rejoicing, and from her earliest days, I think, this lies as a shadow upon her; for to my mind there is a sadness and pathos about the little girls quite different to the masterful looks and ways of the boys, the lords of creation. As it is a part of the Moslem's creed to bow in submission to the will of God, so the parents now, as always, say, "It is God's will" ("Al Allah"), and bow their heads in submission to this new yoke put upon them. Of course there are exceptions, and some love their little daughters very much, but taken as a rule, girls are not welcome—certainly not more than one. If the parents of the girl baby are well-to-do, perhaps they may sacrifice one sheep, but the feastings and almsgiving are done in a much quieter way and with as little ostentation as possible; and if you visit the mother it is not necessary to say *very* much about the new arrival as it is "only a girl," and it is not well to make the poor mother feel too sad.

A GROUP OF PERSIAN GIRLS

Many of these little girls are very pretty and winsome. The one
sitting at the extreme left of the front row is a very attractive child,
and a great favourite of mine. Her name is "Beloved."

So the little girl starts her life, with not too much love and attention. If she happens to be well and strong she will thrive apace in spite of all, but if she is at all inclined to be weak or delicate, the chances are that she will be neglected until it is too late for human aid, and then perhaps, as a conscience salve, she will be taken to the doctor by the mother or some other relative. How many of these little victims have been brought when too late to my husband I should not like to say. Directly the doctor sees a child suffering from some terribly neglected disease he at once says, "A girl, of course! If the child had been a boy you would have brought him long ago." And so, alas, it is true of many cases. It is a convenient way of getting rid of some of a too numerous family of girls, and then the mothers and relations will piously clasp their hands and say, "It is the will of God." The will of God, indeed! This so-called submission to the will of God, or "kismet" or "naseeb," as the Turk and Arab call it, is often responsible for a great deal of neglect by mothers of their little girls. For instance, there was such a nice-looking young widow who used to come and see me. She had two children, both girls, the elder about five years of age, and the younger nearly three. This younger child was a perfectly beautiful child—just like a lovely wax doll; indeed, so much did she resemble a doll that she was often called "l'abbi," which means a doll. Her sweet little face had a complexion which any English mother might have been proud of, and her large brown eyes were full of life and fun, while her dear little golden curls falling over her forehead and forming a halo round her head gave her an appearance of a little cherub. I found out very soon that this child had the beginnings of a terrible disease in her, which, if attended to at once, might be cured, but which neglected would mean certain and sure death. I spoke to the mother about it, and implored her to bring the child to the hospital for treatment; but no, she would not listen; she simply shrugged her shoulders and said, "Naseeb, al Allah. If the child is to die, she will die; if it is written she is to live, she will live," and nothing I could say would induce her either to bring the child or to let us have her to take care of; and I heard afterwards from a neighbour that the mother wanted the little girlie to die, so that she might be free to marry again, as no man would take a wife who already was burdened with two girls. Instances of this kind might be multiplied by the hundred, showing how girl life is neglected, under the blasphemous idea that it is "naseeb."

As a rule it is not considered at all necessary to send a Moslem girl to school, but quite lately the Turkish authorities have opened some schools for girls in Mosul, and have sent women teachers from Constantinople, so this is a step in the right direction. I visited one of these schools, and was very much struck by the happier looks of the girls compared with the faces of the same girls in their own homes. They are taught to read and write and, of course, to recite the Koran. Also, we were shown some very pretty pieces of silk embroidery which the girls had just finished, and really some were quite artistic and pretty. These schools are free, the teachers being paid by Government, and, therefore, girls of all classes sit side by side. The pasha's daughter and the daughter of the pasha's slave may both attend the same school and mix quite freely and happily together.

For the first seven or eight years of a girl's life she may go unveiled and run about pretty freely with only a silk scarf on her head, but when she reaches the age of nine or thereabout a great change takes place in her life. She is prohibited from going out, except occasionally with the mother or other relations, and then she must be closely veiled. Poor children, I do so often pity them—they so soon leave their childhood behind them and become women before they come to girlhood. Of course the great aim and object of parents is to marry the girls as soon as possible to the man who can offer the highest price for her; but the subject of weddings is so extensive that we must leave it for another chapter. Only I will say here that I think the reason girls are looked upon more or less as a nuisance is because they cost so much to get married; for if a father has three or four girls to marry, he needs to be a rich man. From the time the girl is four or five years old he begins loading her with gold and jewellery, so that by the day she comes to be of a marriageable age she shall have a good supply to offer to her would-be husband.

CHAPTER V

THE MOSLEM WOMEN OF MOSUL

Beauty behind the veil—Types of beauty—My dear old friend of 110 years of age—Aids to beauty described—Pretty children—Beauty tainted with sin—Imprisonment of women—Peeps into some hareems—Warm receptions—A visit from the ladies of a select hareem—Love the magic key to open hearts.

"Women are worthless creatures, and soil men's reputations."

ARABIC PROVERB.

"As I told you always, her beauty and her brain go not together."

SHAKESPEARE.

It has often been said that there is very little beauty to be seen behind the veil in Turkish Arabia. I certainly do not agree with this statement, for I have seen some very beautiful faces amongst the Mohammedan women of Mosul. There is beauty, too, to suit all tastes: the winsome blonde, with her pale blue eyes and fair hair; the striking brunette, peeping from behind her veil with laughing brown eyes, which at times are as full of pathos as those of a faithful collie which has lost its master.

I think the chief attraction of Eastern women lies in their eyes. One face comes to my mind as I write. It is not a pretty face in the ordinary sense of the word, but the eyes are wonderful, revealing a soul full of sadness, a longing for something not attainable: eyes that might make you weep as you feel them fixed upon you in unspeakable yearning for love. Another type of face is the bright, vivacious one, seen chiefly amongst young unmarried women—marriage in the East generally having the effect of taking all brightness out of a face or a life. There is also many a sweet face to be seen in Mosul. Perhaps these could not be called beautiful except for the sweetness. One such I can see now as my memory takes me back a few months. A dear face is pressed close to mine, and with pleading blue eyes and such a sweet, expressive mouth which utters words such as these: "Khatoun, I cannot go—I cannot leave you. Will you let me live always with you?"

If only you knew the history of this woman, you would wonder that her face could bear such a sweet look, or, indeed, how she managed to endure life at all.

Beauty of the East is all too fleeting as a rule, a woman of thirty years of age being quite *passée*. Nevertheless, there are some very fine-looking old ladies in

Mosul. One dear friend of mine is proud of the fact that she has reached the grand age of 110! Her face still retains some of its former beauty. Her daughter is a young woman of nearly ninety, her grand-daughter can boast of seventy years, while as to her great-grandchildren, they are countless!

This old lady came one day to the dispensary for medicine, as she wished to be "made strong" enough to take a journey consisting of six hours' riding to a hot-water spring outside Mosul, a place to which she had been in the habit of going regularly for the last 100 years or so! She was also quite distressed because her skin was rough, and asked the doctor to give her some medicine to make it smooth again. Even at 110 she was capable of thinking of and longing for a renewal of her lost beauty. Aids to beauty are much sought after by the ladies of Mosul, as they do not at all approve of becoming "old." It is quite a rare sight to see a white-haired woman. The moment grey hairs commence to appear they have recourse to henna, a dye much in request by Easterns of both sexes. Freckles are a cause of much sorrow of heart to Mosul ladies. One girl, who was really very pretty, was brought constantly to the dispensary by her mother, who implored my husband to eradicate the freckles with which her daughter's face was covered, as, if they were not removed, she might never get a proposal of marriage. However, a man was forthcoming who apparently did not object to freckles, for shortly before leaving Mosul I received an invitation to this girl's wedding-feast.

There are some very pretty children in Mosul, some dark, others fair, with blue eyes and curly hair. However, this latter style of beauty is not as a rule admired. Mothers have a great horror lest their children should have curly hair. If a child possesses it, the women try by all means in their power to straighten out the curls, sometimes even coming to ask for medicine for this purpose.

Very often, however, the children lose a great deal of their beauty when five or six years old. Perhaps it is because their souls at that age become tainted with knowledge of evil, and this knowledge is reflected on their faces. It is heartrending to see pretty little children listening open-mouthed to some horrible tale of sin and wickedness told by a member of the hareem. It is true there is beauty behind the veil, but, alas! it is beauty tainted with the blackness of sin. How can lives be beautiful when the souls within are dead?—as dead as sin and sorrow can make them. Boys and girls grow up amidst surroundings which soon soil their souls; the "innocency of childhood," so dear to the hearts of English parents, is unknown in a Moslem hareem.

Many and many a time have I interrupted a conversation consisting of things which should not be spoken of, by pointing out to the women some boys or girls sitting near by, listening with evident delight to their unclean talk. Sometimes they would desist, but as a rule would only laugh, saying: "What does it matter? They know all about it!" Oh! the pity and horror of it—young lives spoilt and contaminated almost before their feet have started on the difficult and perilous walk through life. Is it any wonder that these children grow up with diseased minds and deadened souls? Then they in their turn become the parents of another generation, to whom they teach the same soul-destroying creeds.

THE CAMERA IN MOSUL

The women love to be photographed, and often ask me to "make pictures of them." These are Christian women, for no Moslem woman is allowed to have her photo taken.

TIRED OF PLAY AT A PICNIC

When all were tired out with playing games and swinging, tea was handed round.

There is no hope for the children of Mohammedan lands until the mothers have learnt a little of the meaning of pure life and conversation. There is no hope for the women while the men are what they are. The whole system is one of degradation and vice. When Mohammed, acting under what he declared to be a revelation from Allah, introduced the use of the veil, he swept away for ever all hope of happiness for Moslem women. By means of the veil he immured them for ever in a living grave. "Imprisoned for life" is the verdict written against each Moslem woman as she leaves childhood behind her. Before the days of Mohammed the Arabs were in the habit of burying alive yearly a certain number of new-born girls; surely the fate of these innocents was better than that of the millions of women to-day who are buried alive behind the veil. "Ensha' Allah" (God willing), in the near future the same Power which raised British women to hold the position they now do will also penetrate through the prison bars of the hareems of Mohammedan lands and set free the prisoners. An enlightened Mohammedan gentleman once said: "The only hope for our women is Christianity." God grant that their "only hope" may not be denied them.

How often I have said to these women, "Alhamd-'llillah (thank God), I am not a Moslem woman!" and the heartfelt answer has always been, "Yes, indeed, you may thank God; but it is naseeb" (fate). The longer I live amongst Moslem women the more my heart yearns with love and pity for them, and the more thankful I am that their lot is not mine.

Let us now peep into some of the many hareems of Mosul. There are some into which I should blush with shame to take my readers, on account of the conversations we might hear; but we will choose some where, in all probability, we shall see and hear nothing objectionable.

Our first visit shall be to a near neighbour of ours. The house is a large one, the owner holding a high social position in the town. As we enter the outside gates we see a large reception-room, in which the master of the house is sitting holding court. We must not look that way, as we are in native costume; so, pulling our veils a little closer, we hurry on till we reach the door of the hareem. This is always kept locked; upon knocking, it is opened by a native girl or woman, who immediately kisses our hands or dress, then ushers us into the presence of the khatoun. In this case the head lady of the hareem has been a widow for some years, and is still wearing her black mourning dress. She rises from her place amongst the cushions on the floor as we enter and salaams low, bidding us welcome to her house, at the same time indicating our seats by her side. We arrange ourselves as comfortably as possible, sitting cross-legged in true Arab fashion. By-and-by the daughter-in-law comes in—a frail, delicate-looking woman, and with her a little girl, her only child. She is sad because she has no boy, and is afraid her husband will divorce her on this account.

Since leaving Mosul I have heard that her fears on this point were not groundless, for her husband has since divorced her and taken another wife in her place. The usual coffee is handed round by one of the many women servants, and our hostess is very much surprised that we will not join her in smoking a cigarette. Sometimes there are a dozen or so women living in the same hareem, wives of brothers, and it is often difficult to know who is who. The relationships are sometimes most perplexing. Even to this day there are houses which I visit frequently, but have not yet mastered the intricate "connections" of the various members of the hareem.

AN ITINERANT COOK PREPARING KABOBS

Kabobs are a favourite dish amongst the Arabs. The meat is chopped very finely, wrapped round iron skewers, and roasted over a red-hot charcoal fire.

Here is another hareem, quite different from the last one we visited. My special friends in this house are two young girls who are not yet married. They are such dear, bright girls, and as I enter throw their arms round my neck and bid me welcome in a most demonstrative way. If I am expected I always find a meal ready, and if my visit is unannounced, a woman is always despatched to the nearest "sook" (market) to buy an impromptu meal. They are poor people, and I always beg them not to do this, but they never listen to my entreaties. The meal consists sometimes of "kabobs," *i.e.* meat minced and pressed round iron skewers and grilled over a charcoal fire; this is placed on a plate and garnished with sliced raw onions and bitter herbs. Another time a sheep had been killed, and our meal consisted of the "interiors," dished in a most tempting manner. Sometimes salads form the principal dish; but whatever the meal consists of, it is always served with love, and is consequently thoroughly appreciated. This house seems always to be full of women, all more or less related. If I get mixed up, as I sometimes do, in the relationship of those present, and show my ignorance of their names, they are quite hurt, and exclaim: "What, you have forgotten me?" "Was I not in the hospital for a week?" or, "Did I not bring So-and-so to see you?" If they have seen me once, they are quite surprised if I cannot remember all about them, and often I have to resort to stratagem to find out their names without exposing my forgetfulness. While we sit and talk the girls are all busily engaged in crotcheting caps. These are sold in the sook at about six-pence a dozen, cotton included. In certain "mahullahs" (quarters) of the town you will see all the women doing this work; in another part of the town they are all occupied with knitting socks, in another cigarette-making is the fashion. Each mahullah seems to have its own style of work for the women, to which it adheres more or less.

In one house where I visit, a basin of delicious "lebban" is always set before me. We all sit on the floor round a diminutive table about five inches high, and each one being provided with a wooden spoon dips out the lebban from the central dish. This lebban makes a delicious food in the hot weather. It is made something after the same manner as "junket," only lebban is more tart and acid. Eaten with grated cucumbers, it makes a very refreshing salad. Fortunately for me, I can eat and, as a rule, thoroughly enjoy native food. In fact, I often prefer it to our own, for almost all attempts at European cookery by native cooks are decided failures. My husband, on the other hand, cannot indulge in this respect, the excessive fat used being too much for his digestive powers.

But to return to our ladies. Not only do I visit in the hareems of the towns, but the hareems very often pay me a visit at our house. The poorer class of women come very freely, and they know that they are always welcome. We have a room specially set apart for women visitors, so that they may feel quite safe from any men servants who might happen to be about. The higher-class ladies do not come so frequently, the idea being that the more strictly they keep to their own hareem, the more select and important will they become in the eyes of the people. There is one family in Mosul who boast that their hareem have never visited any other house. So strictly have the ladies been kept in seclusion, that they were not even allowed to go to the "hammam" (bath) till quite lately. Now, however, they are allowed the luxury of once a month walking a hundred yards or so to the nearest bath. After becoming acquainted with the ladies of this hareem I was very anxious to obtain permission for them to come and visit me. They did not at all hold out any hope that their lords and masters would allow such an unheard-of proceeding. One day, however, my husband told the head of the house that I was very anxious for the ladies of his hareem to come and see me. To the great surprise of all he acquiesced, only stipulating that the visit should be kept as secret as possible. The ladies were very excited, and for days beforehand were talking about the proposed visit and making preparations for it. On the day fixed the way had to be cleared of all menkind. The doctor was banished from the house for the whole afternoon, the men servants were given a holiday, and all doors through which a stray man might happen to wander were carefully bolted and barred.

At the hour appointed a woman servant arrived to know if all was ready.

When she had satisfied herself that no men were visible, nor could become so un-expectedly, she returned to fetch the ladies. They arrived in all the glory of black silk chuddars, which Judy (our woman servant) carefully removed and folded up. The two older ladies were quite simply dressed in print or muslin, but the young wife was decked out in one of her many bridal costumes, and looked very charming. She was then only about sixteen years of age, but was the mother of two pretty children, a girl and a boy. They were all so delighted to be allowed out for the first time in their lives. We began by eating cucumbers and water-melons, followed by tea, coffee, and English biscuits and cakes. These latter they much appreciated, asking permission to carry away some for other members of the hareem to taste. After refreshments had been partaken of they were very anxious to see all over the house. As we went from room to room it was so funny to hear their remarks. The bedroom seemed to take their fancy most of all, as they could not see why we needed a room specially for sleeping in.

They were very charmed with our little harmonium, and listened with great delight while I played and sang to them some of our old English hymns translated into Arabic. One of the ladies trying to play could not understand why it would not "speak" for her, and upon my moving the pedals was overjoyed to find that she could "make music." Their delight at everything was just like that of little children on finding a new toy. Their visit lasted about three hours, and they went away promising to come again soon. This hareem is a most exceptionally happy one. There is only one wife in it, the two elder ladies being sisters-in-law to the bride, and unmarried. They all seem to live together in peace and happiness. Unfortunately, this is only the exception, which always goes to prove the rule, that hareems are not the abode of peace. How can there be peace when the heart is full of jealousy and hatred? One such case comes to my mind. There are two brothers living in one house, one of them being married. After some years of married life had passed and they remained childless, he took another wife, and the first one was thrown into misery and despair. Shortly after this we were awakened one night by hearing most fearful shrieks and yells coming from this house. The following day we heard that the two wives had been quarrelling and fighting, as usual, till at last the husband took the first wife and turned her forcibly out of doors. Fortunately, her mother's house was near by, to which she went, and where she remains to this day.

It has been said, and unfortunately too often truly said, that love has no part in the life of a Moslem woman; and yet it is also true that they are, as a rule, a most loving and lovable set of people. It is because they have so little love and kindness in their own lives that, when it does come to them, their hearts are ready to overflow in response.

Perhaps the Arab women are slow to give their love and trust, but when once given it is sure and lasting. Often these women have said to me, "Why do you love us, Khatoun?" They cannot understand that any one should care for them. Such an idea is outside the range of their experience altogether. One of the first sentences I learnt in the Arabic language was, "Ana ahubkum" (I love you all), and this is one of the most useful and necessary phrases to be learnt. Love is the magic key which opens a way to the hearts of the Moslem women, and which brings forth much fruit in return. It is sad to think that these women, who are endowed with such great possibilities of loving, should be condemned to live their lives, aye, and die too, without one spark of love to brighten and cheer them through the weary years of their lives. Sad, too, that their favoured sisters of England should be content that these things should remain so. Who is to tell them of love if we do not? They know nothing of the God of Love, who looks in pity and compassion on their stricken lives. They only know of a God who is inexorably hard and unfeeling, who holds the destiny of each life in His hand, and against whom it is no use repining, for "What is written is written."

Mohammed says in the Koran, "The noblest of you in the sight of God is he who most doth fear Him."

Truly has it been said that the God of the Mohammedans is an Oriental despot.

CHAPTER VI

MOSLEM FAMILY LIFE

No home life—Women down-trodden—Evils of divorce—Naseeb—The will of God—Truth and falsehood—Honesty prevalent—A thief caught—Swearing and anti-swearing—Fighting, hair-tearing, and biting—Hammams, the Ladies' Club.

"The heart of a woman is given to folly."

Arabic Proverb.

"May Allah never bless womankind."

Quotation from Moslem Author.

"The Very God! think, Abib, dost thou think?
So, the All-Great, were the All-Loving too—
So, through the Thunder comes a human voice
Saying, 'Oh, heart I made, a heart beats here!
Face, my hands fashioned, see it in myself!
Thou hast no power nor mayst conceive of mine,
But love I gave Thee, with Myself to love,
And Thou must love me, who have died for thee.'"

R. Browning.

There is no "home life," such as we understand the term, in Mosul. The word "beit" (house) is the only one in the Arabic language used for describing a home. It would indeed be mockery to call such by the sacred name so dear to the hearts of English people.

In a book lately published in Cairo the author, a well-known and clever Moslem writer, says: "Man is the absolute master and woman the slave. She is the object of his sensual pleasures, a toy as it were with which he plays whenever and however he pleases. Knowledge is his, ignorance is hers. The firmament and the light are his, darkness and the dungeon are hers. His is to command, hers is blindly to obey. His is everything that is, and she is an insignificant part of that everything." This being the sentiment of every Moslem man, is it any wonder that there is no happiness or mutual regard in the family life? The men look upon the women, and treat them, as little better than brutes; then when they become so, turn and revile them. They keep their heels firmly planted on women's necks and then dare them to rise. A man may be as vile as he likes himself, but the moment he suspects one of his hareem of misconduct there is nothing but death, or mutilation which is worse than death, for the offender.

A woman once came to the hospital who always insisted on keeping her face entirely covered with the exception of the eyes; I soon found that the reason of this was because her nose and lips were missing. These members had been cut off in a rage by an infuriated son-in-law, who declared that this woman had intrigued with his wife in allowing another man to enter the hareem in his absence. This is a husband's ordinary method of wreaking revenge on any of his women folk whom he suspects of being false to him. This, or death.

The facility with which a man is able to divorce his wife is a great source of trouble to the women. They never feel secure in the hearts of their husbands, knowing that at any moment he may tire of them and send them adrift.

When a woman is divorced she returns as a rule to her mother's house; but should she have no relation at hand to whom she can appeal for protection, her condition is deplorably sad.

A man may divorce his wife in a fit of anger and receive her back the next day if he so desire; this may occur twice, but if he pronounces the fatal words "I divorce thee" three times the divorced wife may not be taken back till she has been married to another man for a time and *he* also has divorced her; *then* her former husband may marry her again if he wishes. This is one of the good (?) laws of Mohammed the Prophet, and needs no comment.

When a woman is divorced the husband can claim the children if he desires; if not, the wife is allowed to retain them. Should she marry again the poor children are often left to look after themselves as best they can. As a rule the new husband does not wish to bear the expense of the children belonging to his wife's former husband. If, however, he should consent, and the two families are brought up together, the result is generally not conducive to peace of mind. One of our servants in Mosul had a little boy five years of age; having divorced the boy's mother, he looked about for another wife, and finally selected one who had already been divorced and was the mother of a boy four years old. The two boys now live together, and are a fruitful source of friction between husband and wife. A short time ago the mother came to our compound early in the morning looking dishevelled and angry, saying that her husband had turned her out of the house at midnight, refusing to admit her again. On inquiring into the matter we found that the root of the quarrel lay in the fact that the man was jealous of his wife's treatment of her own boy, declaring that he had only married her to look after *his* boy. He divorced her; but acting on our suggestion forgave, and reinstated her in his hareem.

A short time ago a woman came to me in great distress with her tale of sorrow. I had known her for some months, and loved her very much. She was the mother of two fine boys and a girl. When the girl was about eighteen months old the mother became very ill. The doctor attended her for some days, but finally gave up all hope of her recovery. As a last resource, however, some stringent means were used which, with God's blessing, proved successful, and the woman began to recover.

So near death had she been, that the neighbours came to the house inquiring what time the funeral would take place! The husband, a "mullah" (priest), never came near her the whole time of her illness, and the first news the poor woman heard on her recovery was that he intended taking another wife, doubtless thinking that, after such a severe illness, she would not be of much use to him for some long time.

As soon as she could walk she came to tell me her trouble, and to ask me what I should advise her to do. I told her that, if I were in her place, I should leave the man altogether. This, she said, she could not do, as it would mean separation from her children. Finally, she concluded that there was nothing else to do but to go back to her husband and submit to his will. This she did, and I saw her there before we left; but such a different face greeted me to the sweet one of old. Misery, discontent, and anger were depicted there instead of content and happiness. Up to the time of her illness she had been in the habit of frequently coming to see me: now her husband forbade her to do so any more. The week before we left, however, she turned up again with a bad abscess on her leg, for which she gave continual praise to God, saying repeatedly, "Alhamd'llillah. God sent me this bad leg in order that I may come to you"—her husband not objecting to her coming to the hospital to be treated, but only when she came to the house without any apparent reason.

A Moslem woman has very little hope of gaining Paradise. Old pictures by Mohammedan artists always represent hell as being full of women. Their hope of gaining Paradise rests a great deal on the will of their husbands. Some holy men say, "I don't want my wives in heaven. I prefer those provided by God for all good Moslems from amongst the angels." Yet, if you question the women about their hope for the future life, they all fervently express the belief that, eventually, they will have a place in Paradise afforded them.

Poor, blind, misguided Moslem women of Mosul and other Mohammedan lands! How my heart aches for them! Will no one heed the cry of anguish and despair which goes up from their midst? As we think of their lives our cry can only be, "How long, O Lord, how long will these things be?"

Women are great believers in the doctrine of Naseeb or fatalism. To everything that comes to them they bow their heads in submission and say, "Naseeb" (fate).

This doctrine often leads to great neglect of children and invalids, the women excusing themselves by saying, "Maktoob" (It is written). It often rouses our indignation to hear this oft-quoted word misapplied as an excuse for wrongdoing or selfish desires.

For instance, parents will enter into negotiations for the marriage of their daughter with a man known to be an evil liver; then, when the girl is suffering, maybe, for their sins, say piously, "Naseeb—Min Allah" (from God). "Min Allah" indeed! "Min Shaitan" (from Satan) would be more correct!

Then, again, it is somewhat annoying to be told it is "the will of God" that your horse should develop a cough, because the groom neglected to cover him when standing in the rain; or, when your best china tea-set is smashed, you would rather not be told it is "Naseeb"!

Albeit this is an annoying doctrine to the European at times, yet it certainly helps the Eastern woman to bear her troubles and trials, and it is good for her to have this at command, for she has nothing else to aid her. To sorrow, loss, bereavement, and all the ills that human nature is subject to, the Moslem answers always "Naseeb," or, "It is the will of God." Should their children die, or the locusts destroy the crop, it is "Naseeb." Is the weather hot or cold, dry or moist, the remark is always the same, "Naseeb." If the river water is filthy and they choose to drink it, thus contracting typhoid or one of the hundred other ills consequent on drinking such water, they have only to assure themselves that it is "Naseeb," and there remains nothing more to be said or done. It is easier to say "Naseeb" than to take the trouble to filter or boil the water for drinking.

In a thousand ways this belief in fatalism is convenient to the lazy or careless ones, a help to the over-burdened and weary, who know no other succour or helper in time of need or sorrow, while it is, in some cases, a blasphemous libel on God, blaming Him for what is really a sin wilfully indulged in.

As in Persia, so in Mosul, truth plays little part in the characters of some of the people. They have not yet learnt to value God's gift as expressed by the poet Browning—

> "God's gift was that man should conceive of Truth
> And yearn to gain it."

It is strange how even the most enlightened find it difficult to speak the truth always, and correspondingly easy to tell an untruth. A boy was once found out in a fault (quite a trivial one), but, when questioned, he absolutely denied all knowledge of it, until he was confronted by one who had been an eye-witness of the whole scene. Then only did he confess, adding, "I said with *my lips* I did not do it, but in *my heart* I confessed." What can be said to people whose mind is capable of evolving such ideas? We often had to complain of dishonesty amongst the hospital women servants, especially of the cook for petty thefts, such as eating the patients' food, thus causing them to go on short commons, unless I was there to see that each one had his or her proper quantity. One day I was crossing the compound before superintending the distribution of the evening meal to the in-patients, when, as I approached the kitchen, I distinctly saw the cook helping herself most liberally to the food out of the pot. On remonstrating with her, she indignantly denied that she had ever tasted a morsel, until I made her open her mouth and reveal to the amused onlookers proof positive of her lies. Even then she was not ashamed, but only laughed at the idea of the "khatoun" finding her out.

A woman will bring a child to the dispensary and swear that it is her child, all the time knowing that the real mother is waiting outside, too ashamed to be seen coming to the poor people's dispensary, but not wishing to pay the usual doctor's fee. Or some lady from a high-class hareem will dress in her servant's clothes and come to the dispensary, posing as a poor woman who cannot afford a piastre (2d.) for her medicine!

You get so tired of always hearing lies that you begin to feel it is no use to question people at all. I do not wish to imply that there is no truth to be found in Mosul;

but it certainly is a rare and, when found, precious virtue. It is a sad fact, too, that the natives do not trust or believe each other, knowing that, given the opportunity, a brother will cheat a brother or a son his father. Every one is suspicious of his neighbour. On the whole the people are honest, at least with the exception of the many trifling pilferings always to be expected amongst the servants.

Some of them are rather fond of "eating money" entrusted to their care. We had two or three servants who were good at this. They would come to me every day with their accounts, receive payment for same, but instead of handing over the money to the shopkeeper would calmly appropriate it for themselves, till one day the baker or butcher leaves a message at the door politely asking to be paid for past favours. Then the culprit is sent for, and acknowledges having "eaten the money."

Another servant once tried to steal some dolls from a box lately received from England for distribution amongst the in-patients of the hospital. He had helped me unpack the box and carry the contents to the storeroom, pending the arrival of Christmas Day. A few days after I was passing this room, and hearing a rustling inside looked to see what it was, but seeing the door still locked thought I must have imagined the noise. But just as I was passing on the rustling became more distinct, and I went nearer to examine more closely the door, and found that, while the lock was still intact, the door had been lifted bodily off its hinges and then carefully replaced!

Calling my husband, we entered the room and found a poor frightened man trying to hide himself under the pile of paper and sacking which had been removed from the box. He was absolutely shaking with fear, thinking that he would be bastinadoed (beaten on the feet with sticks) or imprisoned. He declared at first that he had come for some string, which he had noticed on a shelf, to mend my saddle; but finally confessed that the dolls had been the object of his visit. About six small ones were found in his pockets; he had wanted them for his children. We told him that if he had only asked he should have had one given him. I shall never forget his astonishment when my husband told him to choose the one he liked best and take it to his little girl. He wept for joy and gratitude.

Swearing is very largely indulged in by men and women alike; it seems to come as naturally to them as swimming to a duck. Originally the words "wallah," "yallah," "billah," were used as swear expressions; but are now looked upon more as ejaculations equivalent to our "good gracious!" "goodness!" &c.; the real swear words being "wallahi," "billahi," &c. Some of the women cannot keep the expression *wallah* out of their conversation, though I try hard to persuade them to do so. For instance, a visitor comes; you remark to her on the extreme heat. "Wallah," comes the answer, "it is hot!" Or you inquire after some member of her family. "Wallah, she is very ill," is the reply.

I was visiting one day in a Moslem house, and the old mother-in-law said to me, "What has happened to X.?" mentioning her daughter-in-law; "she never swears now!" I was indeed thankful for this unexpected tribute to that woman's efforts. We started an anti-swearing society amongst a few of the women; it was quite funny to see how they endeavoured to keep back the old familiar words which had been on their lips since childhood.

BREAD-MAKING

Baking-day is one to be dreaded. The process begins soon after midnight, when the woman arrives to prepare the flour and set the dough. Every woman is pressed into service: one to make the dough into little cakes, another to give it a preliminary roll. She then passes it on to her neighbour to be rolled still thinner, until finally the loaf is as thin as a wafer. It is then placed in the oven on a cushion such as is seen in the woman's hand.

One little boy joined with the women, and he found it hardest of all; but when we left he was still persevering. He learnt the Ten Commandments by heart, so whenever I heard him use a swear word I made him repeat the third commandment.

The women are terribly fond of couching their denials in the form of oaths, as "May my hand be broken," "May I become blind," "May my interior become dried up if I did such and such a thing!" It makes me shiver sometimes to hear them swearing to a lie in this way; and I often tell them that if God only took them at their word, they would be stricken blind many times over.

It is not an unknown thing for women to resort occasionally to fighting as a pastime, but I am thankful to say I have not seen much of it. A woman came to the Dispensary once with a fearful-looking hand: the thumb was about six times its normal size and had become gangrenous. My husband said the only possible cure was amputation; to this the woman would not consent. She said that a short time before she had been fighting with another woman, who had bitten her thumb in her fury. I asked this woman what she had done to her opponent. "Oh," she said, "I only pulled out her hair!"

Another woman once brought me quite a handful of hair to show, which she declared her husband had just pulled out of her head in his anger; while he at the same time exhibited several ugly wounds on his hand caused by his wife's teeth! The man vowed he would divorce her, refusing to listen to any suggestions as to forgiveness, saying, "What would my neighbours say of me if I kept for my wife a woman who would do that?" pointing to the bites on his hand. However, in the end he did consent to take her back, being on the whole an amicably disposed man. Can we wonder that these things should happen when neither the men nor the women have ever learnt to control their passions? We have glanced at the lives of the Moslem women of Mosul. Can we say that they lead an ennobling, beautiful life? Are the home influences such as to foster a happy, peaceful spirit? On the contrary, we have seen that a woman deserves our pity and sympathy for all the sorrow she has to endure.

Have we not seen that at birth she is unwelcome, as a child uncared-for and untaught, as a young woman imprisoned behind the veil, as a wife unloved, as a mother unhonoured; and when her weary life draws to a close she knows that she will go to her grave unmourned. Such in brief outline is the life of a Moslem woman.

A woman's one place of recreation is the hammam. It is indeed a kind of ladies' club; here she throws away for the time being all her home worries and troubles, enjoying thoroughly her few hours of liberty. As a rule the bath takes at least two hours, and often half a day, if the woman has no special demands on her time. She generally goes in the morning, taking with her a complete change of raiment, a mat to sit upon in the cooling chamber, and plenty of towels, also some food to be partaken of after the exertions of the bath are over. I once went to one of these hammams, but the heat was so intense that I could only stand it for a few minutes. I often wonder how ever the women can exist in such great heat for so long; I suppose it is because they are used to it. Many illnesses date from a visit to the hammam; but still they would not give it up for any consideration, thinking it quite impossible to take a bath in the house. Certainly the Turkish bath is much cleaner than the Persian one. In the latter a large tank is used, and as it costs a good deal to warm up, the water is not changed very often. In the Turkish hammam each person has a tap for herself, from which flows presumably clean water. As a matter of fact sometimes this water has already been used, but only in the cheaper hammams. The most expensive baths have river water brought up for the purpose; in the others well water is used, and as this is brackish and very hard it is impossible to use soap, for it will not lather; therefore a special kind of earth is used, which is said to be very good for washing the hair with.

When Judy, our woman servant, returns from the bath, she always comes and gives me a kiss, this being their custom, and we exchange the salutations usual upon any one returning from the hammam.

CHAPTER VII

CUSTOMS OF MOSUL

*Wedding ceremonies — Great expense to parents — Method of procedure —
Funeral customs — Customs at birth — Some other customs.*

"The bridegroom's doors are open wide,
And I am next of kin;
The guests are met, the feast is set;
May'st hear the merry din."

S. T. COLERIDGE.

We have seen that a wedding is a very expensive matter in Mosul, especially to parents who possess three or four daughters; for unless the necessary gold, jewellery, and clothing are forthcoming as a dowry, the marriage will never take place. For this reason a man with a number of daughters will begin saving for their marriage portion and expenses while the girl is yet a baby, and the mothers will often commence gathering together clothing even before the child is betrothed, so that they may be better prepared for the expensive event when it does take place.

Then, too, not only is there the outlay for the dowry and clothing, but also for the feasting of some hundreds, it maybe, of guests during the seven days following the marriage. A man of very fair means in Mosul once told me that the marriage of his daughters cost him at least £200 each, and as he had seven daughters the sum total required was not small. If this man with a good income found it hard work to produce the necessary cash, how much harder is it for those who have no settled income, or whose earnings are small. For instance, a native Christian whom we respected and liked very much had two daughters; both were betrothed and ready to be married. He was earning about £3 a month, and had a wife and six children to support — how could he provide all the necessary gold and other ornaments for his girls? And yet, if he did not, in all probability his daughters would never be married. There was only one way out of the difficulty, and that was to borrow at high interest, crippling himself for many years to come, perhaps for the rest of his life. Instances might be multiplied, but I think enough has been said to show that girls are expensive luxuries in Mosul as regards their weddings! Now as to the "preparations" for the great and eventful day.

When a man makes up his mind to be married, or his parents decide in *their* minds that it is high time their son should take to himself a wife, many are the consultations which take place, and great is the importance of the women folk concerned. They are never so happy as when arranging for a marriage, loving the mystery and secrecy of it; for it would never do for a fond mother to offer the hand of her dear son in marriage to the mother of a possible bride and be refused. The shame and ignominy would be too great; so the mother and other female relations of the would-be bridegroom have to go very carefully to work in selecting the girl and in making any proposal for marriage. Before the actual "asking" is done, the way has to be prepared by very careful hints and indirect inquiries as to the girl's health, accomplishments, and dowry. If all proves satisfactory, then a formal proposal is made. The matter having gone so far, a refusal is very unusual, and, if given, is considered a great insult. I heard of one young man who threatened to murder all the relations of a girl for whom he had made proposals of marriage upon her parents refusing to accept his offer.

I have often been asked by Moslem women to suggest some girl as a suitable bride either for their brother or son. On mentioning some girls whom I knew, their answers were something as follows: "Oh, but she has a white patch on her eye," or "She is too poor," or "She has a bad temper," or "She is not pretty." Their idea of beauty is that of a white, pasty, fat face, without a vestige of colour, except that which art applies! Of course, the man never sees the girl till the day of betrothal, and in the case of Moslems not till the actual marriage takes place. The old custom amongst the Christians of marrying a girl against her will is still extant in some villages. Sometimes it happens that a girl persists in her dislike to marry, even till the priest has arrived to tie the knot: in this case the father would bind the girl's arms and legs till the marriage ceremony was completed, when she was released, it being useless then for further resistance on her part. This is done even now in some villages near Mosul when the girl proves obstinate. As a rule, though, they accept their fate as "Naseeb," knowing it is little or no use to struggle against custom. How often my heart aches for some poor child who is bound to a man old enough to be her grandfather or great-grandfather sometimes. Alas, too often old in sin as well as years!

When the day of the marriage approaches, invitations are sent out to all friends and relations for the specified days of feasting. First comes the day for taking the bride to the bath—this is considered a great function; then follows a week of excitement, dancing, singing, feasting, all forming part of the great event. All thoroughly enjoy themselves, even those who have to work the hardest in preparing the food. The guests are expected to remain from morning till sunset. Three meals are provided each day, the morning one consisting of bread, cream, butter, fruit, &c.; the midday meal is a substantial one of meat, cooked in various ways, rice, chicken, and vegetables according to the season. The evening meal is also a very heavy one, causing the guests to depart perfectly satisfied both with their dinner and themselves.

During the whole of the week the poor bride has to sit in the reception room on a cushion specially prepared for brides, and takes no part in the surrounding gaieties. Each day she appears in a fresh silk dress, and is often covered with golden jewellery. She is not supposed to speak till spoken to, and the guests do not take much notice of her beyond the usual kiss of salutation. At meal times she is "fed" by her relations, a bride being supposed to be too overcome to help herself or eat without assistance.

A MOSUL BRIDE

The girl in the centre of the picture is a Christian bride decked out
in her wedding costume. The gold coins, necklaces, and girdle are
her dowry.

After the days of feasting are over, the bride takes her place in the house as "servant" to her mother-in-law. In a Moslem house the youngest and latest bride always becomes the servant of all for the first year of married life, or till another and younger one is brought to the home. Much depends on the mother-in-law's character as to the happiness or otherwise of the inmates of the hareem. If they wish, they can make the lives of the young wives perfectly miserable, or the reverse.

The same custom of feasting for a certain number of days takes place too in connection with funerals. The guests who come to mourn sit in solemn silence all day long; their mourning does not lessen their appetite, however, for they thoroughly enjoy their "feast" of sorrow. After a death, the "wailers" are brought in. I went once to a Christian house of mourning to see these wailing women. It was a ghastly sight. The professional wailers sat on the ground in the centre of the relations and guests, and worked themselves and others into such a frenzy that I thought some would have fainted from exhaustion; slapping their knees, tearing their hair and clothes, till they resembled maniacs more than women.

A short time ago a very sad and sudden death took place in Mosul in a house very close to us. We were awakened one night, while sleeping on the roof, by hearing the terrible wailing sounds coming from our neighbour's house. At the same time a messenger arrived in great haste, asking my husband to go at once to see the patient, as his relatives were not sure if he was dead or only in a fit. He had been out during the night to some Moslem religious function, and died quite suddenly on his return.

The wailing went on in the hareem for seven days, and was terrible to hear. The sound of the weird wailing of some hundred women is perfectly indescribable, always ending up with a piercing shriek which seems to rend the air and freeze one's blood.

Being friends and neighbours, I paid daily visits to the mourners during that week, but did not sit amongst the guests, preferring to spend the time with the sisters of the deceased in a quiet room above the din and uproar of the courtyard. The wailing has such a hopeless sound, as of a lost soul in anguish. One longed for them to know of Jesus the Living One, and of the time when partings shall be no more.

After death has visited a family, the whole house in which the departed one lived is not swept for three days: this is because they believe that the angel of death is still hovering near, and they fear lest, while they are sweeping, others of the household may be swept from the house by the angel. So the house becomes very dirty, the carpets covered with cigarette ash and ends, but nothing can be touched till the third day is safely passed.

Amongst the Christians it is also the custom after the death of a relative, not to go to the hammam (bath) for six months, and for the men to go unshaven for at least six weeks. The women are very particular about not going to the hammam while mourning, as I found to my sorrow. Our woman servant Judy lost her father just before she entered our service, and she allowed a whole year to elapse before she could be prevailed upon to go to the bath. They are very particular, too, about wearing "deep" clothing—that is, dresses of some dark colour, not necessarily black.

I am sure that the custom of burying a few hours after death is often the cause of many people being buried alive. I have often been regaled by an old woman with horrible stories of how some friends of hers have just escaped being buried alive. For those who providentially escape being entombed alive one is thankful; but what of the many who most certainly are condemned to this awful fate. It is too terrible to contemplate. In a land where no medical certificates are required, and where the body is carried to the cemetery almost before it is cold, how can it be otherwise?

But to proceed to other and more pleasing customs—let us pass from death to life. When a child is born in Mosul, whether Moslem or Christian, the first idea of the parents is to protect the child from the baneful influence of the Evil Eye. The usual custom is to thread a gall, and suspend it round the neck of the infant. Moslems enclose a portion of the Koran in a little bag, and fasten that round the arm of the child or sew it on to the cap. The custom of wearing charms to avert the Evil Eye is very prevalent, and deeply rooted in the minds of the Mosul people.

The kissing of hands is a very pretty custom. Children are all taught to do this even before they can speak or walk. Servants are always very anxious to kiss your hands after they have done something especially annoying or irritating. They make a grab for your hand, and kiss it before you realise what they are doing. In this way they secure your forgiveness before the fault is confessed. I am getting more wary now, and prefer to hear first what they have done before letting them kiss my hand. It is also a sign of gratitude. Upon receiving any backsheesh or present, the recipient is always ready to kiss your hand. Sometimes, when riding through the city, I have had my hand grasped and kissed by some passer-by who has been an in-patient in the hospital, and wished to show his gratitude in this way. It requires a great deal of gratitude or love for a man to kiss a *woman's* hand, so, when by chance it does occur, I feel very much honoured indeed.

There is one custom which is often the cause of a great deal of heartburning, even as it was in the days of Haman and Mordecai. It is usual for a host or hostess to rise from their seat upon the arrival of each guest—that is, if they desire to do honour to that person. As a rule this custom is most carefully adhered to, but it lends itself admirably to any one wishing to be rude to his guest or to shame him before his friends. Fortunately, this is not often the case, but when it does happen one feels very uncomfortable. There is one dear old lady in Mosul, who thinks it beneath her dignity to rise to a Feringhi. But, perhaps, it is excusable for her as she is a Hadji—that is, one who has made the pilgrimage to Mecca, and, consequently, is treated as an exalted being by all her friends and relations.

A rather quaint and pleasing custom in Mosul is that of sending trays containing a dinner all ready cooked and dished to new-comers, or to those returning after a long period of absence. We did not know of this custom when first we went to Mosul, so were very surprised at sunset on our second day after arrival to see two or three men coming into the compound carrying huge trays on their heads. They explained that their master, a Moslem merchant, had sent this meal, with many salaams and good wishes. It was a dinner large enough for twenty people, so we gathered together all we could find on the premises, assistants, catechist, and others, who had been kindly helping us to settle down. Spreading some Persian carpets in the courtyard, we sat down and thoroughly enjoyed our first Arab meal in Mosul.

When any one is leaving the place or starting on a journey, it is customary for the people to send in large trays containing sweetmeats, cakes, and other eatables suitable for taking with you on the road. When we were leaving Mosul, we received quite a large number of these trays—so many, indeed, that at the end of our fourteen days of desert we still had a good many of their contents remaining. Some of these were made of almonds pounded and mixed with sugar; others were made from puff pastry sandwiched with honey: these latter were especially nice.

Distributing food to the poor as a mark of gratitude and thankfulness is another of Mosul's good customs. After recovering from a dangerous illness, it is usual to make and distribute a large quantity of bread, baked in a special way, and flavoured with caraway seeds.

The birth of a son and heir is also celebrated by a generous and lavish distribution of meat and bread. When starting on a journey, too, it is usual to give away to the poor either money or food. On every occasion of life which calls for gratitude to God, this custom of presenting offerings to the poor is carried out. One dear woman, a friend of mine, went even further than this. It was thought at one time that we should be leaving Mosul for good, the Mission being withdrawn. Providentially, this was over-ruled, and when the news arrived from England that the Mission was to be kept on, great were the rejoicings amongst the people. The woman mentioned above immediately desired to show her thankfulness to God in a very special way, so spent one whole day in making a large supply of small loaves of bread, not to distribute to the poor, but to feed the hungry, starving *dogs* of the streets. This by a Moslem woman was, indeed, a work of love, dogs being looked upon as unclean beasts. Surely she "that loveth much shall be forgiven much."

Coffee-making and drinking is associated very much with life in Mosul. It is the custom there to give every one who comes to the house a cup of Arab coffee. This meant sometimes for us giving at least 200 cups in a day. Not only those who come as social visitors receive the coffee, but also all who come to the house on whatever pretext, whether for meetings, classes, or what not. At feast times one servant is always told off to do nothing else but prepare the coffee for the guests. On each of the great feasts, such as Christmas and Easter, it is the custom for every one to call, Moslems and Christians alike. At Christmas the feast lasts for three days, and at Easter a week, the whole of which time coffee must be ready to be handed at once to every caller; also a tray of sweets, consisting of Turkish delight, almond sugar, and other Mosul-made confections.

When a house is "mourning," bitter coffee is given to all callers for six months, and on the first day of each feast for a whole year.

I do not think I have ever visited a Moslem house, however poor, without receiving either a cup of coffee or some sweets. I often beg them not to make preparations for me, but they always insist, as their hospitable instincts are very strong. Indeed, more often than not, they set before me not only coffee or sweets, but meat, fruit, and lebban (sour milk).

A true Arab of the desert takes about an hour to make a cup of coffee. First of all the coffee has to be roasted, then ground to powder, and, lastly, boiled. The Arabs never sweeten their coffee, sugar not being a commodity of the desert.

I once heard the recipe for making Arab or Turkish coffee. Perhaps some readers may like to try their hand at making it.

First roast the coffee to a rich brown, neither too light nor too dark, then grind it to a soft powder. Now comes the art of making good coffee. Half-fill the pot with cold water; bring it to boiling point. Throw in a handful of powdered coffee; allow it to boil; shake down and bring it to the boil again. Repeat this process three times, and the coffee is ready. Specially note: Never wash the pot! Needless to say, this last injunction I do not carry out, but the servants quite believe in that part of the recipe. It is only with great difficulty I can persuade them to wash out the coffee-pot occasionally.

In summer, this reluctance on their part often leads to serious complications. The kitchen, as may be supposed, is not a very cool place during the hot season, consequently it suffers continually from a plague of flies. Dead flies are often served up in puddings and other dishes, to act presumably as an appetiser! Then eating requires a great effort. The coffee-pot seems to serve as a trap for many of these flies, attracted no doubt by the sugar, and there they find a coffee grave. Suddenly a visitor is announced, and the message is conveyed to the kitchen to "Send coffee at once." The cook seizes the pot, never looking to see how many victims are struggling in the dregs at the bottom, adds a little freshly-ground coffee, boils it up, and sends it in to the visitor served in dainty little cups. The visitor takes one sip, and...! I will draw a veil over the sequel. A mouthful of dead flies is not a very palatable drink. My feelings may be better imagined than described.

Sometimes a guest does not approve of the way the coffee is made (even when minus flies); if so, she is not shy, and does not hesitate to hand it back with a grimace, saying to your servant: "What horrid coffee! why do you not make better?" and often demands another cup properly made.

A visit to the bread-makers may not be out of place here. It is the custom amongst some of the people to bake bread once a month, sufficient to last that length of time. Baking-day is a day to be dreaded. The process begins soon after midnight, when the woman arrives to prepare the flour and "set" the dough for rising. The whole of that day every woman on the premises is pressed into service—one to make the dough into little cakes, another gives it a preliminary roll, then hands it to her neighbour, who uses a smaller roller, and finally hands it on to some one else to finish it off. When completed, the bread is about as thin as note-paper and as large round as a child's wooden hoop. The bread is now ready to be baked. The fuel used for heating the oven is chopped straw and goats' dung, which is burnt till the required heat is obtained; then these large thin pieces of bread are plastered to the sides of the oven, and removed as they are browned to an exact nicety. This bread is very nice when fresh and crisp; when stale, it is generally soaked in water before being brought to the table.

We do not make our bread in this way. I tried it once for the hospital in-patients, but found it took far too much time. The daily baking is much more suitable when from thirty to forty people have to be fed daily.

CHAPTER VIII

DREAMS AND VISIONS

Ezekiel's vision by the river Chebar — Our vision by the river Khabour — Rivers identical — "A wheel within a wheel" — Babylonish emblem of divinity — Origin of the cherubim — Dream of a woman suffering from cataract — Effect of dream on her character — Watch and chain recovered by means of a "faked" dream — Illustration of the doctrine of Kismet or Naseeb — "Ghosts" in our compound — Atmosphere of ghosts bad for fowls.

"O dreamer, dream thy dream, and dream it true.

Sir Lewis Morris.

"Did not Heaven speak to men in dreams of old?"

Lord Tennyson.

"... The vision of my soul
Has looked upon its Sun and turns no more
To any lower light."

Sir Lewis Morris.

Dreams and visions have a great influence on the Eastern mind. They believe most firmly that God often speaks by means of these agencies, using them as a warning of impending danger, or as a voice of instruction.

Ezekiel was no exception to this rule, for we read in the words of his prophecy, "That the heavens were opened, and I saw visions of God." This vision was given to him as he stood by the river Chebar in the land of the Chaldeans. The river Chebar is none other than the Khabour, over which we have passed more than once in our "journeyings oft." When on our way back to England we crossed this river, and as we sat near its banks, even as Ezekiel did of old, we too were vouchsafed a "vision of God."

We had travelled through a weary stretch of waterless desert that day, and were rejoicing in the fact that our camping-ground for the night was by the banks of a river — the Chebar. Only those who have journeyed for days through a parched-up desert land can tell the joy with which a river is sighted. We experienced something of that joy on the evening when we saw water for the first time for two or three days. We pitched our camp as close to the river as possible, and, sitting at our tent door, prepared to enjoy to the full the beauties before us. Looking up I saw in front of me a glorious sight. I quickly called my husband, and together we stood and watched this wonderful vision. The sun was sinking as a ball of fire behind the river, when suddenly from its centre there arose beautiful prismatic lights. These gradually resolved themselves into the form of a huge wheel, each spoke of the wheel being of a different colour, merging gradually and almost imperceptibly into the next, as in the rainbow. Within this "wheel" was another and smaller one, also composed of the same prismatic hues. The outer circle of each wheel was formed by a band of bright opaque light. On the top of these wheels was a visionary form resembling the beginning of another wheel, but it was too indistinct for me to say what definite shape it possessed. At either side of these wheels was a large wing, as it were overshadowing the wheels; these were also of a bright white. The whole formed a most wonderful and never to be forgotten sight, and we felt indeed that this was a vision of God.

A WONDERFUL VISION

While in Mosul my husband had received a letter from a gentleman in England, asking him to keep a look-out for any such phenomenon as this. On reaching home it was interesting to find on good authority that the sight we had seen on the banks of the Khabour was one of historical interest. The form of the wheels is almost identical with the emblem which the Babylonians adopted to represent Divinity. On the same authority I learnt, too, that in all probability a vision similar to this was the origin of the cherubims. It is believed by an expert on the subject that the whole of the "vision" is caused by atmospheric influences, the sun acting on the particles of frost in the air, thus forming the prismatic colours. Be this as it may, the result was truly marvellous, and we were thankful that we had been privileged to see "the heavens open," revealing this vision of God.

The whole spectacle could not have lasted more than five minutes, but the sky retained its blaze of colour for about a quarter of an hour after; then darkness covered the heavens.

The natives of Mosul are great believers in dreams, and accept them as good or bad omens. A short time ago a Moslem woman came to the Dispensary suffering from double cataract. She had been quite blind for many years, and was very anxious for an operation, saying if only she could have enough sight to sweep the compound she would be satisfied, as then she could earn her livelihood. The doctor, after examining her eyes, told the woman that he could not promise her a good result from the operation, as her eyes were not healthy. However, as she was absolutely blind, it was worth while to try, and perhaps she might see sufficiently afterwards to find her way about. Accordingly she was admitted to the Hospital to await her time for operation. She was a very affectionate woman, and seemed to be gifted with great powers of intuition. When I went to the door of the ward, even before I spoke, she always called out, "There's my khatoun!" Sometimes I crept in quietly just to see if she would know I was present; she almost invariably did, and sitting up in bed would listen intently, and then say to one of the other patients, "Is not the khatoun here?" Then when she felt my hand, she would grasp it and say, "I knew it, I knew it; I *felt* here" (pointing to her heart) "that my khatoun was in the room!" She was such an excitable woman that my husband feared that she would do something foolish either at the time of the operation or after. He warned her that if she did not keep quiet she might lose her eye altogether; but as the fateful day approached she became more and more nervous. One morning, however, she appeared quite calm, and hastened to tell us the reason of her peace of mind. During the night she had seen a vision which had quieted all her fears and made her trustful and believing.

In her dream she seemed to be walking in the desert, where she met a mullah, who immediately began to revile and curse her. While he was thus engaged the woman saw a form coming towards her which she knew to be that of our Lord (Jesus the Living One, as He is called in Arabic). He began to speak gently to the woman, asking her why she was weeping; she replied by telling our Lord that the mullah had been cursing her. In her dream she then *saw* (although blind) that our Lord turned to the mullah and rebuked him for cursing the woman. Then turning to the wondering woman, He said, "Do not weep, my daughter, for the English doctor is going to give you sight in a few days," and then He left her. She awoke firmly convinced that this was a special revelation from God through Jesus our Lord to assure her that her eyesight was to be restored. From that time she was perfectly calm and quiet, and remained so the whole time she was in the hospital. The day before the operation she was again warned that she might not see any better after; but she smiled and said, "To-morrow I shall see!" Her faith was rewarded, as the operation was successful, and after two or three weeks she went out with very good vision in one eye, and she is waiting for our return to have the other operated upon.

My husband was once travelling "chappa" (post) in Persia from Yezd to Kerman, when one evening he found to his great sorrow that he had lost his gold watch and chain. Both were very valuable to him on account of their associations, so he was very sad at the thought of losing them. The same night he met another Englishman who was returning to Yezd. He told him of his loss, and asked him to make inquiries along the road, offering a reward to any one who would bring back his watch and chain. His friend promised to do all he could, and, calling his servant, explained to him about the loss, and told him to keep a sharp look-out for any news of the lost goods. This servant was a very smart man. The next morning they met a camel caravan on the road to Kerman, and the servant went up to the driver and said to him—

"Oh, my noble brother, may your kindness never grow less; my sleep has been troubled last night by dreams of you."

"*Estakfarullah!*" (God forbid), says the camel-driver. "Why was my lord's sleep disturbed by dreams of me, who am not worthy?"

"Yes; I saw in my dream that you stooped and picked up something."

"Then your dream was wrong," hastily interposed the camel-driver, "for I have picked up nothing."

"And lo! in my dream," continued the wily servant, "I saw that the thing which you picked up was worthless, only a cheap thing which will bring you no gain." The camel-driver here looking sad, the servant continued: "But the owner of that worthless thing is very anxious to find it, as although of no value in money, yet he cherishes it as a thing he loves."

"But I told you," repeats the camel-driver, "that I never picked up anything."

"Then in my dream," continues the servant, carefully ignoring the reiterated denial of the camel-driver, "I saw you glance at this useless object in your hand and then place it inside your *aba*" (cloak).

"No, no," cries the driver, "I never picked it up."

"So if you will let me show you where it is, I can relieve you of this worthless object."

After a little more parleying of this sort, the camel-driver produces my husband's watch and chain, and receives in return a small backsheesh. The servant, highly delighted with himself and his sagacity, smiled as he pockets in imagination the promised reward of five *tomans* (£1). The camel-driver confessed afterwards that he was so taken aback at the idea of his deeds being revealed in a dream to this man that he would not have kept the watch at any cost.

Needless to say the "dream" was only a faked one, manufactured to work on the superstitious mind of the simple camel-driver.

In Mosul the chief of the Seyyids once told the doctor a story relating to a remarkable dream. It was as follows. Two men once called on a mullah to question him regarding a matter which had been troubling them. The cause of their dispute was this. On going to their work each day these men passed a ladder leaning against a wall. One of the two always avoided going under lest it should fall and kill him; while the other said, "No, I will not run from danger, for whatever Allah has decreed must be. If it is written that I am to be killed by the ladder, I shall be." So the two friends, after having spent much time in arguing this knotty question, decided to lay the matter before a mullah and leave the decision to him. The mullah listened to them both, but told them that such a serious question needed much thought. He appointed a day for them to return and hear his verdict. After their departure the mullah fell into a sleep, and in his sleep he dreamed. In the dream he beheld a beautiful boy, the son of a king whom his soul loved exceedingly; then later he met a stranger, who told him that he (the mullah) was to cause the death of the boy he loved so much. The mullah, filled with indignation, repudiated the idea, saying that he loved the boy too much to do him any harm. "Nevertheless," said the stranger, "it must be, for Allah has decreed that the boy is to meet his death through you, and what is written is written." The old mullah returned to his house troubled and sad at heart, but determined that he would do nothing that could in any way bring disaster to the boy. Still dreaming, the mullah received a summons to visit the young prince. Remembering the words of the stranger, he took with him nothing that could in any way injure the boy, contenting himself by taking with him one gift only—an apple. The boy received the mullah in his beautiful island home, and the two enjoyed some blissful hours of converse together.

Finally, ere saying farewell, the old man with extended hands presented the apple to the boy, who gladly accepted it, and proposed eating it at once. The mullah, taking a penknife from his inner pocket, peeled the apple, and returned it on the point of the knife to the young prince, who, boylike, grasped it eagerly. In taking the apple the point of the knife pricked the finger of the lad, with the result that blood poisoning set in, and in a short time the beautiful boy lay dead. The mullah in his sorrow wept aloud, and as he wept he awoke. With humble heart and head bowed in submission, he gave glory to Allah.

On the day appointed the two men returned to hear the verdict of the wise mullah. He received them kindly, but sorrowfully, assuring them that it made not the slightest difference whether they walked under the ladder or not.

"For," said the old man, "if it is written that you are to be killed by a ladder falling upon you, it must be so, you cannot escape. What Allah has written must be fulfilled. His designs cannot be frustrated."

This doctrine, taught to the old mullah by means of his dream, is very prominent in the minds of all Moslems to-day.

When in Persia we had an Indian servant who was a Mohammedan. He told us that three times on successive nights our Lord had appeared to him in a dream, in the form of an old man with a long white beard. So struck was he with the persistency of the dream, that he went to an English clergyman, asking to be taught the Christian religion.

The women in Mosul have often told me of wonderful things which they declared were going to happen to me, as had been revealed to them in dreams. Even now I receive letters from some of these women in which they say, "We see you every night in our dreams."

The first women in-patients in our so-called hospital in Mosul had to be content with a kind of outhouse for their ward. The only place we could find for them which would be hareem was a large room which we used as a wood-house. This my husband had whitewashed and thoroughly cleansed and disinfected. The first unfortunate woman to be put in this ward (?) was a very quiet, gentle Moslem woman, who came for an operation. Her mother came with her to look after her, and these two were alone in their none too comfortable quarters.

Two or three days after the operation, these women declared that in the night a huge form of dragon-like appearance rose from the ground at their side!

Some weeks later this ward was occupied by a little Jewish girl who had been terribly burnt, her mother and grandmother looking after her. There were also two or three other women in the ward. One morning very early, word was brought to us that all the inmates of that room had been terribly frightened in the night. On going out to see what had happened, we found them all lying in the passage, having carried their bedding out of the room. They were looking very unhappy and frightened, and requested to be allowed to leave the hospital at once, saying they would not pass another night in that awful place. Then they all began to recount their experiences of the night at the same time, so it was with great difficulty we could find out what really had happened. It seems that soon after midnight they were talking to one another, when suddenly they saw two soldiers sitting on the edge of their bedsteads. Terribly alarmed, they asked the men however they came to be there—did they not know it was "hareem"? At first the soldiers remained silent, but afterwards told the women that they had come from a village about twelve miles off. That they had been told in a dream to come to the *beit hakeem Engelisi* (house of the English doctor). In obedience to this command they had come. Then, as suddenly as they had arrived, they disappeared. The women, of course, were all fearfully alarmed, some believing that they were real soldiers, others that they were genii in the form of soldiers. They immediately left the room, carrying their bedding with them, and spent the rest of the night in fear and trembling. The next morning we made a very careful examination of the roof, to see if by any possible means soldiers could have entered our compound. We found that next door was the house of the head of the soldiers, and it was possible that some of his guard might have found their way over the walls and down to our house.

Nothing, however, was ever proved; but no one could ever be induced to use that room again, the women declaring that it was haunted by evil spirits. Finally, we made it into a hen-house; but the fowls and turkeys all sickened and died, so there evidently was something very wrong with the atmosphere of that room! Our first attempt at a women's ward was certainly a failure, but "it is an ill wind that blows nobody any good," and so good came out of this evil. As the women would not use the haunted (?) room, other accommodation had to be found, so we gave up our house for them, while we moved into the one next door—the room which was neither good for human beings nor for feathered fowls being now used as a wood-house.

Once when travelling in the desert, a spot was pointed out to us as being the abode of Jinns and Genii. This spot is much abhorred by the muleteers, as they believe that any one camping on that ground is liable to be overtaken by a terrible death. The enchanted ground is encircled by some landmarks, and it is said that any one going to sleep within that magic circle will at once be visited by the Jinns inhabiting the spot, who will immediately come and suck his blood till he is dead.

CHAPTER IX

MANNERS AND SUPERSTITIONS IN MOSUL

Characteristics of inhabitants of Mosul — Social habits — Love of drink — An effectual cure — Gambling — Tel Kaif: a story of Uncle Goro — The Angel of Death and other titles — Difficulties over name and age — Some superstitions — Effect of scent on women — Birds of good omen — Thieves — Sheep-killing — Sheikh Matti — An angel's visit — Medical superstitions — Cure for hydrophobia.

"Nothing has more effect upon the mob than superstition."

QUINTUS CURTIUS.

"To be superstitious is a crime."

ANON.

"Sickness and sorrow come and go, but a superstitious soul hath no rest."

R. BURTON.

The natives of Mosul are, as a rule, a very simple-hearted folk. They are easily amused, easily taken in, and as easily roused to passion. They are, on the whole, good-tempered and patient, and, considering the absolute lack of self-control in their method of bringing up, they give way far less to their passions than might be expected.

They dearly love social habits, and spend much time in company, telling and listening to stories, smoking, and drinking coffee. Unfortunately, they do not confine their drink to coffee, and these social habits often lead to a great deal of drinking. Arak is the favourite refreshment at these times, and is indulged in by both Christian and Moslem alike. It is a pure spirit, and is made by the Christians and Jews of Mosul, and sold by them to the Moslems. No ceremony is complete without the arak bottle. At weddings, funerals, dinner parties, at each and every season of life, it is thought necessary to provide this fire-water. I am sorry to say that the women also drink, but not to such an extent as the men.

It is, of course, considered a great sin for a Moslem to drink either wine or spirit, as both have been forbidden in the Koran: but their love for the arak is stronger in many cases than their love of the Koran. A Mosul Moslem woman told me a short time ago that she did not think there was one Moslem man in Mosul who did not drink either wine or arak. I hope this is an exaggeration, but the tendency to be less ashamed of the drinking habit and to indulge in it more freely is growing more and more. It is sad to think that the Christians of the city are the manufacturers and vendors of spirit and wines, and that they are responsible for introducing them into Mosul.

A story is told of a Sultan of Turkey who, desirous of putting a stop to the ever-increasing drink traffic, made a law by which every Moslem found the worse for drink should be cast into prison. The first morning after the new law had come into action, a Moslem was found drunk lying in the street, incapable of walking to his home. He was immediately taken to prison, and allowed to sleep off the effects of the drink. When he awoke, great was his surprise to find himself in the interior of a prison. On being taken before the judge, he pleaded "Not guilty," and said that he had been suffering for some days from a terrible pain in his tooth, and yesterday had gone to the hakeem (doctor) to obtain medicine to relieve the pain. The doctor had told him that the best cure for his pain was to drink a little brandy, so he had followed his advice, with the result that he fell asleep and only awoke to find himself in prison. The judge then commiserated the man on having such bad pain, but assured him it was easily remedied. Calling to one of his servants, he ordered him to go at once and fetch the barber, who acted as dentist to all such sufferers. The prisoner assured his excellency the judge that it really did not matter, the pain was better. "But," said the judge sympathetically, "it may come back." The barber was brought and told to examine the man's mouth. Finding no sign of decay, he assured the judge that the teeth were sound. The judge began to revile the dentist, saying, "You call yourself a dentist and do not know which is the tooth causing this man pain. Find it, and pull it out at once." Trembling, the dentist took his forceps and extracted a back tooth. "Let me see," cried the judge. "Why, that is not rotten; what do you mean by pulling out a good tooth? Pull *the* rotten one out at once." Then the dentist again operated on his unwilling victim, and a second time the judge upbraided him for not drawing the right tooth, and ordered him to go on till he had found the one that was decayed. The wretched prisoner, feeling he could not bear to lose any more teeth, called out that it was all a lie: he never had had any toothache, and only drank brandy because he loved it, and promised never to touch it again. The judge smilingly bade his prisoner begone, warning him, however, that next time he offended all his teeth might have to come out.

Closely associated with drinking is the gambling habit. This too, alas! is very prevalent in Mosul. In almost every house card-playing forms the chief pastime both in the hareem and amongst the men, and, as a rule, they play for money. Enormous sums of money are lost and won in this way, and, unfortunately, those in good positions are the ones who profit most by this gambling habit. One lady was the possessor of many beautiful jewels, diamonds, pearls, &c., and I was told that she had won them all by gambling.

We are always very glad to take part in the social customs of the people when neither drinking nor gambling is part of the programme, and I, at least, certainly very much enjoy a dinner served *à l'Arabe*, with its attendant native entertainment. The after-dinner story-telling is very amusing when you have mastered the language sufficiently to be able to follow the drift of the tale. Shortly before leaving, we gave a farewell dinner to some of our friends, and, after dinner, entertained them with fireworks, while one of the guests amused us all by recounting stories, some of which were very interesting. One was as follows:—

"There is a village near Mosul called Tel Kaif, in which all the inhabitants are Christians. They are a very original set of people, differing altogether from the Christians of Mosul in language, dress, and customs. They consider they are quite the most clever and important people under the sun, and this idea is apparent in all their actions. Many years ago there lived in Tel Kaif a very clever and wise man called Uncle Goro. If any one was in trouble he immediately went to this man for advice; if any were sorrowful, it was to Uncle Goro they looked for consolation; were any sick, again it was Uncle Goro alone who could heal them. In fact, Uncle Goro was looked upon by the admiring villagers as their one hope and stay in times of need. One day a cow belonging to the village felt very thirsty. Now, the water supply of Tel Kaif is not very good, the villagers being dependent upon a large pool of rain-water, which sometimes dries up during the long-continued season of drought. Doubtless this cow did not approve of drinking dirty rain-water, so, while seeking for other means of slaking her thirst, she espied near the doorway of a house a large earthen water-pot. Into this she looked longingly, but her horns at first prevented her from reaching the water. However, after a little careful manipulation and perseverance, she managed to insert her head into the jar. When she had satisfied her thirst, she tried to withdraw her head, but found she could not, so there it had to remain, while the bewildered villagers looked on in helpless astonishment. At last they decided to appeal to their wise man, so one went off in search of him. When he arrived on the spot and beheld the cow with her head in the water-jar, he considered thoughtfully for a while, and then gave his advice in the following learned manner.

"Oh, my children," he cried, "here is such a simple matter, and yet you could not find a way out of the difficulty. I am surprised that my fellow-men should be so ignorant."

Then they all crowded round Uncle Goro, beseeching him out of his great wisdom to tell them what to do.

"First," said Uncle Goro, "you must cut off the cow's head, then break the water-pot and take out the head!"

This brilliant suggestion was at once put into practice, the owner of the cow being the only one who was not quite so sure of the exceeding greatness of the wisdom of Uncle Goro. When the deed was accomplished and the head extricated from its awkward position, the old man stood and proudly addressed the assembled crowd who had flocked to hear his words of wisdom. "My beloved children," said he, "a day will come when your old Uncle Goro will die, and then what will you do when you have no one to settle such difficult matters as these for you? Pray to God that your Uncle Goro may long be spared to advise and counsel you."

A rather pretty custom exists in Mosul which gives people titles according to their work, or any special characteristics belonging to them. For example, the butcher is called "the father of meat"; the baker, "the father of bread." In the hospital, when I am giving orders for the diet list, we hardly ever speak of the patients by name, but according to their disease, as "Aboo" (father) liver abscess, "Aboo-mai-abiyud" (father of cataract). One of the assistants in the hospital was named "The Angel of Death" by a poor little girl who was brought to the doctor a mass of burns. It was the duty of this assistant to dress the terrible wounds of the child every day, and though as gentle as a woman, he necessarily pained her a great deal—hence the term "Angel of Death." The women are designated in the same way as the men, only substituting "mother" for "father," as "Em haleeb," milk-woman; "Em saba' saba'een," mother of seventy-seven (or centipede), this last simply referring to a girl suffering from hysteria.

This was an interesting case which was in the women's hospital for some weeks. The patient was a young woman about sixteen years of age. She was under the delusion that she had swallowed a "saba' saba'een" (a horny centipede, measuring some seven or eight inches, common in Mosul). She declared she could not eat anything, for every time she swallowed, the saba' saba'een opened its mouth and ate the food just partaken of! She absolutely refused to touch anything of her own accord, so we had to force food down her throat. Two or three women would hold her hands and feet while I fed her with a spoon. As time went on she became worse instead of better, and was always beseeching my husband to operate on her and take out the saba' saba'een. After a time he consented to give her an anæsthetic and operate. On the day appointed she was taken to the theatre and given a whiff of chloroform, while the doctor made a slight incision in her skin. This was stitched up, and she was shown her wound and assured that the doctor had cut her and found nothing. After this she was much happier, and was soon well enough to leave the hospital.

Women never know their age in Mosul. On dispensary days each woman is required to give her name and age. The first difficulty is over the name. Many do not know their surnames at all. When asked, "What is your father's name?" they say, "How do I know?" and then add with a laugh, "Say Bint Abdulla" (daughter of a servant of God). Abdulla is often a very convenient name when the parentage is uncertain.

With regard to their age, women are quite hopeless. I have often seen an old lady, bent double with the weight of many years, come into the dispensary.

"Well, mother, how old are you?" I ask her.

"How old am I? How do I know, my daughter?"

"Do you think you are fifteen?"

"Well, I may be."

"Are you twenty yet?"

"Perhaps I am," replies the fair damsel of eighty. "I know I was born two years before the year that the locusts ate all the corn."

As to how many years ago the locusts destroyed the crop she has not the remotest idea.

Or another woman will come, certainly not more than twenty or twenty-five, the mother of a baby in arms. On being asked her age she replies, "About sixty"! The natives never have any idea when their birthdays are, but keep their name-days instead. Thus amongst the Christians all Johns will keep the feast of St. John as their feast-day, and so on.

Parents have a convenient way of forgetting the date of the birth of their daughters. A girl who is not betrothed will remain twelve or thirteen for much more than one year; for when she has passed fourteen or fifteen years she is no longer considered young, and not very likely to be betrothed at all if her real age is known.

The natives of Mosul are very superstitious; more especially, perhaps, is this true of the women. One curious superstition they have with regard to scent. Now an odour which is filthy and dangerous, such as may be *felt* in most of the houses, is not at all injurious from their standpoint, but a sweet-smelling scent is an abomination to the women. If by any chance I have been using anything in the way of scent (though as a rule I am very careful not to), the first thing I see on entering a room is that the women all immediately apply their handkerchiefs to their olfactory organs. At first this custom appears, to say the least, not too polite; but when you realise \ what it means to them, you understand and excuse them. They firmly believe that a sweet smell brings sickness and sorrow—that it is equally fatal to mothers and young children—hence the great fear of anything in the way of scent. One day our reception-room was full of women who had come to visit me. Suddenly a visitor was announced (a native of the country, but not of Mosul); immediately all the women crowded into one corner, burying their heads in their chuddars. I could not make out what had disturbed them till I discovered that the new-comer was strongly scented. She was left severely alone by all the others, who kept as far away as possible from her, some even leaving the room, fearing lest evil should overtake them.

Another day I went to visit a little patient of my husband's in whom he took a great interest. This little boy was the spoilt darling of his parents, the father especially idolising him, watching over him carefully lest any harm should befall him. Great was his consternation and distress when it was found that an operation was necessary to save the life of the boy. When the little chap was convalescent I went to see him. After talking to the mother some time in another room, she suggested our going to see the boy. No sooner had I appeared at the threshold of the door, when the boy buried his face in his hands, calling out, "Oh, you smell, you smell!" I assured both the mother and the boy that I had no scent of any kind on me, but the boy would not be pacified, and continued crying out, "Go away—you smell!" As he was still weak, I thought I had better depart, as excitement was bad for him. When visiting amongst the women it is better not to use scented soap, as they detect even that sometimes!

Birds have a good many superstitions connected with them. Last year, while we were waiting for the decision of our committee regarding the future of the mission in Mosul, some women informed me that "good news was coming." Good news meant to them that the Mission was to be kept on. On asking how they knew, they told me they had just heard a bird singing which is supposed never to raise his voice except as the harbinger of good tidings. Storks are looked upon as omens of good luck. These birds return every spring to Mosul, hatch their eggs, and migrate in early autumn. The natives of Mosul always hail their return with great joy, especially if they nest on their roofs. Some will even go so far as to put baskets on the roofs, hoping that the storks will be attracted by them and make them their home for the summer. They agree with Longfellow in his love of storks, as expressed in his poem —

> "By God in heaven
> As a blessing, the dear white stork was given."

If there had been any truth in this superstition, we ought to have been very prosperous; for at one time we had no less than three families of storks on our roof. Personally I think they are not altogether too desirable, for when sleeping on the roof they are apt to become very noisy companions. I do not think I like to be laughed at by these birds. In the early morning they stand close by one's bed, throw back their heads till they rest on their backs, and then laugh aloud at the idea of any one sleeping when once dawn has appeared.

The common name for storks in Mosul is "the thieves," as they sometimes steal small articles of clothing hanging out to dry, such as handkerchiefs; and no one would ever dare to go to the nest to hunt, lest they should disturb the birds and cause them to fly away. These birds are rather a convenience sometimes for the washerwoman: when blouses disappear it is easy to lay the blame on the "thieves." They are almost as useful as the proverbial "cat."

Our servant Judy is a little woman full of queer superstitious ideas. While in Mosul I received the sad news of the death of my father: poor Judy was so distressed lest by over-much mourning I should tempt God to take my husband too. As dressmaking is rather primitive in Mosul I decided to have some things dyed black. Judy would not hear of such a thing, saying that only widows must wear dyed clothes, and that if I wore dyed dresses for my father, she was sure something would happen to my husband.

Another thing she never would do, and that is to step over our feet! In the summer evenings we used to sit in our verandah, which was rather narrow, and if by chance we should place our feet on a hassock in front of us there remained no room for any one to pass. I could not make out why Judy would never pass that way when it was necessary to enter the room at our back. At last she told me that if she stepped over our feet, she would be in danger of "cutting our life," and that if we died it would be her fault. After this I often tried to make her step over my feet, by blocking her pathway, but she never would, so strong was her belief that by so doing she would cut short my life!

It is surprising how ignorantly superstitious some of the better-class people are. A wife of a very wealthy Christian merchant in Mosul had a child who suffered terribly from sore eyes. She brought him to the dispensary for some time, but finding that the treatment pained the child and made him cry, ceased to bring him. We heard afterwards that she had resorted to the following superstitious method of healing.

A sheep was bought, killed, and opened: while the blood was still hot the head of the child was inserted into the middle of the sheep's body and allowed to remain there about fifteen minutes. Could any treatment be more revolting and disgusting than this? and yet these people, rich and influential members of Mosul society, really believed that by doing this their child's eyes would be cured. Needless to say it had not the desired effect, and months afterwards they again brought the child to the dispensary, and having learnt their lesson by experience, were content to leave the child in the English hakim's hands, with the result that after a couple of months' daily treatment the eyes were quite healed.

I do not know what virtue is supposed to exist in the killing of the sheep or goat, but it is a custom very much in vogue in Mosul. On our return from Beyrout, after having been absent three months, a live goat was brought out into the desert to meet us, and the moment we alighted from our carriage this poor creature was slaughtered right under our eyes. In Persia the custom amongst the Armenians at a wedding feast was for a sheep to be killed just as the bride and bridegroom were stepping over the threshold of their new home. It was not considered lucky if the bride did not put her foot into the blood as she passed. In Mosul, too, I believe a sheep is sometimes slaughtered at weddings in this way, but I have never seen it done.

When a wife is desirous of becoming a mother, there are various superstitious methods to which she may resort, but perhaps the favourite one of all is that connected with Sheikh Matti. This is a monastery situated some twelve hours' ride from Mosul, on the side of a lonely mountain. The woman makes a pilgrimage to this place, and is then told that she must spend a night in the solitary chapel there. While she sleeps an angel will visit the building, and if her request is to be vouchsafed her, will place an apple by her head. If the angel desires to be especially kind to the woman, he will place two, or even three apples near her, the number of apples indicating how many children God is going to honour her with. Strange to say, these angel visits do not take place unless provoked by a fair amount of backsheesh!

There are a good many superstitions regarding medical treatment of diseases and accidents, but these, I believe, are fast dying out in the face of European learning and skill. The people are learning by experience how much better are the English methods than their own. For instance, it used to be the common custom for those suffering from fever to go to the mullah, who would lay his hands on the patient's head while reading a few verses from the Koran. If the fever did not go at once, well, it was the fault of the fever, not of the mullah. I fancy fever patients are beginning to prefer English medicines rather than to trust to the laying on of hands by the mullah. When any one has been bitten by a mad dog, which, considering the number of street dogs, is of very rare occurrence, he goes at once to a sheikh, who will give him an antidote. This consists of a date from which the stone has been taken, and into which the sheikh has spat two or three times to fill up the gap caused by the removal of the stone. Upon eating this, the man is supposed to be free from all fear of the development of hydrophobia.

These are merely a few of the superstitious customs found in Mosul to-day. Had we time or space they might be multiplied many times over, but enough, I trust, has been said to awaken love and sympathy in our hearts for these simple folk, whose minds are so easily influenced and guided by these useless and often degrading

> "Heart-chilling superstitions, which can glaze
> Even Pity's eye with her own frozen tears."

COLERIDGE.

CHAPTER X

THE YEZIDEES

Gratitude to the English — Persecutions — "Devil-worshippers" — Sun and fire worship — Priesthood — A visit to Sheikh Âdi — Peacock wands — A sacred shrine.

"Whoever thou art, if thy need be great,
In the Name of God, the Compassionate
And All-Merciful One —
For Thee I wait."

WHITTIER.

The Yezidees, or, as they are commonly called, "devil-worshippers," are a very remarkable tribe living in the near vicinity of Mosul. Very little is really known as to their religious beliefs, and whether they worship the devil or only fear him, has never yet been discovered by Europeans.

These curious people are very favourably disposed towards the English, as many years ago the British representative in Mosul was able to assist them very materially. The Mohammedans have always been very bitter against this people, and have done all in their power to exterminate them. A former Pasha at one time captured the high priest of the Yezidees, whose name was Sheikh Naser; he somehow managed to escape, substituting in his place a priest under him in authority. The priest never revealed this fact, and bore with resignation the tortures and imprisonment inflicted upon him. The Yezidees applied to Mr. Rassam, who was the British Vice-Consul at Mosul, and he obtained the release of the priest by paying a large sum as ransom money. This debt was faithfully repaid, and since that time the Yezidees have cherished very grateful memories of the English.

Many years ago these Yezidees were a very powerful tribe. They had two principal strongholds, one in the mountains lying to the west of Mosul, and the other only twenty-four hours' journey to the north. By means of continual attacks and massacres at the hands of the Kurds, their population has been reduced considerably, only about one-third remaining of their original number.

Mohammedans are always very bitter against any sect which is supposed to have no "Book." The Yezidees, coming under this category, receive little mercy from them, and for centuries have been exposed to persecutions from these their oppressors. Of late years the Yezidees have seen the uselessness of rebelling against their fate, and, acknowledging their defeat, are patiently bearing their misfortunes.

These so-called devil-worshippers recognise one Supreme Being, but apparently do not offer any prayers directly to Him. The name of God is often on their lips in the form of oaths, but that of the evil spirit is never to be heard. So far do they carry this superstition, that not only will they not use the word Shaitan (Satan), but any word beginning with "sh" is also shunned by them. Then, again, such a veneration have they for Satan, that it is prohibited amongst the Yezidees to utter any word containing the letter ش (shin), being the first letter of the Arabic word for Satan. Thus they have to find other words to express such commonly spoken of objects as the sun, river, water-melon, &c., as they each begin with the prohibited letter. Layard, in his Travels amongst them, tells of one instance illustrating this superstition. He was standing in the midst of a large crowd of Yezidees gathered to take part in their yearly feast, when he espied a boy climbing a tree at the apparent risk of his neck. He says, "As I looked up I saw the impending danger, and made an effort by an appeal to the chief to avert it. 'If that young Sheit —' I exclaimed, about to use an epithet generally applied in the East to such adventurous youths. I checked myself immediately, but it was too late; half the dreaded word had escaped." He goes on to say that the effect was instantaneous, a look of horror spreading over the faces of all present. Fortunately for him, he was a favourite amongst the Yezidees, and so they allowed it to pass. So great is the horror of this letter, that they have often killed those who use it wilfully. When speaking of the devil they do so reverently, calling him the "mighty angel."

The symbol of their religion is the "Malek el Taous," a peacock, and is held in great reverence by them. Satan is said to be the head of the angelic host, and he is supplied with seven archangels, who minister to him and exercise great influence over the world; they are Gabriel, Michael, Raphael, Azrail, Dedrail, Azrapheel, and Shemkeel. Our Lord is also counted amongst the angels, though not one of these seven, and is acknowledged to have taken upon Himself the form of man. They, in common with the Mohammedans, do not believe in His crucifixion; but declare that He ascended to heaven just before that event took place, some saying that the angel Gabriel took our Lord's place on the Cross, while others say Judas was the real victim. They are looking forward to the second coming of Christ and also to the reappearance of the Imam; this latter being also the Mohammedan's hope. Their patron saint is one called Sheikh Âdi, who is supposed to have lived many years before Mohammed; but very little is known of his history.

They reverence the sun, and are in the habit of kissing the object on which its first rays fall. Fire as a symbol is also connected with their worship, the disciples frequently passing their hands through the flame, kissing them, and then rubbing them over their faces. They have four orders of priesthood, which is hereditary, and consists of the Pirs, Sheikhs, Cawals, and the Fakirs.

The Pirs (from a Persian word meaning old man) are the most reverenced next to their great sheikh or head of the sect. These are believed to possess the power not only of interceding for their adherents, but also of curing disease and insanity. They are *supposed* to lead a life of great sanctity, and are in consequence much looked up to by the people.

The Sheikhs come next in order of rank. These are supposed to know a little Arabic, as their work is to write the hymns which are chanted at their religious services. They guard the tomb of Sheikh Âdi, bring fuel to keep up the holy fire, and provisions to those who dwell within the shrine.

The third rank of priesthood is perhaps the most active of all. These are called Cawals or preachers, and it is their duty to go from village to village teaching the doctrines of the Yezidees. They are all musicians, being taught to sing when very young; they also perform on the flute and tambourine, both of these instruments being looked upon as holy. Before and after playing they often kiss their instruments, and pass them to the audience for them to do likewise. They dress as a rule in white and wear black turbans, while the sheikhs always wear nothing but white. They are generally venerable-looking men with long beards. They act as emissaries for the sheikh, and yearly go forth and collect the revenues. Their emblem of office is a wand, on the top of which is perched a brazen peacock, and they boast with pride that never have their enemies been able to capture one of these staves. They relate how on one memorable occasion a priest, being chased through the desert by Arabs, in the heat of the pursuit stopped his mare, descended, and buried the precious badge of office; then, marking the exact site for future reference, resumed his flight. Having escaped with his life, six months later he managed to recover the buried staff, creeping down by night into the desert from his mountain shelter. Now why should they place such a high value on these emblems? A possible solution was given me by the Rev. Dr. St. Clair Tisdall, who recalled to my mind an old Mohammedan tradition that it was the peacock who admitted Satan into the garden of Eden. This would strengthen the suspicion that the Yezidees really do worship the evil one.

The lowest order in the priesthood are called Fakirs. These wear coarse dresses of black or dark-brown canvas, which reach only as far as the knees. Their office is to perform all the menial work connected with the tomb of Sheikh Âdi, sweeping and cleaning the sacred buildings, trimming and lighting the holy lamps. These lamps are offerings made by pilgrims who have visited the tomb in times of danger or sickness.

A yearly sum is subscribed for the oil necessary for the lamps and for the support of the priests. At sunset each evening these lamps are lit, and give the appearance of a multitude of stars glittering on the side of the mountain; for not only are the lamps placed in the shrine and walls of the courtyard, but they are also scattered about on rocks and ledges and in the dark corners of the woods. As the priest goes from lamp to lamp lighting each one, men and women pass their hands through the flame and smear their foreheads, and those who have children do the same to them. This reverence for fire reminds one of the Parsees of Persia, whom these people in many ways resemble.

Unfortunately I was unable to visit these interesting villages, but I hope to do so on a future occasion. We had intended to spend a month amongst them during the summer of 1906, the sheikh having extended a cordial invitation to us. My husband accordingly went up to reconnoitre, and see if there was any place possible either to stay in or to pitch our tent. He found, however, that it was hardly a suitable place for a summer holiday, as the climate was not very satisfactory, besides which it was difficult to find a place for the tents; so we decided we would not go that year at any rate. Both my husband and the men with him were quite ill for a few hours after visiting Sheikh Âdi, so they were not anxious to return. The natives say that this illness is caused by drinking the water, but that the effect passes off after a few days, when one has become accustomed to the water.

My husband, however, much enjoyed his visit amongst these strange people, and in writing of that time he says:—

"These interesting people dwell in the mountains round about Mosul, the ancient Nineveh. They are ruled over by a sheikh, who claims to be able to put some ten thousand armed horsemen in the field. On account of their suspected devil-worship they are detested by Moslems and Christians alike. The Turks have more than once endeavoured to exterminate them; but, entrenched in their mountain fastnesses, they are very hard to overcome.

"When in Mosul their sheikh called on me and asked me to pay him a visit up in his mountain home. Thus I was able to see their homes for myself, also the sacred shrine, hidden away in the mountains, where their reputed founder (Sheikh Âdi) lies buried, from whom it derives its name.

"The Yezidees, like the Druses of Mount Lebanon, are very reluctant to discuss their religion, and it is said that death is the penalty for any one among them who reveals the truth concerning what they worship.

"On paying a visit to their sacred shrine (Sheikh Âdi), I found it hidden in the hollow of thickly-wooded mountains, and composed of two large compounds, the inner compound containing the shrine in a church-like building with a newly-built steeple. On the right side of the entrance porch is the figure of a huge serpent graven in the stone of the building, with its head uppermost. This serpent is kept blackened daily with charcoal by the two or three old monks who live in the shrine. Upon inquiring the meaning of this symbol, the monk told me it was graven there to remind the worshippers to remove their sandals from off their feet, as the ground around the shrine is holy. If any should be careless or wicked enough to disobey, it was said that they would be bitten on the heels by some of the snakes that were said to infest the place.

"The steeple rises immediately from the room in the church that once contained the body of their founder, Sheikh Âdi. This sheikh was a great Mohammedan teacher who many centuries ago used to preach and teach in Damascus. He gathered around him many disciples, and it is said he was accustomed to vary the monotony of his teaching by drawing a circle on the ground, and, placing therein himself and some favourite disciple, would enable the latter to hear and understand the teaching of another famous mullah speaking in far-away Baghdad.

"This Sheikh Âdi some years before his death retired to this place in the mountains, two days' journey from Mosul, and there he was visited by many, as his fame spread abroad, and in this place he died and was buried. The Yezidees claim that, ere he died, he forsook Mohammedanism and instituted a new religion. The Moslems, however, reverence his memory, and say that the Yezidees, *after* his death, started a new religion of their own.

"In the church there was to be seen a pool of water, said by them to be used as a baptistery, and little else but bare walls. My guide assured me it used to look very different, but fifteen years previously the Turks had captured the place and destroyed all they could lay hands on. On the roof near the steeple are two stones, facing east and west, said to be used as prayer-stones, the Yezidees praying as the *first ray* of the rising sun appears, and as the *last ray* of the setting sun departs, and use these stones as indicators. This, again, is interesting, as (according to Dr. Tisdall) it is a curious fact that Mohammedan tradition avers that it is alone at these two times daily that the devil has power to intercept the prayers of the faithful, and they are, therefore, to be scrupulously avoided by all true Moslems.

"The Yezidees are loath to venture into the city, but a few have already commenced to attend the Mission Dispensary. They are easily recognised by their costume, and by the fact that no Yezidee is allowed to wear any garment exposing the breast. One of these patients informed me that when he wanted to worship he went to the priest (cawal), paid him a small fee, and was placed in a small room, the filthier the better, and made to sit on the floor. The priest would then sit in front of him and make him imagine himself to be in Paradise (the Eastern idea of Paradise—lovely garden, flowing stream, trees laden with fruit, houris, &c.). If (and it is a big 'if') his statement was true, it would point to their priests having some knowledge of hypnotism, but the Yezidees will say anything to mislead an inquirer.

"We had a little Yezidee boy in hospital with his mother. He had been successfully operated upon for stone, but developed jaundice and gradually sank. One evening, ere his mother took him back to her village, a message was brought to us imploring my wife and me to wash our hands in the water our servant brought us; the same water was then to be given by the Yezidee mother to her dying boy that he might drink and live!

"One longs to be able to tell them of Him who is the Water of Life: but they have a language of their own, and understand but little Arabic.

"Will not my readers pray that the Mosul Mission may be strengthened and properly equipped; that the Gospel may be preached to these poor Yezidees, as well as to their Mohammedan neighbours; and that they may learn to love Him who alone has power to cast out devils?"

CHAPTER XI

TRAVELLING IN THE DESERT

Monotony of desert travelling—A puppy and a kitten—Tragedy—Accident by the river Euphrates—Riots in Mosul—Robberies and murder excited by love of gold.

"Of moving accidents by flood and field,
Of hairbreadth 'scapes....
The shot of accident, nor dart of chance
Could neither graze nor pierce...."

SHAKESPEARE.

Travelling in the desert is apt to become rather monotonous when each day goes by with nothing to mark it from the preceding one, so that when some event out of the common does take place it is quite exhilarating. For instance, once during our mid-day halt, which happened to be on the site of a newly-deserted Arab encampment, we heard a cry, and looking about found a wee puppy about two days old. This puppy afforded us amusement for at least two days, much to the amazement of our muleteers. We wrapped it in flannel, placed it in the sunshine to try and instil some warmth into its chilly body, and presently we had the satisfaction of hearing its wailing gradually cease as the sunshine penetrated the flannel. We managed to keep life in the poor little beast for two or three days, but, as milk is scarce in the desert, it was impossible to feed it properly.

One evening we arrived at an Arab encampment, and thought it would be kinder to leave the poor puppy with one of the Arabs, who are supposed to be fond of dogs. So we persuaded our servant to take the puppy and deposit it in one of the tents. He did so very reluctantly, thinking he might be shot at for venturing near after dusk. However, he crept up quietly and placed the puppy just inside one of the tents. Immediately the owner demanded who was there, but Aboo (our servant) fled without waiting to answer. We heard the Arab using some strong language, and then, catching sight of the poor puppy, he took it up and threw it out into the desert. We could hear the little thing squealing and crying, so my husband went to rescue it once more from an untimely end. He found it on top of a rubbish heap, brought it back to our tent, and we tried again to warm and soothe it. The next day, however, the little spark of remaining life was quenched. So the short story of this little forsaken waif ended in a sad tragedy, and my husband undertook the dismal duty of committing its body to the deep waters of the river.

Another day one of our escort galloped up with great excitement to show us a kitten he had just found in the desert—the poor little mite was so thankful to see a human being again, and had evidently been left behind in much the same manner as the puppy when the Arab tribe was migrating.

These are small episodes of the desert which help to break the monotony. I may perhaps be allowed to misquote the well-known lines of S. Gregory:—

> "A little thing is a little thing,
> But 'excitement' in little things
> Is a great thing"—in the desert.

On one occasion we passed an Arab lying on his back and covered with his *aba*, the native cloak worn by all classes. We heard afterwards that it was a case of murder; that the man had been dead three days, and only then had been found by his sons, who were out searching for their father. Hastily covering him with one of their cloaks, they had rushed off to try and find the murderer and avenge their father's blood. We met them soon afterwards, and they told the whole story to our escort.

In the preceding chapters we have seen how often the cry of "Wolf, wolf!" was raised when there was no wolf, till we began to think that the much-talked-of robbers of the desert did not exist at all, or, if they did exist, would not dare to touch a European caravan. However, we soon learnt to our cost that this was not the case.

Two years ago we were travelling from Mosul to Aleppo, and had almost reached our destination when we met with the following adventure.

Having reached the end of our stage one day, we had encamped within a stone's throw of the river Euphrates, just outside the town of Beridjik. Our tent was pitched beneath a lovely spreading tree, under which ran a sparkling stream on its way from the mountains to the river. We thought what an ideal camping-ground it made, and apparently the same thought entered the minds of some others, only from a different standpoint. All round us were signs of the industry of the villagers in the form of huge stacks of corn freshly reaped, now waiting for the threshing time to begin. Ere we retired for the night we were strolling by the stream and amongst the corn, where we noticed two men sitting in the field, who gave us the evening salutations as we passed by. We did not attribute any importance to this fact, as it is not unusual for the villagers to set watchmen to guard their corn during harvest time and afterwards, till the grain is safely housed.

TRAVELLING IN WINTER

A large caravan leaving Isphahan for Yezd while snow is lying on the ground. The man who is holding the horse's head was our servant for a year. He is an Armenian, and is now working as an assistant in the Isphahan Hospital.

So, committing ourselves to the care of Him who never slumbers or sleeps, we retired to our tent, hoping for a good night's rest to prepare us for the journey of the morrow. Our "ideal camping-ground" I found to have at least one great disadvantage—a disadvantage common to all grounds which are used by flocks of goats and sheep for their resting-places. That night these "pilgrims of the desert" were particularly active, and gave me no peace or chance of sleep till the early hours of the morning; then at last, worn-out with the unequal warfare, I fell asleep. I could not have been sleeping long when I was awakened by a movement on the part of my camp bedstead. Sleepily I decided in my mind that our donkey had loosened his tether and was trying to pay us a friendly visit. Often in the night some animal would get loose, and rub himself against our tent ropes till he had succeeded in rooting up one peg, when he would go and practise on another. Thinking this was the case now I promptly fell asleep again, only to be reawakened in a short time by the same sensation. This time I was quite awake, and in an instant flashed my electric torch round the tent, just in time to see a man decamping by the door. I roused my husband (whose sleep is never disturbed by pilgrims of the night), and told him what had happened. He immediately rushed out and gave the alarm to the camp. Unfortunately it was a very dark night, and nothing could be seen a yard ahead, so the robbers had ample opportunity for beating a retreat. Our tent was some little way from the village, so my husband returned to the tent to put on some more garments before going to interview the head-man of the village, who is always supposed to be responsible for the safety of caravans. When he came to look for his clothes, the only article he could find was one shoe, the thieves having cleared the tent of everything available, even to our tooth-brushes! Not only did they clear off everything from the tent, but also emptied a large box which was standing outside the tent, and also took a large valise containing my husband's portmanteau and my "hold-all." Had they been content with these, we should never have known of their nocturnal visit till the morning; but in their desire to secure the small carpet which lay in the middle of the tent, they awoke me, hence the movement of my bed which twice disturbed my sleep. We felt there was nothing to be done till daybreak, so retired once more to rest.

As soon as dawn appeared some of the caravan party rode off in different directions to see if they could find any trace of the thieves, but of course they had disappeared long ago under cover of the darkness. The search party, however, brought back a few garments picked up along the road, which the thieves had evidently dropped in their hurry when the alarm was given. Our escort, a soldier from Beridjik, was sent back to the town to notify the Government officials of the robbery. In a short time the governor of the place rode out with six or seven other officials, all evidently much disturbed in their minds lest they should get into disgrace for allowing any harm to come to a European caravan. The first thing the governor did was to send for the head-man of the village and have him bound and beaten. I was so sorry for the poor man, who had a flowing white beard. I could not bear to witness his beating, so retired to the tent, and tried to shut out the sound as well as the sight of the old man's sufferings. As a matter of fact I do not think the beating was a very severe one, but the victim made the most of it.

This proving of no avail, they all set out for the neighbouring villages, and spent the whole of that day and the next scouring the country for the thieves, returning each day at sunset and renewing the search early next morning. My husband accompanied them the first day, and was very much amused by the behaviour of some of the villagers at sight of the officials. At some villages they would find nothing but women, the men all having fled at the news that soldiers were coming. They found plenty of other stolen goods buried in the ground of the huts, but none of our belongings. In one village a man confidentially whispered to one of the soldiers that *he* knew where the stolen goods were. On being told to lead the way to the place, he led them all to a large field in which were some hundred or more large corn-stacks, and said that the goods were in one of those. I expect he much enjoyed his little joke, for after turning over a dozen or so of these ricks under the scorching sun, the soldiers gave up the task as hopeless. All efforts proving unavailing, we had perforce to proceed on our journey, managing as best we could till we reached Aleppo, where we were able to replenish that which was most lacking in our wardrobe. The fame of our adventure preceded us to Jerusalem, where a month or two later we heard a most exaggerated account of our state when we entered Aleppo.

My husband went at once to our consul on reaching Aleppo, laying before him the whole story. Fortunately for us, Mr. Longworth was a most energetic and painstaking man, having great influence with the Government officials. He asked us to write out an estimate of our losses, which he presented to the Vali, assuring us he would either make the Government pay full compensation or produce the lost goods. After six months of endless work and worry, Mr. Longworth sent my husband a telegram saying that compensation to the full amount had been given. We were very thankful to our consul for his unceasing energy in the matter, and sent him our very grateful thanks. Thus happily ended No. 1 of our chapter of accidents. When we think of what "might have been" that night with those wild men of the desert in our tent while we were sleeping, our hearts go up with great thankfulness to God, who ever watches over His children, and who can keep them as safely in the deserts of Mesopotamia as in the homeland.

The two men we had noticed sitting amongst the corn had probably been hired for the purpose of robbing us, but the real culprit was suspected afterwards to have been one of the leading men of Beridjik—in fact we were told that he was a member of the "town council." Doubtless he wished to procure for himself and his hareem some European clothing, without the expense of buying it.

Another peril from which in God's mercy we were delivered had its origin in Mosul.

The Vali, in obedience to orders from Constantinople, endeavoured to register every woman in Mosul. To accomplish this it was necessary to find out the number and "write" a list of every woman in each house. Moslems and Christians alike rose in revolt at the idea of their women being "written," as it appeared to them contrary to all the laws of God and Mohammed that such a thing should be. The whole town was in an uproar, the shops were shut, no business was done in the sook (bazaar), and men congregated everywhere, talking angrily and making ugly threats. This went on for five days; such a thing had never been known before. Sometimes, in times of trouble, work has been suspended for three days, but no one could remember the sook being shut for such a length of time as five days.

The Christians began to be very much alarmed for their safety, as it was rumoured that, unless the Vali gave way, at the expiration of the fifth day a general massacre of Christians would take place. The French convent was guarded by soldiers; our agent wired to the Consul-General at Baghdad for a like guard for the English, which happily, however, was not needed. When my husband was in the house I did not feel at all nervous, but if he was called out to see a patient after dark I certainly felt very anxious till he returned; for all around us was heard the continual firing of guns and pistols, and I pictured to myself the possibilities and probabilities of some of those stray bullets. "Alhamd'llillah!" nothing happened, and we realised again once more that the traveller's God *is* able to keep, as expressed in those incomparable words commonly known as the Traveller's Psalm.

On the evening of the fifth day the governor recalled his order for the names of the women to be written, and all was quiet once more, at least outwardly. For some time, however, a feeling of unrest was abroad, several murders taking place that week, one of which still remains wrapt in mystery. A Moslem enticed a Jew into the country on the pretext of having some work for him to do; he then made the man dig a grave; after which he stabbed him, and threw the body into the grave made by the victim's own hands. The reason of the murder is unknown.

One evening we were having dinner, when in rushed my husband's chief assistant, in a great state of excitement, to say that his brother had been stabbed in the sook, and they had brought him to our outer compound. My husband immediately went out and found the young man with a wound in his thigh. Had it been a little higher up the result would probably have been fatal, but happily it was a comparatively trivial wound, and a few stitches and a week's rest soon put him right again; but naturally Daoud (the name of the victim) was very much alarmed, and it was some time before he quite recovered his nerve and could walk through that sook again. It seemed such an absolutely meaningless assault, that we could only hope it was a case of mistaken identity. Daoud had been an assistant for over a year, and as far as he knew had not a single enemy in the town.

Matters of private dispute and jealousy are often settled by means of the revolver. An Armenian doctor, a short time ago, was shot when riding home from visiting a case. He was passing under a dark archway, when suddenly he heard bullets whizzing and became aware that he was the target. His horse was so badly hit that he was afraid it could not recover, but fortunately he himself escaped with only a slight graze or two. He attributed the motive of this attack to private grudges borne against him by some of his professional brethren.

There is in Mosul an Armenian woman, whose husband was a doctor who had been celebrated for one special kind of operation. On his death his widow thought she might as well continue her husband's practice, as she had often assisted him with the operations. Accordingly she set herself up amongst the many quack doctors of Mosul. Many of her operations were successful, while the results of a still greater number remain in obscurity. Her charges were tremendous; no matter how poor her patient, she would do nothing till a very large fee had been paid. In this way she made a rich harvest while no European doctor was in the city, but after our arrival I am afraid her income was considerably lessened. Upon our departure from Mosul I imagine she again started her lucrative profession of grinding money out of the poor, for we heard not long ago that she had been stabbed five times while walking in the streets one evening.

Robberies are very common in Mosul. Almost every evening may be heard on all hands sounds of shooting, telling of houses being visited by robbers. Fortunately, so far, they have not favoured us with a visit, and I sincerely hope they never will. One evening we were sitting quietly in the verandah when a woman came rushing in from the women's hospital compound, saying that there were three men on the roof. We all rushed out, armed with anything we could lay hands on, and made a dash for the roof on which the men had been seen, but no sign of them could be found. One of our servants climbed on to the top of the wall connecting our house with our neighbour's, flashing his lantern all round in his endeavours to see any trace of the supposed thieves. Excited voices were at once heard asking "Who is there?" "Why do you throw a light here?" &c.; and the lantern-bearer found to his horror that he was illuminating with his lamp the whole of the hareem of our next-door neighbour, who were all sleeping on the roof, the time being summer. His descent was much quicker than his ascent, as he was in deadly fear of being shot by the irate owner of the hareem.

As a rule thieves only think it worth while to go after gold. Silver is not accounted of any value in Mosul. The natives, especially perhaps the Christians and Jews, always have a great deal of gold in their houses, and in consequence live in terror of the robbers coming to relieve them of it.

Shortly before we left I heard of a very sad case of robbery and murder. A young Christian girl, who had just been married, was awakened one night by a man roughly forcing the gold bracelets from her wrist, holding at the same time a revolver at her head, and telling her if she made a sound he would shoot her dead. For a time she suffered in silence, but an extra sharp wrench from the rough hands of her tormentor made her cry out in pain. Her cry roused her husband, and he immediately made a dash for the robber, who calmly turned the revolver at the man's head and shot him dead. Thus the bride of only a few days' duration was left a widow. Another day two women belonging to one of the leading Christian families were returning from an early service at their church, when they were attacked by a Moslem man, who tore the gold coins from their heads and necks. The terrified women could hardly reach their own homes, so stunned were they by the harsh treatment of the robbers. The strange sequel to this story is, that after a few days a parcel arrived at the house to which the women belonged, which on being opened was found to contain all the gold which had been wrested from them a few days before. Another lady in Mosul, also a Christian, was the proud possessor of a most valuable set of jewels. One day everything disappeared. She neither saw nor heard a robber, but evidently one must have gained admission to the house, for all her jewels were taken; and to this day she has never had a clue as to their fate.

I often say to the women in Mosul who sometimes commiserate me on having no gold: "Which is better — to have gold for the robbers to get, or to have none and be able to go to rest with a quiet mind?" I think most of them would prefer to have the gold and risk the rest, so devoted are they to it and all jewellery. Every woman, except the very poor, has on her marriage, gold coins for her head, gold chains for her neck, a golden band for her waist, gold bracelets for the arms, and the same for her ankles. Is it any wonder that these form attractions which prove too strong for the average robber to resist? I was once visiting at the house of a poor Jewess. She was telling me how poor she was, as her "man" was ill and could not work; but I said, "I expect you have gold?" "Oh yes, of course," was the answer; and going to a cupboard she pulled out a secret drawer and showed me her store of gold coins and bangles, valued at about £200. Before putting away her "gods," she asked me if I thought her hiding-place was secure enough against the invasion of robbers. These people certainly lay up for themselves treasures where thieves break through and steal, the result being that when their "treasures" are taken they are left disconsolate. Having nothing better to live for, are they not worthy of our love and pity?

CHAPTER XII

THE PLEASURES OF DESERT TRAVELLING

Desert blossoms as a rose—Flowers of the desert—Arabs, their occupation and women—Arab dancing—Robbers of the desert—An army of ten thousand—Five hundred armed men—False alarms—Lost in the desert—Delights and disturbances of travelling.

"Truth is truth: too true it was,
Gold! She hoarded and hugged it first,
Longed for it, leaned o'er it, loved it—

Alas!

Till the humour grew to a head and burst,
And she cried at the final pass.

Talk not of God, my heart is stone!
Nor lover nor friend—be gold for both!
Gold I lack, and, my all, my own...."

R. BROWNING.

"O that the desert were my dwelling-place."

BYRON.

It can with all truth be said that in springtime the Desert of Mesopotamia blossoms as a rose. Two years ago we travelled from Mosul to Aleppo by the northern route *viâ* Mardin, Diabekir, and Orfa. We left Mosul about the 20th June, just as the harvest had all been gathered in and the earth had once more resumed its parched-up appearance for another summer. No sooner had we left the neighbourhood of Mosul behind us than we were surrounded again on all sides by fields of waving corn, in many instances still green, and this continued the whole way to Aleppo; the harvest becoming later as we travelled north. Where the land was not cultivated the wild flowers were a perfect delight, and the desert air was filled with their sweetness. In one place the effect of these flowers was peculiarly enchanting. As far as the eye could see, the fields were covered with hollyhocks of all hues, the different shades being grouped together; thus a vast expanse of red hollyhocks would be succeeded by a field of white ones, these again changing to a delightful mauve. I have never anywhere seen such a wealth of wild flowers as we saw in that so-called desert journey from Mosul to Mardin. To try to enumerate the countless tiny flowers of the desert would be futile; they go very near to rival in number and beauty the wild flowers of Palestine. Once we were sitting in a field waiting for our caravan, and my husband said he would see how many different kinds of flowers he could pick without moving. In a minute or two he had gathered over a dozen, all within arm's reach. In that field alone there must have been at least a hundred varieties of flowers.

As we approached Aleppo the flowers became scarcer, and fruit-trees took their place. One day I was riding on the top of the pack mule, when suddenly the animal (who had only one eye) stumbled, and I was deposited on the ground before I realised what had happened. Feeling rather hot and bruised, I looked about for a place to rest in. Fortunately we were near an orchard, so finding a delightfully shady tree, we decided to make this our lunching-ground. As we sat and rested ripe apricots fell from the tree into our laps. The owner of the orchard informed us we could eat as many as we liked — for a consideration!

But desert travelling is not all as pleasant as this. Were we to retrace our steps a month or two later we should see no beautiful flowers or waving corn-fields, nothing but burnt-up desert land.

The direct route from Mosul to Aleppo lies through land almost entirely desert. For two whole days nothing is to be seen save an occasional Arab encampment, and sometimes not even that.

The Arabs of Mesopotamia belong as a rule to the great Shammar tribe. They wander up and down the country living in black tents made from camel or goats' hair. When wishing to seek pastures new they migrate from one place to another with all their flocks and herds, the tending of which forms one of their chief occupations. The Arab women are most industrious: in addition to the ordinary cares of the family, they fetch the water, carrying it home from the well or river in large jars balanced on their heads; they drive the flocks to pasture, milking them night and morning; they spin the wool of the sheep and goat, and weave it into cloth for the men's garments or for the tent canvas. In fact, there is hardly anything the Arab woman does not do, while her lord and master passes the time in scouring the country on horseback, or settling quarrels with his neighbours. Arabs of different tribes are very quick to go to war against each other, and will fight for the merest trifle, though blood is rarely shed, the consequences of a blood feud being so dreaded. With the Arab it must be blood for blood, and once blood has been shed, there can be no rest till vengeance has been satisfied.

The Arabs are very proud of their horses, as they have every reason to be, a true Arab horse being a lovely creature. As a rule they do not shoe their horses at all.

One day two men from an encampment near Mosul were walking along when they saw something on the road which attracted their attention. Picking it up, they examined it very carefully, turned it over and over, but could not come to any satisfactory conclusion regarding it. The object under discussion was a horseshoe, but as neither of them had ever seen such a thing before they could not guess its use. After discussing it gravely for some time one Arab said to the other, "Of course I know what it is. This is an old moon which has fallen down from heaven!"

The Arabs are very hospitable people, and were often profuse in their invitations for us to eat with them. I have once or twice joined the women in sitting round a big cauldron full of "borghol" (crushed corn boiled with plenty of fat) and dipping with them into the one dish, and thoroughly enjoyed it. When you have a desert appetite it is possible to enjoy anything. Once my husband and I accepted an invitation to a meal with an Arab, and were regaled with chicken boiled with a green vegetable called "barmiya," and pillau. Our host would not eat with us, but employed himself brushing the flies away from the food as we ate.

The Arab dance is a very weird performance to watch. The men and women all join hands, and shuffle with their feet, at the same time working every muscle of the body in a most grotesque fashion. As they warm to the dance they get very much excited, yelling and shouting in a frantic manner.

These Arabs are the dreaded robbers of the desert, and our guard always impressed upon us, when travelling, what a dangerous set of people they were. Every speck on the horizon is magnified into a probable Arab; and if by chance one is met in the desert, the excitement is great. On one occasion we were riding in a very lonely spot when suddenly an Arab horseman rode into view. Immediately our gallant guard swooped down upon the unfortunate man, asking him what he meant by spying upon our movements, for they did not think it possible that he would be there alone if it were not for that object. The Arab assured us he had no such intentions, but had only come to meet a friend whom he believed to be in our caravan. However, our escort would not credit his story, so took him prisoner till we had safely passed the dangerous part, and then allowed him to return. We could not help wondering whether, if there had been twenty Arabs instead of one, our guard would have been so brave.

Another time we were crossing a huge track of waterless desert, said to be infested with marauding Arab tribes, when suddenly we saw the escort becoming highly excited, waving their guns about, preparatory to galloping off. Before we had time to ask what it was all about they were off. We were then driving in a carriage, so making inquiries from our driver were assured it was nothing, only he pointed ominously to a long black line seen far away in the distance. Our servant assured us this was the shadow of the mountain, but this was only said to reassure us in case we felt alarmed.

The "black line" appeared to be steadily advancing, every moment becoming more and more like a huge army of mounted men marching straight for us. Our driver, thinking, no doubt, of the probable capture of his horses by the robbers, lashed up the poor beasts into a gallop, urging them on ever faster and faster till they could go no quicker. Our servant, who was sitting on the box-seat, made valiant attempts to draw off our thoughts from the impending danger, as he thought the "khatoun" would be much frightened. But the "khatoun" was not to be blindfolded, and much preferred to see and know what was going on. By this time the "army" had assumed enormous proportions, for as each section appeared in sight, another one loomed behind, away in the distance. Already in my mind I resignedly

(?) bade farewell to all the contents of our boxes, as I pictured the Arabs ruthlessly breaking them open and spreading the contents on the ground for inspection and division. We soon saw that we must give up the race, for every moment brought us nearer our dreaded enemies; till just as we reached the top of a small rise in the ground we came face to face with our "army of soldiers." "Alhamd'llillah!" they were nothing more alarming than a huge cavalcade of about 10,000 camels being taken to water in companies of 500, each company being in charge of a drover, the order and regularity with which they walked giving the impression that they were regiments of mounted soldiers. I fancy the alarm of the guards and driver was only assumed for our benefit, for on our return journey they began the same story at the identical spot, and there again, sure enough, was the steady advancing line; but this time we were wiser, and could laugh at our would-be alarmists.

Another time we had just crossed a river at the end of a long day's march, and were enjoying a well-earned rest and cup of tea, when our escort came up in great distress of mind to say that he had just heard that a band of 500 armed men had that morning crossed the river with the avowed intention of lying in wait for the Feringhi caravan and attacking it. We were getting used to alarms of this kind, and at first only laughed at their anxious faces; but they were so persistent in their entreaties that we should not remain on that side of the river, that we began to think that perhaps, after all, *this* time they might have foundation for their fears. So we made a compromise to the effect that, if they wished, we would pack up and move on to some village, although we were very tired. So with this they had to be content, and it was arranged that at midnight we were to start. However, just before turning in for a short rest, the guard again made their appearance, this time to say they had considered that it would not be at all safe to travel by night, and that we had better wait till daylight, adding in the usual way: "But do not be afraid; we will watch all night long." So we all retired very thankfully to rest. It was a very hot night, and being unable to sleep I went outside the tent door for a little air, and found our gallant guard all fast asleep and snoring. In the morning they assured us that they had never closed their eyes all night, but had sat up watching for robbers!!

We had experienced once in Persia the pleasant sensation of being lost when alone in the desert. In the Turkish-Arabian desert we, in company with the whole caravan, were once lost, and spent many weary hours wandering about seeking for our right road in vain. It was a day or two after leaving Diabekir; our escort, reduced to one soldier as the road was considered fairly safe, was quite sure he knew the way. Our muleteer and servants had never travelled that road before, so we were completely in the hands of one man; but as he seemed quite sure, we did not trouble about it, knowing that these men are always on the road acting as escort. But we soon found that we were trusting to a broken reed, so far as his knowledge as a guide was concerned. We started one day on what we supposed to be a short stage, but to our surprise it seemed to lengthen out into a longer one than usual, till we began to despair of ever reaching the end. At last, when sunset was a thing of the past, we began to suspect that our guide was not too sure of his where-abouts; and this suspicion soon changed to certainty when we suddenly found ourselves on the top of a steep bank, down which it was impossible for the animals to climb. Our clever guide then confessed that he did not know where we were.

It was now quite dark, and we had been riding since early morning, so felt pretty tired; but our muleteer said it was quite out of the question to stay where we were, as there was no water for the animals, and the hills with which we were surrounded were known to be full of robbers. So we wandered on and on and *on*, listening in vain for some sound of habitation and hearing none, longing even to hear the joyful sound of the barking of dogs or croaking of frogs, telling of life and water; but our longings were not to be realised that night. At last, about ten o'clock, we said we could not possibly go any further; so, amidst much discontent and fear on the part of the men, we dismounted and declared our intention of staying where we were till dawn. The animals were all tethered, and we all sat round in a circle, so that if the robbers came we should be able to show a good front. The men appeared to be quite frightened, and declared they would not sleep, but each would take his turn at watching. We were too sleepy to care much whether the robbers came or not, so wrapping ourselves in blankets we were soon fast asleep. Awaking about half-an-hour later, I looked out to see how the "watchers" were getting on, and saw that they were all fast asleep, covered up in their *abas* or long cloaks. I soon followed their example and slept till morning, no robbers having come in the night to disturb our slumbers. We discovered that we had wandered a good distance out of our way, but found the right path soon after nine o'clock, and very thankful we all were to obtain water to drink—the animals more so than any of us, perhaps.

Travelling in the desert is very pleasant if the stage is not a very long one. To start about sunrise or a little after, ride three or four hours, then have a lunch of bread and melons, and finish up with another three hours' ride, makes a very pleasant picnic; but when the stage takes twelve or thirteen hours to do, the pleasure becomes a burden. At the end of a short stage it is delightful to sit outside our tent and enjoy the cool breeze of the desert, and watch the stars peeping out one after the other. Sometimes, however, the weather is not such as to allow of this form of enjoyment. When we were coming home in 1907, in crossing the desert we came in for some tremendously heavy thunderstorms. One night we were simultaneously awakened by a tremendous gust of wind which threatened to bring down the tent. We sprang up and clung to the poles; but thinking the whole structure was bound to fall, and preferring to be outside, I forsook my pole to which I had been clinging, and rushed out into the pouring rain. My husband went to call some of the men, and found them all happily asleep in the carriage: with great difficulty he awoke them, and together they made secure all the tent-pegs. By this time the great fury of the storm was over, and we crept inside the tent, wet, cold, and miserable. Wonderful to say, neither of us caught cold after our adventure. The next morning we spread all our wet bedding, &c., in the sun to dry; and just as it was nearly ready, down came another storm and soaked everything again. Such are some of the joys of travelling in the desert.

CHAPTER XIII

PIONEER MEDICAL MISSION WORK IN MOSUL (NINEVEH)[6]

Winning the confidence of the people—Native surgery—Difficulties to be overcome—Backward patients—Encouraging work—Prevalent diseases—Lunatics—Possible future of Mesopotamia.

"... My soul is full
Of pity for the sickness of this world;
Which I will heal, if healing may be found!"

Sir E. Arnold.

It is often thought that in the East, whenever an English doctor arrives at a city, patients throng to him from all quarters. This is only partially true, at least in the near East. If medicine and attendance are granted free indiscriminately, doubtless at first crowds will attend the out-patient department, many coming merely out of curiosity. If good work is to be done, it is better to make some charge, however small, exempting only the very poor. This principle has, I believe, been adopted by all our medical missionaries, and fees thus earned go to help in making the work self-supporting.

The European doctor in Persia or Turkey has first to win the confidence of the people, and this is sometimes no easy matter. On our arrival in Mosul we rented a house in the centre of the city, which had two compounds. We lived in the inner compound, and made the outer into a dispensary and small hospital. At first everything looked rather hopeless, the house being an old one and nearly in ruins. However, we made a big stable into a waiting-room for the patients; other rooms were patched up and transformed into consulting-room, dispensary, operating theatre, and wards, all of a most primitive kind. In this great city of 60,000 to 80,000 people our staff consisted of my wife and me and two native assistants, who had been trained in our Baghdad Medical Mission.

There was no lack of physicians in the city, but excluding two or three Turkish army doctors, and one or two others with Constantinople diplomas, the rest were quacks of the most pronounced type. Nearly every old lady in the city thinks herself competent to treat diseases of the eye, the barbers are the surgeons, bone-setters abound, hereditary physicians are by no means scarce. These latter inherit

---

[6] By Dr. A. Hume-Griffith.

"herbal prescriptions" from their forefathers, and though now forbidden to practise by the Turkish Government, yet contrive to visit many houses as a "friend"
after dark, and earn enough for a livelihood. The Dominicans (who have a large
Mission in Mosul) also give away many medicines, and have now a qualified native doctor. But though there is much "physicking" in Mosul, but little surgery
is done, and that gives the opportunity for the European doctor to step in. Arab
surgery is of the crudest description. Let one sample suffice. A poor Arab woman
was brought to the dispensary, soon after we started work, by her father. She complained of not being able to breathe through her nose. On examining her throat I
found that the upper air passage had become shut off from the back of the throat
as a result of old inflammation. Upon further inquiry I elicited the following history. Two years before, the patient had developed a bad sore throat. Her father took
her to the native surgeon, who had the poor woman's mouth held forcibly open,
while he proceeded to cure the sore throat by rubbing it with a red-hot flattened
piece of iron!

Gradually we commenced to win the confidence of the people: they came in
ever-increasing numbers to the dispensary. Gathered together in the waiting-room
would be a crowd composed of many different nationalities—Christians, Moslems, Jews, Kurds from the mountains, Bedouins from the desert, Yezidees (the
so-called devil-worshippers), a motley throng, listening quietly and without in-
terruption to the reading and exposition of the Gospel, ere passing one by one
through the doctor's consulting-room, for the treatment of their multitudinous
diseases. The medical missionary is called upon to do his best to cure every ailment; he must be ready to accept heavy responsibilities, there are no "specialists"
to consult, often he is without the help of any trained nurse, and in pioneer work,
at least, he has no properly equipped hospital, and must perforce perform most
serious operations under the worst possible conditions. In addition to all this, in
lands under Mohammedan rule there is always the risk of a riot if a patient should
die in a Christian hospital, especially on the operating table. Yet despite all these
drawbacks, it is a grand life, revealing to a man his own utter weakness, and making him rely more and more upon his God.

Soon we were able to commence admitting in-patients, being forced to limit
admission to surgical cases. At first there was considerable difficulty in getting the
patients to come on the actual day fixed for the operation; each one was anxious
for his neighbour to be the first. Finally I was compelled to threaten to put a black
mark against the name of any patient who had agreed to come in for operation and
then failed to put in an appearance, adding that *that* patient would have to wait a
long time before having a chance offered a second time. This had the desired effect, a woman needing a small eyelid operation being the first to brave the terrors
of the Feringhi hospital.

In due course, instruments and dressings all having been prepared, the patient, in a condition of mortal terror, was led into the operating room, and induced
to lie on the table. But alas, her fears gained the mastery, and she instantly jumped
up, ran out of the room, and disappeared from the dispensary. This was not encouraging, but a few days later a little Jew boy suffering from vesical stone (a very

common disease in Mosul, especially amongst children) was brought to the hospital by his father. We persuaded him to enter the hospital with his boy, and thus finally gained our first in-patient. The stone having been removed, and the boy making a good recovery, we had no further difficulty in getting in-patients. Our six wooden beds soon all had occupants, then we added six more beds; finally, obtaining a neighbouring house for our own residence, we made our old house (the inner compound) into a small hospital for women and children. Thus we were able to accommodate twenty-four patients, and as each had at least one friend, we often had over fifty people resident on the premises. It is this in-patient work that gives the most encouraging opportunities to the medical missionary. There in his little hospital he has patients of all creeds, lying side by side; many have been relieved or cured by operation, and will listen gratefully to all the teaching they can get. Each patient before the operation hears the doctor pray a short prayer, asking God to bless the operation and cause it to be successful. Day after day, week after week, he receives instruction, and gains an entirely new idea of what Christianity really is, and when he leaves the mission hospital and returns to his home, whether in the city or in a distant mountain village, all his old bitter opposition to Christianity has disappeared, and often he will send other patients for treatment to the English mission. The following statistics, for two years only, may prove interesting, as showing the far-reaching influence of even a badly equipped, undermanned medical mission:—

Total attendance of out-patients		24,519
Operations performed $\left\{ \begin{array}{l} 197 \text{ Major} \\ 372 \text{ Minor} \end{array} \right.$		569
Total number of in-patients		288
Number of villages and towns, *excluding* Mosul, from which patients have come to the dispensary		348

This last item is especially interesting; excluding Mosul (from which naturally most of our patients are drawn), 348 *different* towns and villages (some as many as ten days' journey) have sent us patients, and yet the work is barely started!

To illustrate the effect of a medical mission in disarming opposition, I may add that, in 1907, when it was feared that, owing to the need for retrenchment, the Society would have to close the work in Mosul, a petition, signed by most of the prominent Mohammedan residents, including the chief mullahs, was brought to me, asking that I would remit it at once to the Society. It was a request that the Medical Mission should not be withdrawn, as it had been such a boon to the inhabitants of the city. In a very wonderful manner God heard and answered our prayers, and the Mission is not to be closed, but rather it is hoped to equip it more thoroughly.

The operations most frequently called for in Mosul are those for "cataract" and vesical stone, but patients come with many other diseases, both surgical and medical. The city is full of phthisis; the insanitary conditions under which the vast majority of the inhabitants live favour its rapid dissemination. Smallpox and typhoid fever are very common, and once these diseases have been definitely diagnosed, neither the patient nor his friends will permit any further medical treatment. For the latter disease the patient is kept on fairly strict diet until he "perspires." This to the native mind denotes the end of all possible danger, so he is then pressed to eat anything and everything, with disastrous results. Malaria, dysentery, hepatic abscesses are also rife; there have also been epidemics of cholera and plague, but not of late years. Once the projected Baghdad Railway (which will pass through Mosul) is an accomplished fact, we may expect the importation of plague from the south, unless the most stringent precautions are taken.

The Bedouin Arab can rarely be persuaded to stop in the city; after the freedom of life in the desert, he feels stifled within the four walls of a house. Ere leaving Mosul I had a curious demonstration of this fact. An old blind Arab was brought to me by his son, suffering from double cataract. I told him that by means of a simple operation he might once again be able to see, but that he would have to stay in the hospital for a few days. He indignantly refused, saying he would rather remain blind the rest of his life than sleep beneath a roof. In vain did his son plead with him, and finding that I would not operate at once and allow him to be treated as an out-patient, the old man went sorrowfully away.

Every in-patient admitted had to bring a friend to help to nurse him, as we had no proper hospital equipment and no trained nurse. Only twice in the three years did I break this rule, both times with disastrous results. The first was a poor old man from a village some days' journey from Mosul. He was poor and friendless, also blind with "cataract"; reluctantly I allowed myself to be influenced by his pathetic pleadings, and admitted him without any one to look after him. Prior to his admission he had been bitten on the calf of one leg by a dog, and complaining of pain from this wound, we dressed it with a simple boracic fomentation. Unfortunately this dressing was forgotten and left on the leg. The eye was in due course operated upon successfully, and the patient received the usual strict injunction to lie still for twenty-four hours. At the first dressing everything seemed all right; two days later I found to my sorrow that the eye had suppurated, and that there was no hope of saving the vision. The strictest inquiry was at once instituted, but for some time we could discover no clue as to how the eye had become infected; then the truth came out. It appeared that the second night after the operation the old man commenced to feel a slight pricking pain in the eye that had been operated upon (not an uncommon symptom after "cataract" extraction, with no bad significance as a rule). The pain seemed similar to that which he had felt in his leg, which had been relieved by the application of the boracic fomentation. The patient reasoned thus with himself: "It is night time, I had better not call for the doctor; but the medicine on my eye is evidently doing no good, while that put on my leg cured a similar pain to this at once, so I had better take off this bandage from my eye and replace it with the one on my leg"! This he had proceeded to do, and consequently lost his newly acquired sight.

The other case was somewhat similar, but the patient was a fanatical Moslem priest, whom I afterwards found out was a well-known "majnoon" (madman). He also had been admitted alone, and we had but little trouble with him until after the operation (also for "cataract") had been performed. A few hours later my assistant came running to me, and said: "Doctor, that old cataract patient declares that he must and *he will* say his prayers. We have done our best to prevent him, but in vain." Now a Mohammedan, before he prays, performs certain ablutions, which include washing his hands and face; so I at once ran up to the ward, but, alas! we arrived too late. The old priest had taken off his bandage, washed his face and hands, said his prayers, and was quite unable to understand why the Hakim Sahib should be angry! We gave the poor old man some lotion and a shade for his eye, and sent him back to his home (as he lived in Mosul), refusing to accept any further responsibility. Some weeks later my assistant met the old priest in the bazaar, quite pleased with himself, for he had actually obtained sufficient sight to find his way about alone.

Fortunately the majority of the patients are more reasonable, and quickly learn to submit more or less to "hospital regulations." Children sometimes proved troublesome, especially boys, when accompanied by a crowd of relations. I remember one morning, when making my daily round, coming across a group of people surrounding a little boy six years of age. He had been ordered a dose of castor oil, and had made up his obstinate little mind that he would *not* take the nasty stuff. Being a boy, and only son and heir, he had been spoilt most royally. Father, mother, aunt, grandmother, and friends each in turn tried persuasion, varied by gentle threats, all in vain. He beat and (I am sorry to say) cursed the women, his mother included, and sullenly refused to accept the medicine from his father, despite sundry promises of sweets, money, &c.

After watching the scene with some amusement I stepped forward, took the cup containing the obnoxious castor oil, and forcibly administered the dose without regarding the boy's shrieks and tears. Then I read the parents a little lecture upon the evil result of spoiling their children, which I fear had but scant result.

Often do I feel ashamed as I note how patiently pain and diseases are borne by these poor people. It is always "the will of God," and therefore there is no use complaining, and little use rebelling. Time after time have I had to gently break the news to some poor patient, who may have come long distances to see the English doctor, that his blindness could not be cured by operation, being caused by what is popularly known as black cataract (glaucoma). A few (usually women) would go away weeping, but the vast majority both of men and women would quietly respond, "Alhamd'llillah" (Praise be to God), with but little sign of emotion.

So far as I know there is but one asylum for cases of mental diseases in the whole of the Turkish Empire, and that one is at Asfariyeh, near Beyrout, and belongs to an English society. The usual method of dealing with lunatics in Mosul is, if they are apparently harmless, that they are allowed to wander about freely and treated kindly; but once they develop symptoms of mania they are treated as wild beasts, put into a dark room, and chained to a wall. But we possess a specialist in "mental diseases" in Mosul, belonging to an old Mohammedan family, who has a great reputation for the treatment of "lunatics." In the courtyard of his house he has had dug several deep wells, and beside each well is placed a large tub, having a hole in the bottom which communicates with the well. The poor madman is made to work from sunrise to sunset, drawing water from the well and pouring it into the perforated tub, being told that he may leave off *when* he has filled the tub. If he refuses to work, he is unmercifully beaten. Several cures are said to have resulted from this treatment.

There is nothing so potent as the in-patient work of a hospital in overcoming opposition. Amongst our numerous "cataract" patients was an Arab from Singar (a mountainous district near Mosul). He came armed with a perfectly unnecessary introduction, in the shape of a letter from one of the chief Mohammedans in the city. After he had regained his sight and had left the hospital, ere returning to his mountain home he went to this "big" Moslem to thank him. He found himself the centre of a large and curious throng, who questioned him severely upon his experiences in the "Christian" hospital. Some of the more fanatical (it was in the early days of the Mission) did not scruple to speak against the hospital and the English hakim; but, like the man in St. John's Gospel, this Arab was not afraid to testify of what had been done for him, "for," said he, "you can say what you like—one thing I know, before I was blind, now I can see."

But enough—I fear to tire my readers; but ere closing I would like just to refer to the possible future of Mesopotamia. One thing is certain, a few years more will exhibit great changes. I have already referred to the Baghdad Railway. As I write it is rumoured that the German Government have at last obtained a further concession from the Sultan of Turkey, which will allow them to continue the line another five hundred miles, piercing Mount Taurus and reaching near to the city of Mardin (some ten days' journey north of Mosul). When this is accomplished the rest of the work is quite simple. The line from Mardin to Baghdad (passing through Mosul) should present no difficulties, and Mosul (with the ruins of Nineveh) will become easy of access from Europe.

In the next place there is the question of the navigation of the Tigris. Ere long there is no doubt that boats will be allowed to come up the river from Baghdad to Mosul, and possibly on up to Diabekir (300–400 miles north of Mosul). This will mean an enormous increase in trade, both in imports and exports.

Finally, there is that fascinating problem of the irrigation of the Mesopotamian desert. The remains of old canals are still visible, and it needs nothing but an energetic government willing to spend a comparatively small sum, plus the services of a capable engineer, to transform the whole of that desert between the two great rivers Euphrates and Tigris into a veritable Garden of Eden, even as it must have been in the days of old, when huge armies were able to find sufficient provender for man and beast throughout the whole of that vast region. The "finale" of that great province, containing the ruins of so many ancient cities, has not yet been written; and there are many signs which tend to suggest to the thoughtful observer that, ere another century has passed, Mesopotamia may once again take its place, and that no mean position, amongst the kingdoms of the earth!

INDEX

A

B

T

U

V

W

Y

Z

Lector House believes that a society develops through a two-fold approach of continuous learning and adaptation, which is derived from the study of classic literary works spread across the historic timeline of literature records. Therefore, we aim at reviving, repairing and redeveloping all those inaccessible or damaged but historically as well as culturally important literature across subjects so that the future generations may have an opportunity to study and learn from past works to embark upon a journey of creating a better future.

This book is a result of an effort made by Lector House towards making a contribution to the preservation and repair of original ancient works which might hold historical significance to the approach of continuous learning across subjects.

HAPPY READING & LEARNING!

LECTOR HOUSE LLP
E-MAIL: lectorpublishing@gmail.com

www.ingramcontent.com/pod-product-compliance
Lightning Source LLC
Chambersburg PA
CBHW051430130726
47987CB00005B/1996